Table of 'Coon-Tents'

Introduction

THE BOOTLICKER'S GALLERY

Clarence Thomas, Supreme Court Justice

- Introduction
- Transcription of the Debate (October 19, 1991)
- Letter to Omaha Chamber of Commerce re: Clarence Thomas Visit (November 18, 2001)
- Conclusion

Jesse Owens, 1936 Olympic Champion

- Preface
- Introduction
- Confusion By Any Other Name: Quotes From Jesse Owens
- *Blackthink: My Life as a Black Man and White Man*: A Chapter-by-Chapter Case Study

  - Chapter 1: I Know the Trouble They've Seen
  - Chapter 2: Henry Owens' Torture
  - Chapter 3: But Equality is Here
  - Chapter 4: Negroes Have Human Hang-ups
  - Chapter 5: Anatomy of a Militant
  - Chapter 6: Blackthink Won't Win
  - Chapter 7: I Know Because I've Been There
  - Chapter 8: Showcase the Good
  - Chapter 9: Black Man, Heal Thyself
  - Chapter 10: Open Letter to a Young Negro
  - Chapter 11: Open Letter to All Whites
  - Chapter 12: We Shall Overcome - If

Candace Owens, conservative commentator
Rev. Al Sharpton, Host – "Politics Nation"
Iman, super model
Ezola Foster, conservative politician and spokesperson
O.J. Simpson, Hall of Fame NFL running back

Omarosa Manigault-Edwards, Trump supporter/critic
Diana Ross, superstar singer, Motown records/actress
Raven-Symone, actress/talk show host
Stacey Dash, actress/conservative commentator
Kanye West, rapper/songwriter
Whoopi Goldberg, actress, host of "The View"
Diamond and Silk, conservative commentators
Robert Griffin III, NFL quarterback
Charles Barkley, Hall of Fame NBA star, host, "Inside the NBA"

Conclusion

Introduction

As a people, African-Americans are in deep trouble. No leaderless people can survive for a long period of time. Up to this point we have survived the holocaust of enslavement, eked out an existence through massive migration and sharecropping, burned cities down in order to get basic civil rights and then all of that went to Hell in a handbasket: we lost our sense of purpose, identity and direction.

Today's Negro Leadership: Made and Manufactured in America. Because of the 400 year dehumanization process during enslavement, no statement could be more germane in these days and times of the black sellout, the treacherous Quisling and the duplicitous race betrayer. Some call this "post-racial America"; this book will prove that the black overseer, the "house negro" as Malcolm X called them, are alive and well and living in America.

This book is not about name-calling but about "defining." At a time when there is a dearth of Black leadership in America – perhaps the lowest in the history of blacks in this country – there is a need to ask questions and investigate into why this is the case. My main concern is how influence peddlers – known to most of you as "leaders" – are being pawned off as power brokers, when nothing could be further from the truth.

In this book I name people whose comments, actions and attitudes have filtered down and influenced hundreds of thousands – perhaps millions – of impressionable black folk, young and old alike.

Among those mentioned and discussed in this book are Clarence Thomas, Supreme Court Justice; Jesse Owens, winner at the 1936 Olympics whose perpetual butt kissing is still being held up by the system as some kind of "model"; Raven-Symone and Stacey Dash (both who have publicly rejected their own blackness); Rev. Al Sharpton, a professional poverty pimp; Omarosa Manigault Newman, the biggest sellout since Ward Connerly; Diana Ross, Charles Barkley (who hides his personal life but has the gall to speak out on black issues), Whoopi Goldberg and several others.

I once read where Audre Lorde wrote, *"When I dare to be powerful – to use my strength in the service of my vision, then it becomes less and less important whether I am afraid."* You have your views and I have mine. Mine are published. So read and enjoy.

THE BOOTLICKER'S GALLERY

Clarence Thomas, Supreme Court Justice

INTRODUCTION

Cynthia Jackson is an intelligent young lady, a strong writer and a single parent. We dated for a while and were involved in community events (all organized by me, of course). When it came to politics and race issues, we were usually in agreement, but when it became known that Clarence Hill was vying for a seat on the Supreme Court, and that a young black woman opposed it because he had sexually harassed her, Cynthia and I had some different views on the subject.

Since I had a hit radio show in Milwaukee at the time on WNOV-AM, I invited her on because she had finished a brief paper on the subject and I had just written a column for the black newspaper that I was editor of, The Milwaukee Courier.

On that day -- October 19, 1991 -- Cynthia and I debate "The Clarence Thomas Hearings" on WNOV, and then head back to her house to listen to the tapes.

TRANSCRIPTION OF THE DEBATE

THE DEBATE: Matthew Stelly vs. Cynthia Jackson. SUBJECT: Clarence Thomas and Anita Hill. Following is a full transcription of that debate:

Matthew:
Good morning Milwaukee, today is October 19th, 1991 of course, and this morning in the studio with me is Cynthia Jackson of the University of Wisconsin-Milwaukee, Communications major and, of course, profound political thinker – (or so she thinks) – NOW, (laughter) today we're going to talk about the Clarence Thomas nomination and also the Anita Hill situation and we'll be presenting some pros and cons and of course you can call in with your decision, your information, your perspective, at 799-1668. Cynthia has done a lot of research into this area, and she has a statement and also some interesting view points on some things that were written by some other people as well, so we're going start off first of all stating our general theses. I'm going to be reading from my column this week in the Courier, it's called, "Clarence Thomas: Getting Over on 'The Hill'" (laughter). Then, she'll be reading her perspective and we'll be more or less exchanging ideas, viewpoints and then you can call in, okay? So if you're not taping the show, you should be, if you are taping it, then you're in for a classic, I guarantee it. Now. "Clarence Thomas: Getting Over on 'The Hill':"

Clarence Thomas made it to the Supreme Court by the skin of his teeth and the black community should be reeling from one of the most embarrassing televised events since Ben Vereen danced in blackface at Ronald Reagan's first inaugural ball.

First, the Senate looks like it really cares about women's rights and the issue of sexual harassment. By providing this 'mock forum,' white males can now can now act as if the amount of time they spent is now synonymous with real concern.

Secondly, by convincing many that they were really concerned about women's rights, they can now proceed to dog women as never before. Just like in the post-Bakke decision days, expect to hear statements like, 'Well, we did what we could. Now I'll stay in my place and you stay in yours.' Translation: more disparity in pay and less resistance to the still male-dominated workplace.

Third, the entire nomination process has been and will continue to be criticized. With such criticism, the process shall be overhauled. This society owes this much needed change to blacks and women, in that order. Once again, our groups 'humanize' a system which has erroneously boasted of being concerned about the welfare of all.

Fourth, black people have fulfilled our traditional role: that of providing dramatic, sexual entertainment for the majority population. What fun it must have been to watch a black man and woman chew each other up on national television.

Fifth, men now have the fear of women that is necessary in the workplace. Fear? Yes fear. For only in being afraid of retribution will the "hound" see the woman as a human being who has rights, and who exercises those rights. Yes, fear. For only when our own jobs are threatened will we appreciate the value of a woman having and keeping hers.

Sixth, the polygraph issue that has been dealt with and rightfully, debunked. How many black people are doing time because of the white man's flawed technology? Even the much vaunted voice-stress evaluator must be reassessed. As it was during institutionalized slavery, pseudo-science was used to promote the myth of black inferiority. Today's polygraph experts and VSE users are a throwback to V.K. Vaardeman, Virey, Camper and William Shockley.

Seventh, the Senate appears as if it cares about black rights at a time when there is increased racial tension all over the nation. What timing! People like Joe Biden, Ted Kennedy, Strom Thurman and Hank Brown can all feign ignorance of 'black culture' or 'black thoughts' and then pretend as if they are interested enough by asking questions, questions that have been answered decades ago.

Eighth, the hearings brought to light the existence of real black-on-black disunity. We argue using the superficial premises of conservative, liberal and the like, we demonstrate a clear lack of political understanding of cultural background. We show that we do not understand. If Thomas wins, that does not mean that we will; if Thomas loses, we do not necessarily lose. He will be one cog in a white institution that is inherently anti-black. He will be but one voice.

Ninth, raises the new stereotypes and magnifies the old one regarding black males. These will be used to justify continued exclusion of the black male from the workplace, just as the Persian Gulf War fanned the flames of racism against individuals from the Middle East.

Tenth, the fiasco took attention off the upcoming Middle East summit which could have placed attention on American-Israeli relationships, and concentrated, instead, on the issue of black male-black female insensitivity.

Eleventh, Anita Hill's beauty can now be more appreciated at a time when light skinned, almost white is gradually creeping back into the mindset of non-white America. Anita's physical appearance served to offset the Vanessa Williams-Paula Abdul-Latoya Jackson Syndrome which is dominating the black aesthetic, especially black music.

Twelfth, the Senate showed the American people, and blacks from all walks of life, that racism is no respector of black persons, whether conservative, liberal, moderate or neutral.

Thirteenth, the confirmation reinforced the power of the white male and his technology. From the televised sophistication and rapid transcription of testimony, to the legal background and wealth of information available on all those who testified, the white male showed the world his data bank mentality. This could also be known as "The King Solomon Syndrome," or "The Sitting in Judgment Mental Disorder."

Fourteenth, the hearings demonstrated that blacks, regardless of how much financial assistance or education you receive in white schools, are still children to be watched closely, even by the most well-meaning of white folk. Merely note the absence of blacks on the Senate panel; the run-and-tell-mommy approach used by Anita Hill, and the my-buddies-can-vouch-for-me approach used by Thomas.

Fifteenth, the hearings pointed out the inadequacies and, in some cases, the outright backwardness of the local media coverage by the Milwaukee media. Clips from hearings were supplemented locally by interviews with the uninformed or investigations into lie detectors. What a waste!

Sixteenth, Anita Hill will now become richer again, thanks to Clarence Thomas. Just as he wrote her recommendations that gave her jobs in the past, he is now going to make her rich as she writes books on the subject, hits the speaking circuit and perhaps makes a TV-movie.

Seventeenth, the white-dominated women's movement will get a touch of "color" which it needed so badly. Such groups now have the façade of caring about black women, something they have not convincingly demonstrated in the past.

Eighteenth, the hearings validated the existence of the concept of "black conservative."

Nineteenth, the integration paradigm achieves a major victory through the use of such terms as, "role model," "African-American," and "achievement" and so on. Now all these can be associated with striving to integrate into the system. That is, those who make it through the educational system and other obstacles placed in the inner city.

Twentieth, election year eve becomes more important with the majority of the electorate being female, and with white women threatening to retaliate.

Twenty-first, the 'high tech lynching for uppity blacks' comment made by Thomas. Though it was somewhat late, the comment proves what I've been saying all along: that even the even the most bootlicking of Uncle Toms can turn black when his life-chances are threatened.

Twenty-second, women who have been the victims of sexual harassment can and will now come forward. And when they do, a lot of people – male and female, black and white – are going to be subjected to the kind of public scorn that is only further going to tear this nation and community apart.

Let the battles begin.

Those are my views on the subject and opening comments, and now, Cynthia Jackson from the University of Wisconsin-Milwaukee has some comments of her own. Good morning Cynthia and you may now continue.

Cynthia:
Good morning, Matthew. I chose to focus on Clarence Thomas. I have something I wrote, I'd like to share with you, "Clarence Thomas: A Fade to Black."

While many people viewing the confirmation hearings were aking themselves whether Anita Hill or Clarence Thomas was telling the truth, I was asking myself what I felt was a more pertinent question: when did Clarence Thomas become a black man? After hearing Clarence Thomas accuse the special committee of lynching him for being an uppity black, I wondered when this metamorphosis occurred.

Many of you are now wondering if I am sane. Mr. Thomas is obviously a black man; look at his skin color. But you see I believe there's more to being black than skin color. To be black in America is to acknowledge that there is a different standard of living. Until these charges of sexual harassment were brought up, Mr. Thomas was operating under the ideology that blacks had equal opportunity in America; if there were not successful, it was because they had not worked hard enough to achieve that status. So it knocked me for a loop when the very same men that he embraced politically were now being accused of being racist. Could it be that Clarence Thomas knew that saying this publicly would put the Senate on the proverbial hot seat?

Lynching in this country did not historically happen to black men who felt as Thomas does. Lynching occurred among black men who failed to accept their second-class status. Men who acknowledged that America was not a haven of opportunity, but a well of disparity if you are born of color.

When I think of lynching, I think of men like Martin Luther King and Malcolm X, who sacrificed their lives for what they believed was right for all blacks. I definitely don't associate the word with the Clarence Thomases of the world who conveniently become black when the chips are down. When is the black race going to stop embracing people who disassociate themselves from our struggle? People who prostitute our race by accepting it only when the majority has cast them aside.

Clarence Thomas says he now knows what it feels like to be mistreated. Well, good morning to you, Mr. Thomas, and where have you been for the last 43 years? To be a black man and face racism at 43 is a godsend. I wonder where Mr. Thomas was when blacks took to the streets to provide opportunities for the next generation, opportunities that conservative blacks have so conveniently refused to maintain for the next generation?

Many blacks feel because Clarence Thomas is black in color, we join him in his quest for the Supreme Court. These blacks think that once he's in office, he will change his views and defend their rights; that he is only faking his political beliefs. Well, Mr. Thomas was in charge of one of the most powerful organizationsn in the country, the EEOC, and during his tenure he not only defended Reagan's assault on blacks in the workforce, but failed to set any new agenda to help black America.

During the confirmation hearings, we were also subjected to Senators, such as Orrin Hatch, who were appalled by the hearings and thought they were a travesty of justice. Give me a break! I wonder where these sensitive Republicans came from? They supported legislation that literally killed black men, but all of a sudden they are enraged when Clarence Thomas is called to the carpet. I guess it's okay to kill someone as long as you don't have to look at the body.

As we quibble over who is lying about what, I'll still be wracking my brain about what I feel is the more important question: when did Clarence Thomas fade to black, and if Clarence Thomas did fade to black, is the change permanent?

I also have some comments to make about an editorial I read in the Milwaukee Courier. It was written by Walter Farrell, a professor at the University of Wisconsin-Milwaukee.

First of all, let me tell you how I feel about conservative blacks. Like I said in my column, I think that they prostitute the black race, they use blackness when it's convenient. And I want to read one of his points: 'Black citizens across every gender and occupational grouping indicate that Judge Clarence Thomas deserved a seat on the Supreme Court. However, the strongest support emerged from black working men and women who constitute the core of the African-American community. They are the ones who form the troops for local and national civil rights initiatives and took pride in the achievements of those blacks for whom they have opened doors.'

First of all, Clarence Thomas doesn't represent the black race, and those people who supported him seen his skin color only. I think that they supported him because they didn't want to seem un-unified in the white community. And to [tarp] on that is bunk in the first place.

*Okay, the next point that Walter Farrell made, 'Professor Hill was being used by larger forces to sabotage a black man's rise to the pinnacle of his profession.' What about the rise to the pinnacle of **her** profession? I think that black men look at black women and think that we're their helpers instead of an equal. And for him to say that Professor Hill was used by a larger force is to say that black women have no brain of their own, that we always have to run behind our men and never use any of our own intelligence.*

*Okay, my next point, 'completeness or truth of her story' (giggles). First of all, I don't think that Anita Hill was lying, and for someone to go publicly and say that she is a liar, they have to refute it by presenting some truth – which Clarence Thomas didn't do. What he did was come up and start using excuses, saying, "Oh, you're lynching me." It's funny that he can say they're lynching him now, and before he said there was no racism in America. He said this was like the place to be; that if you worked hard, you could pull yourself up. Which I don't understand, because the reason why they selected him was because they needed a black for the position, so actually he was elected off of **affirmative action.***

Okay, the next point that Walter Farrell made, 'white conservatives, on the other hand, saw Judge Thomas' appointment as a referendum for a new direction on social welfare and affirmative action change.' Here we go, with black people worried about what white people think about us. Well, first of all, they don't care about you. So stop worrying. And he says that by supporting these conservatives that we present a kind of unity. What kind of unity is that when we're the poorest in America and we go behind people who don't give a damn about us?

Okay, the next point that he makes: "White conservatives like Senator Strom Thurmond and Orrin Hatch vigorously campaigned for the appointment throughout the process." Think about it: Strom Thurmond and Orrin Hatch. They never supported any legislation giving blacks any kind of power in the workforce, but all of a sudden they rally behind this man. Sounds kind of suspicious, doesn't it?

The next point: "Since president Bush was only going to appoint conservatives, they felt it best that they support one of their own." I want you to think about that: **one of their own.** *Not one of* **us,** *but one of their own. So when you look up there and you see him, that skin color doesn't hide the fact that* **that's one of their own.** *And President Bush mentioned in the paper yesterday that he hopes to garner some black votes from this. So you see what their objective was.*

And last point that Mr. Farrell made: "But the mass community has chosen to place its bets on Judge Thomas' in hopes and expectations that he will do the right thing." He probably will do the right thing in his eyes: get a house, live comfortably and screw black people."

Matthew:
The number here is 799-1668. We're going to talk a little more about Anita Hill and also the Clarence Thomas situation. I'd like to shift focus a little bit to the Anita Hill situation, sum up my views on her presence, because a lot of people have been making her the real focus of the issue when really, she's not really – in my book, worthy of that much focus. She came forward and did some things, said some things that might have happened to her ten years prior. They said she confided in her friends when it happened, but see, that's the problem with black people now: we wanna take a situation that's of importance, confide in a few of our buddies, and meanwhile the majority of people get dogged. Now, how many women got dogged out in the workplace by her just confiding in her buddies then years ago? If she would've went national ten years ago, that could've been ten years less of women getting dogged in the workplace, don't you think?

But see, the idea is even if she did come ten years later, she should've came when Bush first nominated this guy, Thomas, because I didn't know him from Adam's house cat. When he first nominated him, she could have came forward and did it then, nip it in the bud, nip the process in the bud. But what did she do? She waits until he goes through the process, then comes forward claiming the FBI approached her about the issue, she says that she was just responding to FBI reports, but the bottom line basically is that during the interim of those ten years, she was in contact with Clarence then. If she wanted to be, get it known, get it out there, what she should have done is said, 'look, I'm going to go ahead man, and tell these people what you did to me ten years ago.' But that's not what happened. What happened was when he hears about it again, its been in the white man's media, she's dogging him out just before it gets to the Supreme Court.

Now personally, I think something happened between the two of 'em, more than what they're saying in there, more than what they said at the hearing. I think they actually had a relationship. He married a snow bunny, she got mad, and decided to wait until he gets his crowning glory and more or less dogs him out. Now, both of them are toms in my book; but the idea basically is that on a national level, she comes forward when she should have come forward when she should have come forward ten years earlier. If I kick you in the butt, you gon' wait ten years to say 'ouch'?

Cynthia:
*Oh here we go, Matthew, the old saying black women are always jealous of white women. No, I don't believe that, I do not believe that. She was 24 years old when she had that job. She had a degree from Yale. And the women in the office wanted her to go out and eat donuts with them. **She's his intellectual equal.** When are women gonna accept other women as people of power? Now, I just don't agree that she waited to dog him out. I've been sexually harassed, and I've talked to other people who have been sexually harassed. You don't just go and yell to everybody, you tell a couple of people, you hope to put it away, but it'll come up sooner or later. Now I agree that it does seem strange that she waited for **ten years.** But I know a lot of women out there who have waited longer.*

Matthew:
Well if you've been sexually harassed, and you just tell a few people, that mean's that the person who sexually harassed you is still out there, you haven't done anybody any justice. Basically what you've done is you might have solved your own personal examples of it, but you haven't any service until you expose the person who harassed you at that point. That's the same attitude Anita Hill has; she wants to deal with it on a personal level, but when it comes down to helping out a large group of people, she doesn't do anything.

Cynthia:
Let me just say this: when you get hit, do you worry about going and hitting everybody for everybody else? You're worried about the person who directly hit you. You don't go out there and go on some bandwagon for the whole world when you're a 24 year old, and you're facing this one person. He's big enough to you. The whole world is hard to take on.

Matthew:
*First of all, that is exactly what I do. That's why nobody hits me. Because the conditions under which such conflict takes place is what I always address. And if you listened to this show, you'd know that. Now, 799-1668's the number, we'll be going back and forth as we have been this morning, so just feel free to call in, give us your opinion, your views, try to stick to the subject, but if it's real important, we'll handle the issue. But the main thing here is the Anita Hill-Clarence Hill situation, sexual harassment as **alleged** by Ms. Hill and Cynthia Jackson (laughter). We'll take a call now. Good morning you're on the air ...*

Caller #1:
*The first thing I want to talk about is the fact of her coming forward. If she came forward ten years ago, she could have stopped sexual harassment, that's a lie. It doesn't work that way. It would have got no attention, just as many sexual harassment cases do. Right now, the only reason that it got attention was because it **was** in the public eye.*

Matthew:
Why didn't she sue?

Caller #1:
*Sue? **That is bullshit**. There's many women out there who sued. It won't go anywhere.*

Matthew:
Did it go somewhere this time?

Caller #1:
The whole idea of sexual harassment being an issue is bullshit anyway!

Matthew:
Well, make up your mind now, you're contradicting yourself. Either it's not or it is. Now is it or not?

Caller #1:
What, bullshit?

Matthew:
Is it B.S. or not?

Caller #1:
It's bullshit. Nothing's going to be done about it. And most women know that. Men are going to be put on the hotseat, 'I won't touch somebody at the workplace.' **That** *is bullshit.*

Matthew:
Well first of all stop saying that word. And second of all, you're a hypocrite. Now either it's B.S. or its not. Which is it?

Caller #1:
It is.

Matthew:
Okay, now that's your position, right? Okay good. Now you're making sense. Now hang up so somebody else can get on the line, okay? Bye. Now, the number's 799-1668. Now, what do you think of those comments, Miss Jackson?

Cynthia:
I think she was right on the buttom. I think for someone to bring up sexual harassment, I mean, if you tell some else about it, I think that's enough. To sit up here and have to go on a soapbox and tell the whole world about it is pretty hard to do. She did it, knowing what she had to risk. And ten years ago, imagine, 24 years old, here this man is in a position of power, and you're going to say, 'oh well he sexually harassed me.' She knew she would have been out of work and her legal career ruined. Sure, she was worrying about her own position but at 24 years old, I don't know very people who wouldn't.

Matthew:
You're lookin' at one of 'em. But here's the point I'm makin'. If we would have had the same attitude along racial lines, there never would have been a Civil Rights Movement. Now when Rosa Parks came forward, true she did come forward based on being fatigued, etcetera, but the idea is this: individuals who feel strongly about something move on it based upon, and the way they move on it, shows you how strongly they feel. If I'm really concerned about something, and its offending me, then I have to assume that its going to offend everybody who's like me. As a result, I move accordingly.

Now you might justify it on an individual level, she's 24 years old, but look at the whole idea of what she could have done, what good could have been done. Now you say no good could have been done. With that attitude, that kind of projectionary attitude, if we would have believed that taking on the white man in Montgomery, Alabama was negative, we never would have marched. So again, I'm right as usual. 799-1668 is the number, you're on the air.

Caller#: Mr. Borum
Hello. Good morning. I'd like to address Thomas. We all know what conservative mean, black conservative. And now, going back to Miss Hill, Miss Hill should be looked at .... Hello?

Matthew:
Yeah, we're listening.

Mr. Borum:
Miss Hill should be looked at, I really think she's a role model. Let me tell you what a role model – I think all black young people should take a look at Miss Hill, and she is a role model. She's well-educated, she comes from a poor family, and she has dignity and you look at her hair, her hair's not red anything like that there. And she do have nerve, but to address and to come forward – she's not going to commit suicide getting' the job. Everybody know Thomas had power. And Matthew, you know Thomas got power, and you know the procedures what it takes to get a good job. You know you have to have an education. If that young lady would have come forward at that time she never would get a good job. C'mon Matthew, give that young lady a break. And thank you.

Matthew:
Yeah, and thanks for the doggin' as usual. But here's my point: you don't sit around thinking that a job's more important that a moral principle. I mean most of **you do**, *and I can see why you would. Cynthia does, she's still a student. You do, I don't know why after the way the state dogged you for your dough. I don't. The principle is more important than the job, the principle is more important that the paycheck, the principle is more important than your own individualistic needs. To think black is to think collective minded. If what you believe is so important and it hurts you so much, then its going to hurt a lot of other people, too. Now most of you are cowards and I can understand where Anita Hill came from. But the fact that she finally did come forward, the timing of it has got to be taken into consideration: how many people got dogged in the process? Just because she waited until he got ready to get nominated, that says something right there. She didn't really accomplish that much anyway, all this stuff is is a façade. Nobody really cares about sexual harassment any more, the white man's gonna be a dog*

*no matter what happens, male-female relationships are gonna continue to
deteriorate – it was just a circus! Don't you understand? Oh – Miss Jackson?*

Cynthia:
*I'd like to get back to that comment you made, that she could have told somebody
like her. First of all, where she was at, there's very few people like her. She's
dealing in Washington, where it's very conservative, mostly white, and even other
blacks have a problem with their identity as we seen with Doggett. I think the
gentleman that called is right on the button; it takes a lot to get a job and to keep it
– I don't think you have to give up your identity, but I think she had to deal
realistically with what she had. She knew to be 24 years old and walk up to
someone in a position of power and say, 'well, you sexually harassed me. I'm
going to go tell everybody,' he could have not only had her job, but ruined her
legal career.*

*And about those women on the panel, those women on the panel, I just think that
that was a travesty of justice in itself. I think that for them to try to analyze her
sexual life, at the same time she acted like she was better than everyone else, well –
a degree from Yale! I'm not saying that you have to act like a snob, but it should
your decision whether you want to go and eat donuts with the girls or go out for a
drink or something. She separated herself from them and I think they were very
resentful of it. She was a nice-looking woman, now just imagine ten years ago,
being 24, new to the workforce, with a law degree.*

Matthew:
*I still don't excuse the idea – see again, what you guys are saying is right based
upon your perspective because most of you have the same [methods of acting] as
her: you go to school, you get degrees, then you go out and try to find a white man
to adopt you. As a process of looking for somebody to adopt you, you naturally
become cowards because you wanna keep that mortgage payment, that BMW
payment bein' made – but that don't make it right, though. Because the majority of
people don't come forward on the job workplace is the issue, the fact she didn't
come forward on the workplace, 24 years old or not – I was coming forward when
I was 20! The idea is what? The idea is the principle. Everybody's missing that
because she has a law degree and she's young, a career. Black people are so
messed up, sitting around talking about a career, is in and of itself an insult! How
can you talk about a career unless you control your own business? If you don't
have your own business, then you ain't got no career, because the white man – if
he don't get no bootie the night before, he can fire you arbitrarily and you won't*

do nothin' about it, just like SHE didn't do nothing about it. 799-1668's the number. You're on the air.

Caller #3:
I agree with you, Matthew. Ten years ago, he rapes her, she should have spoken out then. I think that, like you said, kick me in my butt ten years ago and I wait ten years later to say ouch, then it really didn't mean anything. And I think that she was jealous because he married a white woman. And if he did rape her, I'm not saying he raped her, I'm not saying he didn't, but there was something that happened between them, and I think all it is was jealousy. I think she should have spoken out. That's all I have to say.

Cynthia:
*Oh boy, here we go, here we go again: the poor, ugly black woman's jealous of the beautiful, illustrious white woman! Here we go again! I think it's very sad that a black woman would make a comment about how we're jealous of white women instead of looking at the issues; you should have looked at the brothers who were **dogging** a black woman on TV! Talking about her physical appearance, whether she was **worth** him losing his job over. You should have looked at that. But we live in a country where you're fourth-class citizens, you would obviously take on the views of white males and now, **some uppity black males.***

Matthew:
*First of all, there's no such thing as a fourth-class citizen. You're either a first-class citizen or a ward of the state. Second of all, you're drawing conclusions that are not in evidence. She didn't say anything about the ugly black woman – as a matter of fact, by you making those comments twice in a row, **you** must perceive it that way! Nobody said anything about the black woman being ugly, nobody said anything about the black woman being jealous of the white woman. You drew those conclusions! Now, we'll break for commercial, let you gather your thoughts. The number here is 799-1668. Give us a call. We'll be right back.*

COMMERCIAL BREAK

Cynthia:
I'd like to address those last comments made by Mr. Stelly. First of all, the lady didn't come out and say that black women were ugly, but what else can you perceive from that comment? The comment that she was jealous, what else can you get from that? It's hard for me to believe anybody viewing the hearing and

saw how Doggett talked about Anita Hill's physical appearance could not get this meaning from it. And, I just want to know what you have to say.

Matthew:
*What I have to say is that you're drawing conclusion from information that's not in evidence. Black women being jealous of white women is not so much the issue on the collective case as it is in this case here. I'm the one who said that I think these people were jealous because he married a white woman, and gave the white woman all this prestige, he had drug her along with him everywhere he went, she followed with a true police-dog like loyalty, got dogged at the end, decided she was gonna get payback. It ain't got nothin' to do with black women being ugly or being jealous of white women – **although a case can be made.** When you sit around talking about a career, when you sit around talking about wanting to work for somebody, when you sit around waiting for a white man to adopt you, indeed you want the same thing that the white woman wants which is her man evidently. Or else you'd create your own business. Now. Chew on that. 799-1668, you're on the air.*

Caller #4:
Hi, I'm calling in. I want to make a comment about the young lady who wrote that about Clarence Thomas. I think she's right on the button about him all of a sudden becoming black. You know, fading to black. Because if you really think about it, you work hard you do this you do that and be this wonderful person in this white America. And also about Anita Hill, why did she continue a relationship with this man who sexually harassed her? Most women shy away from those – (inaudible) I would have gone to another – I'm sure there are other things she could have done. And why didn't she come out sooner ... I know she was only 24. I'm 22, and if something were to happen to me like that, I know I'm not in a political position or anything – I definitely would stand up. I'm a beautiful black woman, I don't think she was jealous of this white woman taking her man because – I think it was just totally irrelevant to the point. I think they did have a relationship, also. Those are just my points. Thank you.

Matthew:
*Comments appreciated. And also the whole idea really of somebody being harassed and then following somebody after that. That **is** probably taking place all over society, but it goes back to my original point. My original point is, without police dog-like loyalty, we follow our master wherever he goes. Put that into macrocosm: four hundred years of being dogged out to a system called slavery, and we're still kissing his butt, following him wherever he goes. Sharecroppin' –*

*we so-called get emancipated, don't have anywhere else to go, we sharecrop. We do the same thing today; no matter how many degrees you've got, no matter how much skill you have, ultimately speaking, most black people want to do nothing more than sharecrop. That's what we're talking about here; people who want a career at the expense of themselves. They won't take a stand on any issues. They might sit around in a bar and tell a few people, 'yeah, I got sexually harassed,' and then therapeutically purge themselves of the responsibility of **acting.***

But I'm talking about movements start because people care enough, to a great degree. There is a direct correlation between how much you care about something and how far you take it. And also, the immediacy with which you act. You ain't gonna sit around here waitin' no ten years talkin' about, 'well, my kid got killed,' so I'll wait ten years before I address the issue? It's the same way with me: when I see something, an injustice being committed, I don't just take that one individual case, I elevate that case to the level of social observance. And then, let the principle stand on its own.

Cynthia:
*Matthew, many people are now doing what Anita Hill did; they're working every day even though they know facing the best conditions. You know why? Because they gotta eat. Just like she had to eat; coming from **a family of thirteen.** What she saw in her job was a way to move up in the echelons. Despite your feelings on moving up and working for the white man, I strongly believe that she worked because she wanted to get ahead and pull her **family** up.*

Matthew:
Yeah, next time describe those echelons, because we know whose echelons she's moving up in, don't we. And I really appreciate you proving my point. 799-1668's the number. Good morning, you're on the air.

Caller #5:
Hello, Matthew? Keep up the good work. Maybe some of these black people will open up their eyes and understand what you're doing. It's all for a good cause. And I wanted to make a comment. They're talking about Miss Anita Hill and this other guy, why don't they talk about some of these pastors that's here seducing women right here in these churches, huh?

Matthew:
I agree.

Caller:
And it's not only them. There's a lot of innocent women out here that's being seduced by men that are in good positions, you know.

Matthew:
Okay, but we have to differentiate between seduction and harassment, although the way you described it at the end is harassment because they're in superior positions to them. Seduction is a two way process, you know you submit and you're seduced, it can be done between people on the same level. But when you get in a situation where somebody can use power over you, that's supposed to be what makes it harassment – although I can make the argument that the person whose being harassed has all the power.

*See, when white people sit around trying to dog us out all day long, when men attack women trying to get to them, that gives **you** the real power. Now you might not have the legislative recourse to get redress, but you have the power because you're the source of the attention. What I say is take that attention and turn it against the person who dogged you out in the first place, like I do the white man on a regular basis, see? That's what she should have done. You don't do it sittin' around in a bar talking about 'yeah, I got harassed' to your girlfriends. What you do is you take it, that attention you're getting on the individual level and you use it so that the person who harassed you will never harass anyone again. That's what she should have done. She didn't do it. That's my point. I believe she got harassed. But my point is that it must not have been very much harassment because she didn't act with **immediacy**, and she didn't act in a profound way where a lot of people could have benefited. That's my definition of what a person does when they get dogged.*

Caller:
I think you're right.

Cynthia:
*When someone gets **dogged,** they don't immediately look at what other people would look at. What happened to Anita Hill was this: she looked back at the situation, she realized that he was not in the position to have any type of dominance over her career, so then she made a decision to go ahead and press charges against him. I don't understand how come anybody can't get the meaning in this. What she was saying was 'look, this man hurt me, I'm gonna get him back.' Everybody looked at him and said, 'oh, she's hurting his career.' She put everything on the line. Matthew made a comment in his column about how she's*

going to be able to write books and she's going to go here. Who controls all that? This is a male-dominated world, and after she stood out there to get lynched, I doubt if they're going to come back and ask her to write a book or get hired or anything like that.

And another comment about the brothers, the so-called brothers. They sit up here and they made her look like nothing. And you talk about going to a white man and telling him 'I got sexually harassed' **when your own brothers** *won't even believe it's harassment. The comments I heard from a lot of men were, 'Well you know, black women are used to hearing that type thing, so I don't see why she had to dog out another brother'. They didn't even look at Clarence Thomas: he's not a real brother. His income is not going to go to help the black community. So I don't* **even** *understand that position.*

Matthew:
Yeah, a UWM student defining what's a real brother and what's not. But here's my point: my point is that you're not dealing with the reality of the situation, you're dealing with your own imposed reality of it. Now we've already made it clear – you're talking about her putting her career on the line. She waits ten years when she's **tenured.** *Do you know what tenure is? Tenure means its very difficult to get fired. So you wait 'till you're safe – see, that's what the problem is with black people now: we wanna wait until we're safe and distant before we start caring about other people. What she should have done is done it then. In fact, I can make the argument that the time and the conditions were* **more** *conducive then dealing with sexual harassment than now. Because we're talking about 1981 – we're talking about a time period when black people were at least trying to do something in the area of Civil Rights. Not any more. We're talking about the first year under Reagan. We're talking about black people all across the country resisting Reaganism. So she was in a perfect situation to do something then. Now, you can say that, you know, 'she had to have a job, and she had to eat,' but I'll say this; in the final analysis, its what you do in your* **daily life** *that defines and demonstrates your real views and values. Your daily life, not a life ten years after you feel safe, not upon making sure everything is cool with you and then all of a sudden you lash out or strike out when somebody's going to do something that has a lot of visibility and notoriety attached to it. It's what you do in your* **daily** *life. And what I see this woman doing is more or less benefiting from a lot of what Thomas has done, including jobs, follows him all over the universe,* **then ten years after the fact** *she all of a sudden wants to become some kind of a Civil Rights hero and say, 'look, this stuff that he did hurt me.' Well I figure it like this: if it hurt a lot, she should have responded in kind, the way somebody does when they get hurt a lot. With*

*immediacy, all deliberate speed, and with a great deal of intensity and public support, which she would have had during that time period – as a matter of fact, she would had even **more** support being only 24 then, because she would have been young, hadn't entered the workplace, took on a monolith – she would have had even more support. Now.*

Cynthia:
Obviously this shows, Matthew, that you don't know anything about being a black female.

Matthew:
Right! (laughter)

Cynthia:
*I just want to say that ten years ago, it would have been no better for her than now. Men still felt the same way they did then, and the Reagan administration was just starting out, it was more unsure for her. It wasn't weak, it was stronger than ever. People were on their way to vote for a new administration that would **dog black people.** So it was stronger than ever. So what was she going to do, stand up and make some charges about it? I'll tell you one thing, you think its easy to prove a sexual harassment case, just go down here to the EEOC and see how it is to prove a **racial** case, let alone sexual harassment. Anita Hill – I'm **very proud** that ten years later that she went up and talked about this. I'll tell you why. Because I know **lots of blacks** who ten years later, once they get comfortable, they forget that they're black, or they forget that they're female, they forget what they are. She put herself on the line and she went out there and said something for all women, which she didn't have to do. Look at Clarence Thomas: once he got a comfortable position, what did he do? **He dogged all black people.** If you don't believe me brothers, when you're driving down in your car and the cops ask you to look in the trunk, you say 'thank you Mr. Thomas,' because he supported that bill, the Privacy Act.*

Matthew:
Inaccurate information about the Reagan administration, though. In its embryonic beginnings, we were just getting out of the Carter situation so it would have been a lot safer. Reagan didn't have his program until like, startin' in '82 onward. Right now it's rockstrong. The idea coming forth now, as a matter of fact, really works in Thomas' favor. The idea is make it appear as if this society cares about women. Have a mock forum – I knew he was going to be confirmed. The idea is she helped his confirmation. The implication by coming forward anyway, assumes that the

*white man has the kind of understanding and **compassion** for women that will enable her case to be heard and Thomas to be voted out. You guys believed in him; you guys thought the white man really cared; you guys thought he was going to vote for Anita Hill, she got her day in court, and America was going to be one big happy family. Wrong, as usual. Good morning, you're on the air.*

Caller #6:
Yes, I'd just like to say to the sister that's in the studio with you I mean, I'm listening to everything that she's saying and she said that ten years if Anita had spoken up, it wouldn't have done her any good. I think it would have done her a lot of good, because I know what it is to be sexually harassed, okay? If I had 'a waited ten years to say 'this man did this to me,' or 'this man did that to me,' what good would it have done me? I mean they would have never caught him because first of all, I probably never would have seen the man again. I mean, for her to get up there and wait ten whole years, I mean, after ten years a wound heals. I mean, she can't still be hurtin' because he raped her, if he did. Okay. I think it's because she can't hang around with him any more. I mean he dumped her, I'm not just saying for a white woman, it could have been a black woman, okay. So jealousy over a white woman is really not the issue, I mean as far as I'm concerned. This could have been a black woman, but the simple fact that Clarence didn't want to have anything else to do with her. She could have spoken out. I mean, this lady in the studio, said I'm proud of her because she stood up, but she waited too late to stand up. Because she just could have sat down, you know. She waited too long to stand up.

Cynthia:
You're sadly mistaken if you think that five years ago they would have treated her any different. Everybody's talking about this time factor. Think about it. Ten years ago? It wouldn't have made a difference if she came up three years later. Men felt the way they're going to feel about her. And the only difference it's made now is probably about five or six years ago, black men felt a little more compatible to us. But ten years later we're seeing the strain in our relationships. That's the only difference.

Matthew:
Yeah. Anyway, 799-1668's the number. You're on the air. Good morning.

Caller #7:
Yes good morning. I'm calling to give my opinion. I have been looking at this Anita Hill thing and Clarence Thomas, and this thing goes way back and it's time for

black women to stop using excuses, just like black men. We're going back to the same old thing. And it's time to get up and face reality and do what's right.

Matthew:
Thanks for the general truisms. But anyway, we have some more callers. Hope you call again.

Caller:
Yeah.

Matthew:
799-1668's the number. Let's shift gears a little bit and talk about the two of them, the relationship between Thomas and Hill. What are your views on that? Was there a relationship there? What is your theory behind this relationship with the EEOC and later at the Department of Education? Do you have a theory on that?

Cynthia:
*I do. I believe that he seen a young, pretty attractive woman and he used his position to try to date her. But she found him unattractive, and she didn't want to date him. He kept pressuring her. I think that the women who were in the office who said that he didn't treat her any different than he treated them **contradicted** themselves, because the lady at the end said that she acted above that, and she acted like she was better than them. He tried to date her, when she turned him down, I think that he later went to white women.*

Matthew:
So then, him coming over to her house and stuff like that, that was just strictly business, and him fixing her stereo, that was just strictly business?

Cynthia:
I can believe that.

Matthew:
And I can believe that a meteor's going to smash into the station any minute now, so everybody duck! 799-1668's the number. You're on the air.

Caller #7:
Good morning. Anita Hill and Thomas got trapped. They found two black people trying to play the white man's game, beat him at his own game, and lost. And, it's not important who told the truth, the important thing is that you can't play the

white man's game and hope to win. You have to play your own game and keep your own identity. They played the white man's game, tried to lose their own identity and they ran into a buzz saw.

Matthew:
Okay, thank you for the call. Appreciate your comments. You're on the air.

Caller #8:
Hi, I think their relationship just went bad, and I think there was something going on there and someone got hurt in the process. So someone went to tell ....

Matthew:
Thanks for the call. Also, the caller before, though, that's the point I've been trying to make at least as far as the whole idea of – it's like two pit bulls fighting, it's like the old days of the gladiators, these two black people vying for top dogsmanship in somebody else's system. So it's like the brother said, it doesn't matter who told the truth because the truth is still a lie because of what the truth leads to. On the one hand it leads to somebody black getting into a white Supreme Court, where there will be a black body there but very little viability. On the other hand, on the other side of the truth, this person got sexually harassed at a job where both of them were working at a department whose very existence proves racism is a key factor. There would be no need for the EEOC if there wasn't racism in America. So, like the brother said, it's like two rats on a cylinder: movin' but no going anyplace. Good morning, you're on the air.

Caller #9:
*Hi, first of all I would like to say that she, she kept in contact with him over ten years, she's the one who kept in contact, or records **show** that she did, they didn't show that **he** kept in contact with her. And then if, if she – hold on, I'm nervous now – she's just gonna say its her word against his, if she was that smart, the woman graduated from Yale with honors, to me you think she would have had documents, she would have had videotapes, recorded tapes of him doing this. I mean, I'm not that smart, but I would have thought that much to at least blackmail the brother!*

Matthew:
(laughter) Good point!

Caller:

I would a' had me five thousand every month, I could even pull the tape, when he got ready to marry the white woman, he could've had her, but he still would have been paying me (laughter). Thanks a lot.

Matthew:
I agree.

Cynthia:
*I don't agree because even if she **had** came up and spoke about it ten years ago, no one would have believed her, so why should you tape – and let's face it, most of the sexual harassment things that she talked about, how you gonna videotape right quick of someone touching you or holding you or someone saying something to you? That's very hard to do. This is the same thing they ask you to do when you have housing discrimination laws, they ask you to go back and ask the person – she has to prove that he did it. And that's very hard to do. I mean, I know women out there right now who can't prove that someone's sexually harassing them, but they are harassing them and for us to always have to prove that someone is sexually harassing us is sexist within itself!*

Matthew:
Yeah. Okay, 799-1668's the number. You're on the air.

Caller #9 again:
It's me again, and like I'm saying this chick could've got a camera, they make cameras to put in a pen tip, and she had money, she could afford these things …

Matthew:
And tape recorders as well.

Caller:
And so, I mean if she really wanted to get him, and she was that worried about some harassment honey, and if he harassed her that much, then she would have done something ten years ago, whether it was then, twenty, thirty, if you hurt, you hurt now and you fight back …

Matthew:
That's right, and when he came …

Caller:

.. you just don't wait ten years, you just don't wait ten years for something like that.

Matthew:
I agree with you. Thanks for the call. And when he came to the apartment to fix the stereo, that was a perfect situation to set him up in. You know something about that, don't you? 799-1668, you're on the air.

Caller #10:
Yes, I'm sitting here and I'm listening to all this, about time, about whether he raped her or whether he didn't, whether or not she's jealous over him marrying a white woman or not, I mean, it's so many issues here. But I really think that for a person to hold a grudge against another person, because – what I see is forgive and forget. She had power, just like he did – it may not have been as much. She had money just like he did – it may not have been as much. I think what she should have done after ten years is just went on about her life and not try to bring this brother down, whether he raped her or not, because she didn't holler out 'help' when he was raping her, so obviously, he didn't rape her, okay? But I think she should just go somewhere, assume her career, you know, do whatever she's doing, and let bygones – I think she should have just let it go because after ten years, I mean, it would be just like the boy that cried wolf, and then everybody's running out and then there's no wolf. And then when the wolf comes out, he cries wolf, and nobody wants to hear it. So that's what it sounds like to me.

Cynthia:
*Let me tell you, now this is how far it can go. Now this is to believe that she was raped, and she would let **that** go. You see, black women have problems accepting power over their lives. Now why should she let it go? She's the person being hurt, he should have stopped it. She's the one who has to prove herself **all the time.** And I think that if you don't believe – what I call this is the new assault on black women. If you don't believe it, if you listen to an Arsenio Hall show at night, if he describes the ugliest woman he can describe, you can believe she has black features. You better believe that the Bulls basketball team has women who almost look like they're white. It's the new assault on black women, and if you don't believe it, you better listen to the media or look at the videos. And a lot of brothers out there are saying, 'well, she shouldn't have said this,' or 'she should have kept – what about your allegiance to us? **Black women are always responsible for keeping the black race together.** When are black men going to be responsible for doing the same?*

Matthew:
Well first of all, your point about the new assault on black women, its not a new one. But the idea is, I agree with you one hundred percent, that's why I believe that if you get assaulted, you do to the assaulter what they did to you. Thank you for proving my point again. 799-1668, you're on the air.

Caller #11:
Hello, Matthew.

Matthew:
Good morning.

Caller:
*Hi, I want to make a comment on the sister that called earlier about the cameras and everything. Now, if Anita Hill was assuming that he was sexually harassing her, and this was going on, she could have planted videotape or a microphone or whatever. And another thing, when she was saying that he was making these comments to her, now this was going on for some time. Don't you give a person some kind of indication that it's okay to talk to you that way? If you do, they'll keep talking to you, if you don't, then they'll say, 'okay well cool, I can't talk to her like that.' So I gather that she gave him some kind of indication that it was okay to talk to me like that. First of all, we don't know if she was talking to **him** like that, we don't know what was going on. All we know is what the people are saying in the media, we don't know what was going on. They could have had something going on all along. So, I don't agree with nothing the lady in the studio is saying because I feel **she** has an identity problem **herself.** Thank you.*

Matthew:
*Well, thanks for the call, but let me give you an example. About a year and a half ago, this cop busted this 17-year-old kid in this bar out here. She was probably fine, and I don't know what happened, but he kept meeting with her. SO what happened was she went to the police chief and set him up. They gave her a fake house on the east side, the brother came in with some tequila and some coke to give to her, the cops were hiding in the closet, she gave them a code word, and they came out and busted this guy. This was a 17-year-old girl, in this city, who felt – now that's taking your life in your hands taking on a cop. See? Now, I know that if this could be done on that kind of a level, it could have been done then. And with the benefit of superior resources, a lauded background, and certainly – if nothing else, she could have went to **Thomas'** boss, she could have went to somebody **external** to the agency; she was right in the same area as the FBI; they could have*

*rigged it and set him up if she really wanted to do something. She didn't want to do the right thing. There's a difference between wanting to do the **right** thing ten years after the fact and seeking an opportunity at the time of the commission of the act and then remedying the situation so that everybody benefits. Oh, I think we have a call, don't we? You're on the air.*

Caller #12:
*Uh yes, Matthew I want to ask you a question. The lady that's in the studio with you, is she good looking or what? Because she keeps harping on this **'ugly'** thing.*

Matthew:
Well, she's pretty but she has low self-esteem (laughter). Okay! Okay!

Caller:
*Nobody's saying that Anita is ugly. I mean, everytime somebody calls in and says that she was jealous because he married a white woman, she assumes that they're calling Anita ugly. Nobody's calling her ugly. I mean, we're just saying that, I mean, like the lady who called in and said about crying wolf, if you're going to cry wolf, make sure there's a wolf there before you cry. And when you see the wolf, **then** you cry. Don't wait 'til later to say, 'wolf'.*

Matthew:
I agree with you. Appreciate the call. You're on the air.

Caller #13:
Yeah, I'm back again. I just wanna say that black women never had anything to say about sexual harassment until the white women started talking about it, and these white women are unhappy with their marriages, they're unhappy with their own identity, and so if a man says 'good morning' to them, they get upset and say, 'you sexually harassed me.' Black women who want to be white and want to take on that system they holler sexual harassment, the same way as their white sisters. So that's what Anita Hill did, and shame shame on her! She got what she deserved.

Cynthia:
*Here we go again, another black man saying, 'well you should never yell sexual harassment because black women should be used to men talking to them that way.' Why don't they try giving us the same respect that they **so willingly** give to white women? And about the sister who said I have a problem with my identity, I know who I am. I'm a black woman who doesn't have to be swayed by the fact that men are making the decisions. If Anita Hill had went running from office to office, you*

know who she would have found at the other end? White men. And then probably some kiss-ass black man.

Matthew:
Well according to you, that's what Thomas is.

Cynthia:
That's true.

Matthew:
Well then, she's damned if she does, and damned if she doesn't?

Cynthia:
I don't believe it's damned if you do, damned if you don't. The thing is is that she operated off of principle. She went ten years later and she told everybody what happened to her. There are women right now who have been dealing with this for twenty years and won't get up and do the same thing.

Matthew:
If you have principles, you don't delay acting upon those principles, you act immediately.

Cynthia:
She did act immediately. She told people around her. She had her witnesses up there. She had her witnesses, but nobody believed her witnesses because they didn't come out yelling.

Matthew:
Well, you can take the side of the issue that you choose to take the side of. We ran out of time, it was a great show, of course. Cynthia Jackson is a student at the University of Wisconsin-Milwaukee, and she'll be joining me again in the studio in a couple of weeks and we'll be dealing with another important issue that I'm sure will pique your interest.

Now, whatever side you come down on as far as the Thomas situation goes, one thing is clear: black people, again, played moral conscience to America. Now people talk about sexual harassment in the workplace, there are people coming forward now. Black people had to do it. My position is this: every sickness ain't death, every goodbye ain't gone, and every big man ain't strong. So when you get dogged in the workplace, what you wanna try to do is to affect as many people's *lives as you can **then**. You don't wait, down the road, and then talk about moral principle all of a sudden. If Black people like King and Malcolm would have had that **delayed** moral principle reaction, we'd be still in the days of slavery, institutionalized slavery at that.*

I'd like to thank Cynthia for coming on the show this morning, and we'll be back again next Friday with another edition of "The Matthew Stelly Talk Show." Bye.

LETTER TO OMAHA CHAMBER OF COMMERCE: NOVEMBER, 2001

Ten years later, almost to the date.

As if I didn't have enough to worry about, the Greater Omaha Chamber of Commerce decides that they want to bring that Uncle Tom motherfucker Supreme Court Justice Clarence Thomas to town. Well, this is one brother who wasn't going for that.

So I sat down and wrote a letter to the president of the Chamber of Commerce in an effort to explain what was going on and why he was making a major mistake:

Dr. Lou Berger, Chairman
Greater Omaha Chamber of Commerce
1301 Harney Street
Omaha, Nebraska 68102

November 18, 2001

Dear Dr. Berger:

Although you have been in office less than three months since the retirement of former chairman Bob "Methusalah" Bell, you have already committed a mistake that the former chairman would NEVER have made: displayed a blatant hatred and disregard for black people such as that displayed in your decision to bring Clarence Thomas to speak at your Annual Banquet.

Following is information on: (1) Why you should NEVER bring this conservative curmudgeon to Omaha; (2) an overview of the "Negroes" on your board who obviously agreed with the decision and (3) what I plan to do to make your decision one that Omaha will remember for a l-o-o-o-o-o-ng time.

Clarence Thomas: The 'Wallace' of the New Millennium?

In case you don't know it, the riot of 1968 that took place here in Omaha was started because racist right-winger George Wallace of Alabama was running for President and came to Omaha. He and his cronies staged a speech at the Civic Auditorium and then, with the help of the Omaha Police Division, instigated a riot which made national news.

I mention this because although Thomas is black in hue, he could not be more white if someone dumped his fat ass into a vat of acid. Like Wallace, his visit is political, comes at a time when Omaha is at its racial nadir, and paves the way for even more tension because of the simmering passions because of the police auditor position. You should come to grips with the fact that black people all over the nation harbor a great deal of disdain that black people have for Thomas. And this disdain goes beyond opposition to his political views; it goes to his arrogance and his deceit by claiming that he got where he is WITHOUT affirmative action. Not only is that an absurd lie (since he was, at one time, chair of the Equal Opportunity Commission), but he now votes AGAINST these kinds of programs now that he is seated in a position that he cannot be fired from.

It was called "the charade in September" – oh, don't you remember? The year was 1991 and at the time, I was the editor of the Milwaukee Courier newspaper. As a black editor, I joined more than 200 other blacks around the country who took turns lambasting this caricature that white folks seemed to love so much. We watched as he lied on Anita Hill after trying to sneak through without admitting that he stalked her. And don't forget there was another woman – Angela D. Wright (assistant editor of the Charlotte Oberver) who said Thomas pressured her for dates, asked the size of her breasts and appeared at her Washington apartment one night, unannounced and uninvited.
We watched as he paraded his white wife, Virginia, to hearings, proving that there were no black folks in his inner circle: his friends were all white, and he turned his back on his own family, bonding with white nuns and then never looking back. And white people, being as naïve as they are, sat back and listened as he talked of being a victim of a "hi-tech lynching."

In October of that same year, after 100 days -- Thomas was confirmed by a 52-48 margin (one of the thinnest margins of victory in court history) -- USA Today conducted a survey that was reprinted in the October 1991 issue of Black Enterprise magazine. In response to the question, "Does Clarence Thomas Reflect the Views of Most Blacks?" 52% of those questioned said "no;" 24% answered "yes," and 24% answered "don't know." In November of 1993, Emerge magazine charged that Thomas was "betraying the nation's African American population" and claimed that, "Thomas has voted against minorities every time."

Since I have two Master's degrees and one of them is in political science, the "brothers" who sit on your board might want to remember that a former Supreme Court Justice, Hugo Black, was a one time Klansman, but ended up one of the nation's most liberal justices. Many blacks felt Thomas could be converted, that once on the Supreme Court, he would change. Put it this way: Thomas changed for the worst – he is a follower of Antonin Scalia, the "Italian" justice – and Scalia HATES black folks. Do some research and you'll see what I mean.

The all-white, all-male United States Senate Judiciary Committee confirmed him after a public spectacle where even super-racist Strom Thurmond voted for Thomas. This is the man you wish to bring to a city that is already rife with racism, permeated with perversions of various kinds, and inundated with ignorance. The Chamber of Commerce is supposed to be about "elevation," not popularization.

And do not forget that the racist World Herald was right there, once again trying to define "de good nigrahs" from "those radicals." Here is what those Nazis with notebooks, those Klansmen with copy paper had to say about Thomas in their July 31, 1995 issue:

Thomas is a reasonable man who has questioned and revised some of the convictions of his younger days (sic). That doesn't make him an Uncle Tom. On the contrary, it puts him in good historical company (sic) (p. 6).

What's "good" for the white goose ain't necessarily "good" for the black gander. Ultra-conservative, pro-Thomas columnist George F. Will proves my point and also proves the "good ol' nigrah" image that Thomas immediately reinforced once confirmed. Here is how Will showed how "worthy" Thomas was:

Three months after the failure of the smearing of Clarence Thomas, Justice Thomas has participated in a case that perfectly demonstrates why he deserved to be confirmed. The case involved an apparent injustice – an act of racial discrimination. But the court had the courage to let the injustice stand rather than resort to judicial overreaching. This is a story of the court to be judicial and self-denying rather than political and self-indulgent (Chicago Sun-Times, 2/2/92, p. 31).

Remember to tell the "coloreds" on the Board: "It is a wise warrior who acts with caution and discretion when an enemy throws bouquets in his direction."

What Thomas represented was a successful "check-mate" of the black community by then President George Bush, who USED Thomas' skin color as a shield.

"But We Have a Diverse Board ..."

Diversity, as I have said throughout my presentations around the country, is a joke as long as the white man is in control. To you, diversity can range from a room of tanned and untanned white folks to a room with a few "negroes" in it. A "Negro" is someone that you've handpicked to represent "the nigrah point of view." And as it is with any endeavor where race is involved and whites are in a decisionmaking position, you fail in this selection as well.

Ten years ago almost to the day, and then you and your misguided cronies dig up those memories by inviting this "Gunga Din" to speak here in Omaha, a city already rife with racism that you ignore on a daily basis?

Since no one on your board, white or black, could carry my jock strap intellectually speaking, let me deal with Thomas and how he has impacted upon people with dark skin – like the ones you have on your Board. For the information of those reading this letter, those people are: Paul Bryant, Dick Davis, Michael Green, Johnny Rodgers, Jim Swoopes and Will Thompkins.

Let me extract two examples form my exhaustive file system. In one case called Presley v. Etowah County Commission, Thomas joined a 6-3 majority in allowing two Alabama counties to strip powers from black officials after their election. In Hudson v. McMillan, Thomas voted that prison abuse of a handcuffed black convict was not an Eighth Amendment (cruel and unusual punishment) issue. Oh, why was it raised? A black man was shackled and handcuffed in Louisiana and two prison guards punshed out his teeth, cracked a dental plate and left his face bruised and swollen. Keep that in mind next time one of you "brothers" is pulled over by one of these racist ass Omaha cops.

Do those selected to sit on the Chamber of Commerce represent the city of Omaha or black folks? I say the former. "Having lived someplace" means nothing unless you represent what the needs of the people are. Paul Bryant – I wrote his term papers for him thoughout his undergraduate and graduate work and I still retain copies of several of them. And we all know about the debacle when he tried to run against Senator Chambers after white folks – including some of your buddies at the Chamber – prodded and financed him into doing so.

Don't know much about Mike Green except that he's about as middle of the road as you can get. North Omaha gets no representation from him. Ditto for Dick Davis. Johnny Rodgers' claim to fame is that he played pro ball and bought attention to the NU program. What kind of inroads has he made for the Malcolm X Memorial Foundation – which I helped bring into fruition, by the way? Will Thompkins inherits a position from a man, George Dillard, who stole more than $60,000 from the Urban League. What will he do about THAT? Jim Swoopes is a good brother who always ends up working for some all-white institution that doesn't appreciate him. That says more about him than it does about white folks, however.

I don't need to lambaste these brothers to you, because you're white and you could care less. I just want you to understand that visibility is not necessarily viability. They might hail from North Omaha or party there, but look at the condition of it: what have they done for us LATELY? And the same goes for you and your jive-ass Chamber of Commerce: why would YOU want to bring a black man to a racist and segregated community, UNLESS that black man is more white, than black? Don't play stupid – you know what I mean.

Action vs. Rhetoric

I suggest, Dr. Berger, that you NOT bring Clarence Thomas to this city. Part of your Hippocratic Oath pledges you to "do no harm." Well, that doesn't just apply to the medical setting or the surgery table; it applies to the context under which people live, and you have to respect that context. Black people make up 1/5 of this city's population, and you need to be steering that Chamber in that direction – toward true urbanism, not continued "Roy Rogers-ism."
Since you probably think that this is some kind of bluff, let me now say that Triple One will extend its full resources, through both the Neighborhood Association and the Parents' Union, to expose the decision you and your board have made. We have contacts in the black media across the region, including the Chicago Tribune, the Kansas City Star-Times, the Denver Post and the St. Louis American. We will be putting the word out to make Thomas' stay here feel much longer than it really is.

We will be contacting other civil rights groups around the city, one of which you apparently already control, since its director is on your Board. But I will attempt to contact Bro. Thompkins (of the Urban League of Nebraska) anyway, because he can probably see the writing on the wall. And if he can't then I shall make it my personal responsibility to make sure that his constituents know about that shortcoming.

A series of community forums and debates will be sponsored where the topic will be, "Why is Clarence Thomas Coming to Omaha?" An integral part of those information sessions will be documention of how LITTLE the Chamber has done for North Omaha, and how LITTLE its leadership cares about black people in general.

Invite someone who reflects the silly, sectarian and racist interests of Omaha and your bourgeois board: perhaps Don Rickles or better yet, Antonin Scalia himself? Or perhaps invite one who best reflects the mentality of your constituency; perhaps Ronald McDonald, Barney the Dinosaur or a doctor, much like yourself – Dr. Seuss!!   You'll be hearing more from various community members regarding this horrible decision to bring Clarence Thomas to Omaha, in the days ahead. Of this I am most positive.

Stay tuned.

Sinceramente

Matthew C. Stelly, director

Cc: Clarence Thomas, Supreme Court
        Kweisi Mfume, National Director - NAACP
Omaha black leadership
Omaha black community
        Omaha media
        Others
        Files

Jesse Owens, Olympic Champion and Oreo (A Chapter-by-Chapter Assessment)(Formerly titled: "Coon in Cleats")

Preface

I have written hundreds of thousands of pages of analyses in my lifetime as a student, a journalist, an (national award winning) essayist, and race theorist. I have read the accommodationist and conservative writings of black people ranging from Booker T. Washington, Martin Luther King, Jr., and various bootlickers in Omaha, Nebraska, Milwaukee, Wisconsin and Dallas, Texas, to Armstrong Williams, Clarence Thomas, Shelby Steele, Ward Connerly and a host of other race traitors.

I have never read anything as mind numbingly "tommish" as Jesse Owens' book, *Blackthink: My Life as a Black Man and White Man*. What I have to say goes beyond mere intellectual differences, which he and I surely have. I was at the point after reading this book that I shook my head and concluded, "This nigga needs his black ass kicked."

I started to name this response to Owens' book "Spook in Spikes" or "Coon in Cleats." I also thought about "Treacherous Trackman" and "Bootlicker from the Boondocks." But I settled on the current title because Jesse Owens was like an Oreo cookie: black on the outside and white on the inside. This point will be proven throughout the pages of this book.

While there is no doubt that Owens was an Uncle Tom and sellout, he did not write Blackthink. The white man who gets co-authorship credit, Paul Neimark, was the writer. Owens almost admits it in the book and I will share that with you. You don't give someone co-authorship credit unless that person has made major contributions to the book that is being written in your name. The only reason Owens' name was placed first was because he was the one with the fame; Neimark was a professional writer and as such, had a lot to say about Jesse's views. As tommish as those views were, Neimark is still a white man first, and that is why Owens allowed him to be involved. Owens is the kind of nigga who seems to have always believed that the white man's ice is colder than any black man's ice.

Even the titles of each chapter sounds like something that only a sellout would write. Titles ranging from, "I Know the Troubles They've Seen," "But Equality Is Here," "Negroes Have Human Hang-ups" and "Blackthink Won't Win," to "Showcase the Good," "Black Man, Heal Thyself" and "We Shall Overcome – If." He is making excuses to the white man for the protests of young blacks, he blames black people for problems "making it" and he attempts to absolve the white man of the racist system that he has created. Owens, like Harry Edwards once said, "is a bootlicking Uncle Tom."

He offers case study after case study, example upon example of black being fucked up or having "changed" after the white man came along and rescued them. He praises Martin Luther King, Jr. but only has negatives to offer the brothers from the 1960s that scared whitey into giving Owens what little he was able to get before he died. He doesn't know shit about black women and his favorite reference materials are from peckerwoods and novels.

And there's a good reason for that: he didn't write the book by himself. He explains this toward the end of the book:

> You probably noticed another by-line on this book in addition o
> mine. It's the name of the writer I've worked with for over ten
> years, the fellow who helps make my thoughts into words. He's
> often pretty militant, but I've been able to work with him for that
> long a time and forge a closer friendship year after year because
> he's more free of prejudice than just about any white man I've ever
> known. But he's still bigoted as hell sometimes. And he knows it
> (pp. 164-165).

In my book, Jesse Owens allowed his white "co-writer," Paulo Neimark, to help him put this bullshit on paper. And he had thought about it. Here's how he explains it on page 22:

> If I had to sum up what I'm going to try and say here, it's that.
> people have been after me to write this book for quite a while. I've
> wanted to. A number of times I stated putting my notes together.
> But then I became dissatisfied, felt I needed more time to polish
> certain thoughts, just as I always used to tell my coaches how I
> needed "one more practice race before I'm read." Life doesn't give
> you all the practices races you need, though. Not long ago I
> became very ill, as sick as I'd ever been in the little room in
> Oakville I shared with my six brothers and sisters. I began
> *Blackthink* for good after that.

I believe that like most athletes of that time, Jesse was barely literature. He could function well enough, but not well enough to write a book and use the types of words that appear throughout. He's just not that smart. Not that the white man is much smarter; but the white man had a plan and a vision about where he wanted that book to take the reader. And the words are those of a black man who is so confused and fucked up, he titles the book, "My Life as a Black Man and White Man." Jesse has never been white physically; that would have been a dream come true. What we can draw from that title is that he may have been black *physically*, but *mentally*, he was definitely a peckerwood.

And who is the book dedicated to? Not his wife or family. Not another black person. It's dedicated to, "To a young man whose color I do not know." What? That sounds just like something one of those self-appointed white liberals would attempt to pawn off as a compliment. I f you don't see another person's color that is a bias in itself! That means that all you can see that person as is as a fellow white person no matter what his color is! This is an act of racism!

Most of the negative quotes in the book have to do with black men who are conscious, who Owens' refers to as blackthinkers. The profound, deep thought come from quotes from peckerwoods, dead as well as alive. His selections for pre-chapter quotes, his on-going references to white writers and their books (which I don't believe he could have possibly read –but Niemark may have), and the statements he made which challenge his own humanity and manhood, are the marks of a straight up bootlicker, a water carrier – a Gunga Din. Even the black people who he holds most dear, from Willie Mays and Joe Louis to Martin Luther King and others, are black men who kowtow to white people.

So since Jesse Owens is now long dead (he already was mentally and spiritually when he was alive), I will dish out that much needed ass whipping post-mortem using logic, intellect, facts, history – and his own words (and those I believe were put in his mouth by co-writer Paul Niemark). And there is a final note I'd like to share with you, the reader.

On page 173 he writes,

> Well, I'll tell you something: I don't even think most negroes have
> been getting the message. That was my first purpose in writing
> Blackthink – not only to help the white man know the Negro but,
> equally as important, to help the Negro to know himself (p. 173).

Jesse Owens was not qualified to do either. He wasn't the kind of black man who was intelligent or conscious enough to help any other black person do anything but learn how to kiss ass. And white people weren't going to listen to him: you can see that throughout the book they treated him like shit. He was in love with having white friends, but they only used him in return. From his coaches to Olympic competitor Luz Long – a Nazi – Jesse Owens wanted to be white but since he couldn't, he did the next best thing: worshipped and associated himself with them.

He's not finished. Also in the final chapter titled, "We Shall Overcome – If," he adds the following explanation as to why he bothered to write *Blackthink*:

> This was my second purpose in writing this book – *to drive the
> first real nail in the coffin of blackthink.* Oh, most people are
> against it, but they're unknowingly against blackthink on
> blackthink's terms, or on the old Establishment terms. For what
> blackthink is threatening to do, even to those who disagree with it,
> is to further alienate the Negro from the world in which he lives. I
> wanted, in an emotional way before any other, to help bring my
> people back to the human family – back to my other people, if you
> please. (p. 174 – emphasis added).

I have been a high quality (and high volume) writer for more than fifty years, for as long as I can remember. I wrote 20 page papers even in elementary school, and I've written plays. I've won two national essay competitions and my newsletter was recently (2016) selected as a finalist in the Neighborhoods USA competition. I have more than 200 manuscripts and over 2,400 articles in print. Therefore what I am about to say is being stated from a position of expertise.

I don't think Jesse Owens wrote this book. Don't get me wrong: I do believe he was an Uncle Tom and a big enough coon to believe in what appeared in the book. But there are too many slogans, phrases, psychological assessments and so on to make me think that this bumpkin could arrive at these conclusions and remain as invisible as he did. The fact is, I believe that the Jews were the driving force behind his ideas, behind the editing of the book and its final conclusion. This book was a message to black people to calm down and to turn away from black nationalist thought. It was a message that there is such a thing as "black bigotry" and that on every level, it is as negative and destructive as "white bigotry.

The book is an on-going litany of assumptions about what Owens calls "blackthink" (if he even coined the phrase) and the black men who stood strong against racism. While kissing Martin Luther King's ass – as most negroes do – he has nothing good to say about people like Stokely Carmichael, Rap Brown, Cassius Clay (Muhammad Ali) or any black men of relevance. He praises white people throughout the book and, by giving them the benefit of the doubt, he also manages to side-step racism and lay the concerns being shouted by black people to nothing more than low self-esteem and on-going scams.

When white people name a building after a black man, you know the black man is either (1) a super-tom who did their bidding, or (2) a black man so beloved by black people that white folks did it as a concession. Sometimes the two are one and the same. But when you see or hear the name "Jesse Owens" being bandied about and placed on buildings or streets or even gymnasiums or track stadiums (as in Lancaster, Texas), there is no doubt in this writer's mind that it is a tribute to one of the biggest Uncle Toms who ever drew breath.

One final point: back in 1990 when I was editor of The Milwaukee Courier newspaper, I received a copy of and reviewed a book by Shelby Steele titled, *The Content of Our Character*. As I wrote in my review, Steele was the biggest Uncle Tom that I had ever read the writings of. At that time. Since that time I have had the chance to read Jesse Owens' book, *Blackthink*, and I paraphrase the late Frederick Douglass:

> Go where you may, search where you will, roam through all the suburban neighborhoods, porn stores and segregated college campuses of America, , travel through the Deep South, Ferguson Missouri, L.A. New York or racist Texas, search out every lynching, cop killing and rape of a black woman that you can, and when you have found the last, lay your facts by the side of the everyday practices of this nation's white folks, and you will say with me, that, for revolting barbarity and shameless hypocrisy, America and its trained lapdog Jesse Owens, reign without rival.

With that having been shared, on the following pages I will prove that Jesse Owens was just that: a straight up Uncle Tom.

Introduction

A major motivating factor that pissed me off about Jesse Owens as a man and about *Blackthink* as a book is that this man makes the claim that "the race crisis" is not real. Let me share with you his exact words:

> But that doesn't mean there aren't some things that should be said,
> and that aren't being said, things that can show how "the race
> crisis" going on in America right now is for the most part the
> biggest hoax in our history. And possibly the cruelest – for in its
> seeds is another crisis of infinite proportions. Harry Edwards, my
> name is never been Tom. But I *am* old enough to be your uncle. I
> know the trouble you've seen. Now can I make you – and
> everyone – see that it's nothing, absolutely nothing, next to the
> trouble and your *blackthink* are about to make? (pp. 22-23 –
> emphasis original).

But not only is Owens an idiot, but he's also a liar. In the guise of case studies of people whose first names he uses, he sets up these racial situations and scenarios that he claims exist. Anyone with a brain could see that Owens is lying his horse-racing ass off . I will point these prevarications out as they appear in this book.

As if this is not enough, throughout the book, in an attempt to buttress his contention that most black people think the way he does (read: like sellouts), he quotes from and gives continual attribution to various white writers and scholars, quotes from white studies which were evidently biased in favor of quelling the racial tensions that permeated America at the time, and generally gives kudos and compliments to white folks in an attempt to show that when all is said and done, the white man is trying his garsh-darndest to help the poor negro people.

What a crock of shit.

Now would be a good time to introduce what might be called "The Process of Brainwashing and Negro Psychology as Employed By White Folks." The reason is that Jesse Owens is the type of black person that white folks would just love black youth to imitate. He is the kind of Uncle Tom that white folks feel comfortable with and enjoy being around. Owens was the prototype of what Malcolm X would call "the house nigger."

As evidence of this, just look at the embellishments that usually accompany the athletic accomplishments of Owens. There is no doubt that he was a great performer in track. But then white people begin adding to his accomplishments the kinds of political "accomplishments" that simply did not exist at that time and do not exist today. White Americans hated Hitler and the Nazis and that hatred leads them and their Jewish friends to never pass up a chance to make Hitler look like an asshole. From their one-sided movies and lie-filled books to TV shows like "Hogan's Heroes," Jews use the media and their white lackeys to make it appear as if America saved the world from "Aryan supremacy." But what they don't say is that it was replaced with a different from of white supremacy – this time America would be in charge.

Owens was a tool used to make it appear as if America was number one. All of a sudden a black man, one who wasn't allowed to eat in white restaurants back in the U.S.A., was an "American." They used Owens to "knock Hitler down a peg or two" and put a mark on his "white superiority" rhetoric.

Following are some of the historical statements that white folks cling to when it comes to Owens. Wikipedia, for one, offers the following:

> Jesse Owens
> Track and Field Athlete
> James Cleveland "Jesse" Owens was an American track and field athlete and four-time Olympic gold medalist. Owens specialized in the sprints and the long jump and was recognized in his lifetime as "perhaps the greatest and most famous athlete in track and field history". His achievement of setting three world records and tying
>
> …

Take note that he was "recognized in his lifetime" as "perhaps" the greatest and most famous athlete in track and field history." But again, they don't tell the entire truth: if he was so great and famous, why did white people in America treat him like shit? Why did he end up having to run against horses to promote baseball? Why wasn't he given money and a major job with an American corporation the way they do marginal white athletes? Because of white racism, that's why. And while a black man can be accepted as a "gladiator," to white folks, "a nigger is still a nigger." What you read above is called lying by omission.

But there's more:

> His achievement of setting three world records and tying another in less than an hour at the 1935 Big Ten track meet in Ann Arbor, Michigan, has been called "the greatest 45 minutes ever in sport" and has never been equaled. At the 1936 Summer Olympics in Berlin, Germany, Owens won international fame with four gold medals: 100 meters, 200 meters, long jump, and 4 × 100 meter relay. He was the most successful athlete at the games and as such has been credited with "single-handedly crush[ing] Hitler's myth of Aryan supremacy" (Wikipedia, 2016).

There are a number of important race- and politically-based points that should be made here before we can move on. In other words, this is a teaching moment with focus on the previous excerpt.

To begin with, who were the people who called what Owens did "the greatest 45 minutes ever in sport"? Don't they mean perhaps the "greatest individual accomplishment ever in sport"? Maybe that would make more sense. Because track is a bullshit sport and the Olympics only come every four years.

Therefore, when it comes to "sports" you would have to include professional sports, and I can name a number of events that had 455 minutes that were far greater (at least to me) than some coon running and jumping on behalf of the United States.

Secondly, it may not have "been equaled" during the time it was done, but it certainly has been equaled –and surpassed – since that time. I would say that the accomplishments of Mark Spitz, Carl Lewis and Michael Phelps were more rewarded and therefore reflect more greatness. And if you add up the collective time of their accomplishments, they don't even take twenty minutes, let alone 45!

Third, the reason why such statements are made: again, go back to where the Olympics took place and who was the host. Jews were calling the shots behind the scenes and they were the primary focus of Hitler's hatred. Therefore it only stands to reason that anyone who could make Hitler look like an asshole would be able to curry favor with the Jews in particular and white folks in general.

Fourth, and finally the biggest lie of all is where the passage makes the claim that Owens "has been credited with single-handedly crush[ing] Hitler's myth of Aryan Supremacy." How could that be? If it's a "myth," then it cannot be crushed with a single act. Just because I tell a room of kids that Santa Claus is a white muthafucka who is guilty of theft doesn't destroy or hurt that myth one little bit. And Aryan supremacy is nothing but a subset of white supremacy and even though it's a myth, it is one that is well-publicized, widely held, and backed with Jewish-led propaganda machinery. One black man with speed and hops could not possibly crush the myth of Aryan supremacy.

This "introduction" then, paves the way for the racial politics involved with the book *Blackthink,* but more importantly, provides us with the chance to explain the difference between the thinking of an Uncle Tom like Jesse Owens and the thinking of ordinary black folk. This is not to say that the majority of black people are not Uncle Toms because in my view, based on what is being said and done today in 2016, I believe that they are. But there remains a difference even in that, and in the self-negating thinking of Jesse Owens.

Let me say that *Blackthink* is no autobiography (that would be written 10 years later in 1978 with the same peckerwood under the title, *Jesse, a Spiritual Autobiography*) and then again in 2007 by a sister named Jacqueline Edmondson, *Jesse Owens: A Biography*. The latter is a little 136 page book by a woman who is an Associate Professsor of Education at Pennsylvania State University. She's also written biographies of Condoleeeza Rice (2006) and Venus and Serena Williams (2005).

What I want the people reading this book to understand and remember – especially the young people – is that *you can be a great athlete and still be a piece of shit as a human being.* One need look no further than the likes of Terrell Owens,

Michael Jordan, Marion Jones, and others, all great in their own right but who are selfish sellouts who don't give a shit about anyone but themselves. Jesse Owens was one up on these people because he was also stupid – he loved the white man more than the white man loved himself.

With that having been said, let the lessons regarding the "politics of race" begin.

Confusion By Any Other Name: Quotes From Owens

In this section of the book I am going to offer some information that came from Jesse's own distended lips, thus providing the perfect contextual background for the Uncle Tomfoolery that you are going to find in the book Blackthink. This section includes some essential background and concludes with some selected quotes from Owens himself.

My concerns about Jesse Owens' anti-black consciousness attitude, which he has dubbed "blackthink" is partially linked to the fact that he should know better. He grew up poor and his father worked hard just like most other black fathers during his time. He therefore had to know what the source of their condition was: it was the white man. Check out what Jesse complains about as an adult:

> There were seven children for my mother to take care of (two had died) but she still hired out as a cleaning woman several hours a day. Even so, there were weeks when we came close to starving. Beans and onions. Potatoes and onions. Bread and onions. And never enough of them. Years passed, and the best my father could do was find a few weeks to temporary work here and there (p. 20).

His father did the best he could to raise Jesse right. He sure didn't raise him to kiss some white man's ass. And in fact, as you read the rest of his book, you will see where his father decided he wasn't going to take the abuse of sharecropping any longer and stood up to the white man who had ripped them off. That's more than Jesse ever did. And yet those who did stand up to the white man decades later – people like Harry Edwards, Tommy Smith and John Carlos – he puts them down throughout his book. He condemns "blackthink" and implies in his writing that white people are somehow in the same boat as we are.

That's not all. Throughout the book, as I will point out, Owens offers these "case studies" that consist of first name only people who he uses to make his respect points. But it is on page 56 of the book where he actually describes what I view as the uncle tom/sellout/defector prototype. Here is how he describes it:

> These blacks, fifteen million strong of them, are where it's really at
> with the negro people. The Richies and J.'s and Peters and their
> families are the silent black majority that has neither spoken nor
> been spoken for …

Who does Owens think he is? He knows nothing about the black population other than what the white man tells him. And that is another key point about the book: his white co-writer must have put ideas and words in Jesse's mouth and mind. Ideas like the one just quoted sound an awful lot like those white liberals who paint lies about black people, lies that make black people sound submissive, happy and complacent. *Lies that make white people feel safe.* And it's niggas like Jesse Owens who white people see as 'the perfect nigga.' Or, as the white man used to say back in the day, "An educated black man is a good field hand, spoiled."

So because he's an Uncle Tom he believes most blacks think the same way. As he puts it,

> I'm one of them. I've always been one. And I'll tell you two things
> about us. First, we don't' always agree with one another on what
> should be done about Vietnam, nuclear war, violence in the streets
> and all the rest. In fact, I am often as opposed to what our leading
> "moderates' have said as I'm against the rantings of Rap Brown,
> Jim Forman or Harry Edwards. But, second, not one of us, not a
> one, would any more riot, any more think of revolution, than we'd
> board a boat back to Africa because of what was done to our great-
> grandfathers (p. 56).

Jesse Owens is not a member of any group of black people except for those who we would classify as sick, sellout niggas. He was that way in the 1960s when black consciousness was at an all-time high. If you can tom in the 1960s surrounded by Afros, bubas and niggas speaking Swahili, then you have to be a super sell-out, plain and simple. But let's go over the previous paragraph so you can get the snippet of an idea of what a true race traitor sounds like.

He talks about not agreeing with what "moderates" say. There is nothing moderate about a white man. Oh, they talk a good game and some of them can even get to the point of "befriending" (read: "tolerating") black people. But when push comes to shove, a white man has a long history and it seems to be a part of his genetic code. Don't take my word for it: read Michael Bradley's The Iceman Inheritance or Dr. Frances Cress Welsing's "Cress Theory of Color Confrontation" and you'll get an idea of how deep their race hatred runs.

Moderate? These are terms that a white man – like Owens' "co-writer" would use. They put words in Owens mouth, ideas in his mind and beliefs in his value system. And that's why he grew up to be an Uncle Tom despite the trials and tribulations that his family went through. He is a race traitor. And the next tidbit from the previous quote bears me out.

He writes that, he is "against the rantings of Rap Brown, Jim Forman or Harry Edwards." Why does what the black man have to say have to be reduced to the level of a "rant"? Do you know what a "rant" is? It's a tirade or as Webster defines it, speak or shout at length in a wild, impassioned way." The English language is packed with synonyms for the word "speaking." Owens could have selected any of them. But along with his pal the white man, they intentionally make black speakers who confront the white man sound as if they are insane. This perpetuates the stereotype of "the crazy nigger" that so many white people believe truly exists and which is why they support police incursions into black communities. That is what "to protect and serve" has come to mean on the side of those police cars: to protect white people from niggas and to serve those same niggas up to the courts and the prisons!

Then, as if he speaks for all black people, take note of where Owens writes the following: "But, second, not one of us, not a one, would any more riot, any more think of revolution, than we'd board a boat back to Africa because of what was done to our great-grandfather." Owens is a lying sack of shit. Even as his book of drivel was being published, black people were kicking this white system that Owens loves so much all up in the ass.

Blackthink was published in 1968, although the William and Morrow version is dated 1970. But let's give Owens the benefit of the doubt in regard to black people not agreeing with revolutionary actions, returning to Africa or race riots. Really, asshole?

Well there was the Kent State shootings in May of 1970 when four kids were killed after the National Guard were called in. That led to a week of rioting. How about the Jackson State shootings a few weeks later where two black kids were killed. More riots. In 1971 the Wilmington riot took place and then there was Attica in September of that year where black inmates fucked up the prison so bad they had to drop tear gas on them and gun down a bunch. As I was discussing with my daughter most recently, the Symbionese Liberation Army shootout took place in May of 1971 and the cops massacred a group of black revolutionaries. That also led to riots in the Bay Area, and in 1973 the Native Americans confronted white boys up in Wounded Knee and that incident in South Dakota got national attention.

No riots Jesse? And I'm not even dealing with the riots of 1965 through 1969 where the REAL damage was laid out. Owens doesn't speak for black people because he cannot relate to us. He is a full-fledge member of the "I-Wanna-Be-A-Peckerwood" club and he died that way. They used him as an athlete, degraded him when he got back to the states, brought him up on tax evasion and he died penniless. Such is the fate of the bootlicker.

With that having been said, let's look at a few quotes from Owens which he had the gall to post prior to the introductory section of the book I am about to analyze. These eight (8) quotes speak volumes, but I will share them with you (his words are italicized), one-by-one, with my analyses of each one filtering in and out.

The only bond worth anything between human beings is their humanness.

What? Those "bonds" that Owens alleges exist are defined and determined by the people who make the rules, the ones who hold the power. Do you see any of them talking any shit about "humanness"? They are the ones who divided humanity into "Racial groupings" which, in turn, made it easier to rank and rate each group based on their closeness to how "white" they are (racially and mentally speaking). Furthermore, to talk about "any bond that is worth anything" is a preface to stupidity: who is he to define the one, sole "bond" that people should hold dear? Christians don't even agree with Bible principles; capitalists don't agree on the distribution of wealth principle; politicians have ideological differences.

Jesse Owens: you are an idiot.

Life doesn't give you all the practice races you need.

Practice races? This asshole has track and field on the brain! The "practice race" is how you fare in a race that has been defined by this system. This system has made education "Compulsory" and that is the race that everyone is forced to enter into . The ones who win are not the ones who come out like Jesse Owens: first place in the turd-eating contest. It's what you do with your education that elevates the race, helps the community and develops the nation. That's my definition – and I'm sticking to it.

We need to stop lining up and engaging in competition for the white man's enjoyment. We need to deal a hand of our own choosing since we know that muthafucka has stacked the deck. We need to stop dubbing those who graduate from college as "the best the race can produce." We need to stop acting as if whitey's game is the only game in town and develop a deck of cards and a hand of our own choosing. That's the kind of "practice" I'm talking about.

And finally, if "Practice might make perfect", as the maxim goes, it is my contention that you should approach life assuming that there will only be limited time to get practice in; so therefore be ready to kick ass at a moment's notice and after you've studied your opposition.

We all have dreams. But in order to make dreams come into reality, it takes an awful lot of determination, dedication, self-discipline, and effort.

This is a fact. But Owens' version is to aspire to be as much like white as possible. Nowhere in his book does he offer up a single idea that black youth can use as a basis for self-determination. Nowhere in his book does he talk about Black Studies, although the time period in which the book was published was the heyday of the advent of African-American studies all over America. All he does it pay homage to those civil rights coons who were so busy begging for integration that they allowed black women and children to be subjected to police dogs, fire hoses and beast-like cops.

The "determination, dedication, self-discipline and effort" have all been channeled into a little compartment that is known as "individualism." America has driven home a belief that being on your own, doing for self, fuck the group and get as much shit as you can for yourself are the only options. As a result individualism has become the order of the day. As Karenga (1967) wrote, "Individualism is a white desire, cooperation is a black need" and more importantly, "Individualism means being yourself at the expense of others."

If you don't try to win you might as well hold the Olympics in somebody's back yard.

What does he think the rotating sites for the Olympics is geared toward doing? After all, they are not held in America every year, are they? And not only that, but this nigga is comfortable in "somebody else's back yard;" on white campuses, in white corporate boardrooms selling out the race and so on. And it's not about "trying" to win; those who "try" in the Olympics don't get shit and are rarely heard from. If you win, you might be able to carve out a lifestyle – if you're a peckerwood or a black man who can box. Otherwise, you end up like Jesse Owens: competing against race horses and writing books so you can make an utter ass out of yourself.

A lifetime of training for just ten seconds.

If this is what your life has been focused on, you've got a fucked up life. And it is no wonder why this Uncle Tom ended up the way he did: dead and broke. Training to run a race for white entertainment and a few Olympic medals that couldn't even translate into cash? There are far too many athletes who have a philosophy like this, basketball players who "live for the game," football players who "eat and sleep football" and so on. That's why black women are dumping these niggas and engaging in lesbian behavior or going it alone.

The battles that count aren't the ones for gold medals. The struggles within yourself - the invisible, inevitable battles inside all of us - that's where it's at.

If he knows this, then why does he remain such a bootlicking Uncle Tom? Why does he come to such specious and spurious conclusions when it comes to issues of race? Everybody knows that the "battles that count" are not about gold medals – it seems that Jesse Owens is the only person stupid enough to even consider such an assumption. His self-struggles revolve around cognitive dissonance and personality disorder: that's why the sub-title of Blackthink is, "My Life as a Black Man and White Man." A more appropriate title would have been "My Rejection of My Life as a Negro and My Failure To Become a White Man."

One chance is all you need.

Bullshit. That's why life far too often comes down to "trial and error." To stumble is not to fall, but to go forward faster, as the African proverb teaches us. As the late painter and writer Walter Anderson once wrote, "Our lives improve only when we take chances and the first and most difficult risk we can take is to be honest with ourselves." Jesse Owens was therefore wrong on both counts.

For a time, at least, I was the most famous person in the entire world.

Bullshit. He might have been the most famous person in the world of SPORTS. But Jesse Owens was never the most famous person in the world. In America, he might have had a glint of fame, but it was short-lived as I will prove in the following analyses. If you were really the most famous person in the world, wouldn't you be able to market it in some way? Even Hitler, as notorious as he was, is still remembered to this day. Fame is based on what it is you are "excelling" in at the time. And even that Nazi asshole had a plan and tried to carry it out. And that is why he is remembered.

Who's going to remember a nigga that ran a sprint, held the broad jump record and won four gold medals? Nobody outside of the world of sports. And again, what took place is kept on the downlow because in order to deal truthfully with Jesse Owens' life, you have to talk about the white folks and the Jews that screwed over his family. And if you do that, the logical question would be, "what did Jesse do about it"? And the answer would be, "He didn't do a god damn thing."

Blackthink: My Life as a Black Man and White Man: A Chapter-by-Chapter Case Study

The chapter begins with a quote from "Harry Edwards, black militant" who would later Dr. Harry Edwards, a professor at the University of California at Berkeley, author of several scholarly books and respected contributor to black people and black thought. But at the time of Owens' book he is described as noted and the quote that is attributed to him is, "Jesse Owens is a bootlicking Uncle Tom!" In my viewer, *truer words were never spoken.*

And so it begins …Chapter 1 is titled,

<u>Chapter 1: I Know the Trouble They've Seen</u>

It is clear throughout this book, and particularly this chapter, that Jesse Owens doesn't understand race relations. Even during the tumult and turmoil of the 1960s, he remained a sellout and spokesman for white folks. Just like the Ward Connerlys, Shelby Steeles, Star Parkers, Clarence Thomases, Condoleezza Rices, Ben Carsons , Jesse Lee Pattersons and other sellouts of today, we've always had them in our ranks. As a Native American sister once told me, "On every plantation, there's a happy camper."

Owens saw and was a victim of racism and racial segregation. And he just didn't get it. This book shows that he appears to believe in the white man more than he believes him himself. For instance, the book opens with the following statement as he and another "negro" are driving on their way to a college track meet:

> The rest of the team, the white part, was traveling ahead in five other autos. Shinier ones. It had taken Dave Albritton and me two years to save the $32.50 for the Ford, a minor fortune to a couple of Negroes just a memory away from the nightmare of sharecropping in the South … (p. 11).

So Owens is willing to admit that there was a "white part" of the team? That means that he had to acknowledge that he and Albritton represented the "black part." And in all his racial blindness if he can admit that much, then he has to acknowledge not only the existence of racial segregation, but also the driving force behind it: white racism! In fact, without even mentioning the word "racism," he describes the symptoms of it as he shares the following:

> Dave and I had been able to run a little faster and jump a little
> better, so we'd gotten the jobs and the incredible chance to be the
> first members of our families to ever go past the beginning of high
> school, let alone to a genuine place of higher learning (pp. 11-12).

Run a little faster and jump a little higher. Ain't that just like a nigga? And then have the gall to brag about it without criticizing the fact that this is the only way a black man can get into college. And that seems to be the same way that this country is steering education today: on far too many of these elite college campuses, the majority of black people walking around them are athletes, male and female! In 1973, I was the first one in my family to ever go to college, so we're talking about a 40 year gap between Owens' reality and mine! Where are all these buttheads who are still walking around here talking about how race relations have gotten better and/or how racism has "subsided"?

Instead of addressing or dealing with the racial duality, this coon in cleats instead gives white people undeserved credit and then paints a picture that smacks of "black ingratitude:"

> There were no athletic scholarships at Ohio State University then,
> not even if your marks had been good, nor even if you'd learned
> how to use your legs to become "the world's fastest human" the
> year before. Today, a young Negro like Harry Edwards can climb
> out of the ghetto and go to a tuition-free university, become an
> articulate leader, and then use his articulation against those who
> taught him the words (p. 12).

So what if there were no athletic scholarships? You know what did exist? Niggas like Jesse Owens, people so starved for acceptance that they worked and sweated just so they could get on a campus where, as in outside life, they would be segregated. You had the black dorm and the white dorm; you had the table in the cafeteria where the black students sat and where the white students sat. And do you know what? This shit still exists on college campuses today, although white kids blame black students for "wanting to sit by themselves." I wonder why?

Owens, the spook in spikes, makes it look like Harry Edwards is somehow "ungrateful" or "wrong" in dogging out higher education. When Harry wrote books, he talked about racism and how black students were being maltreated. Look at their titles (and then read them!): *The Revolt of the Black Athlete* (1970*), Black Students* (1970), *The Struggle that Must Be: an Autobiography* (1980). He founded the Olympic Committee for Human Rights; he got his doctorate from Cornell University and then returned to Berkeley to teach. What did Jesse do? Do the accomplishments of Edwards sound like the actions or values of a black man who was biting the hand that fed him? He turned higher education on its year, got his credentials and continued to fight for the defense and development of black people.

Owens did *none* of this. All he can do is talk about "the good ol' days" and how his daddy worked so hard for this and toiled so hard for that. And believe me, Jesse had it hard: which is all the more reason why he should have been more committed to fighting for freedom for *others*!

Read on:

> Still, it was nothing compared to what it took for my father to get out of the South fifty years ago, Harry Edward and those like him didn't just leap out of their poverty and ignorance in one easy vault. You didn't wish yourself out of the East St. Louis jails where the Harry Edwardses finally landed because they couldn't stand drinking drainage ditch water and eating from white garbage cans, the jails where their brothers and friends still are. It took grit, the same kind of grit that was at work when harry later threw the discus almost two hundred feet for his school's record (p. 12).

There is no doubt that those who came before us were great men who were subjected to a great deal of degradation and racist action by white folks. Owens is not providing any new information here. But what he is trying to do is make it look like Harry Edwards was some kind of hardened criminal who stumbled onto the college campuses. He makes it appear as if Edwards was a jailbird. Let me stop and tell you, the reader, something right here: some of the most crooked, deceptive and evil-minded people I know have never spent a single night in jail. And on a more political level, those white Congressmen and Senators and Washington whose policies hurt so many people – they commit crimes, through policy and legislation, that are far worse than anything Harry Edwards could ever do.

What Owens has written above (with the help of his white "co-author") is paint a picture of having a monopoly on black oppression. Harry Owens, Jesse's father, was one of tens of thousands of black men who were forced into sharecropping in order to care for their families. I think it is disingenuous of this Uncle Tom to use his father as a barometer to compare with the black men that he considers to be "militants." Since he cannot compare himself without intelligent people dogging him, he chooses his father, he selects an entirely different time and context, a different set of conditions and then juxtaposes it with the most tumultuous era in American history as far as race is concerned.

And he's not finished:

> But when he shouts in one breath that every white man on earth is no good and in the next tacks up a picture of me on his wall with the words "Traitor of the Week," Harry Edwards is saying that the

> jails and alleys have claimed some important part of him – some
> organ of his soul, is the only way I can put it (p. 12).

That's not what Harry Edwards is saying at all. What he's saying is quite simple: the white man is a piece of shit and Jesse Owens, the white man's biggest supporter, is also a piece of shit by extension! It's very simple. This has nothing to do with Edwards having had some part of his soul taken; the fact of the matter is, by defending and developing his people, by becoming a part of and organizing groups that help black athletes and others, Edwards his showing that he still HAS a soul. On the other hand, it is clear that Jesse Owens sold his soul a long time ago.

Owens cannot speak for black people unless it's in the negative. When he does interject the variable of race, he wants to include peckerwoods and everyone else in his warped analyses. As he writes on page 12, "I'm not a great man. What I've done is no more than countless other Negroes (and Jews and Poles and Greeks and just Americans in general) have done" (p. 12). This nigga is wrong in so many ways. Let me share a few.

To begin with he is correct when he says that he is not a great man. He could not have been more correct. Just because you can jump and run (which a huge percentage of black men can do) doesn't make you great – not in the real world where people's lives are affected. Somewhere down the line Owens recognized this but instead of keeping his fuckin' mouth shut and being a quite Uncle Tom, he decides to act as if he's some kind of race relations expert or civil rights advocate.

Secondly, he shares that what he has done is no more than what countless others have done (you see he includes his white pals, the same ones that lynched black people in the South, harassed black families in the North, and passed and enforced racial segregation all over the nation – those so-called "white ethnics"). Again, he is correct. But as I point out, black people never oppressed any of those white "others" that he mentioned. They used their lack of skin color to join with the American white man to kill off Native Americans, exploit Chinese in the building of the railroads, run Mexicans out of the country and of course, import African slave labor. He includes the plight of the racial oppressor with that of the racially oppressed.

Third, by admitting that he had "done no more" than these groups, he still falls short of the facts: he hasn't done a god damn thing! Running a sprint and long jumping ain't gonna make a dent in the racism that permeated America at that time and continues on, unabated! Jesse Owens was just another nigga with speed as far as I'm concerned. And I haven't seen or heard about one yet that ended up being worth a shit as far as the struggle for human rights is concerned, and that includes Florence Griffith Joyner (with her fine, steroid takin' ass), Marion Jones, Carl Lewis, Usain Bolt, Jackie Joyner Kersee or any of them. They go to the Olympics, win some medals and then come back to the U.S. and move to a suburb where there are few if any, black people. Jesse Owens was among the first to pave the way for this wicked *modus vivendi.*

True idiocy raises hits head in the following statement by Owens:

> It had happened a hundred times, maybe a thousand. I lost count long ago. But I do remember riding in the Ford that day and not being able to keep down the bitterness that all Negroes had to be in one car. Not that it wasn't "natural" in a way. At the university all the negroes lived together in one old house. But was *that* natural? (p. 13 – emphasis original).

The gap between something happening "a hundred times" or "maybe a thousand times" is almost as large as the one between Owens' ears! But such a generic statement is an indicator and reflection of the lack of research and study that went into this book. He's not writing about himself: he's taking political, social and economic positions on the black condition which it is clear he is not qualified to do!

Another point is his reaction when he personally witnesses discrimination and/or abuse of black people. He calls it "keeping down the bitterness." Isn't this the problem with black people, both past and present? Do we not have a right to be bitter? Isn't it bitterness that can serve as the basis for both revolution and recovery? It was Frederick Nietzsche who wrote, "Growth in wisdom may be exactly measured by decrease in bitterness." So then, *an increase in bitterness* can be measured by the outright lack of wisdom in a person. A person like Jesse Owens, for instance.

Then, as evidence that this negro believes that black life is moot unless white people are somewhere around, he writes that, "At the university all the negroes lived together in one old house. But was *that* natural?" The implication of this statement and question is that whites and blacks living together IS the natural way. Is it? Where in society in the 1930s and 1940s did this black muthafucka see black people and white people living side by side? For that matter, there are few places TODAY where you can find it unless it's in some upscale community or some ghetto area where peckerwoods are filtering back in and taking over housing and taking over the neighborhood.

What is natural about "integration"? In order for me to truly drive home the point, let's go back five years from the time that Blackthink was published (1968) and deal with the March on Washington and a speech that Malcolm X gave after the March was over. The speech was given in 1965, and Malcolm links integration with civil rights, selling out, white fear of black people rioting, white media control and black leadership – just as I intend to do in this rebuttal to *Blackthink.* However, remember how Owens implied that black people living together was somehow not natural? Here comes a teaching moment. Bear with me.

The question in response to Owens and as information about "integration" is this: How did we (black people) get so brainwashed? To begin with, we were never "de-briefed" following four hundred years of enslavement. We were just "set loose" complete with that "slave mentality" that programmed us to believe that the white man's ice was colder than our ice. And there were other strategies and tactics that were employed, some of them outlined by Malcolm in the following passage:

> The slavemaster took Tom and dressed him well, and fed him well, and even gave him a little education -- a little education; gave him a long coat and a top hat and made all the other slaves look up to him. Then he used Tom to control them. The same strategy that was used in those days is used today, by the same white man. He takes a Negro, a so-called Negro, and make [sic] him prominent, build [sic] him up, publicize [sic] him, make [sic] him a celebrity. And then he becomes a spokesman for Negroes -- and a Negro leader.

Using "tom to control" the black masses continues to this very day in 2016, and as you can see so far, it surely worked on Jesse Owens. Although the "dress" may have been modified, the approach to using black people to do white folks' bidding is still alive and well. Making black people into celebrities is easy enough to do in this day and age of social media, and then, no matter how ill-informed, these celebrities – from actors and athletes to high profile black politicians – they become spokespersons for the people. We are the only racial group in this country who, when the issue becomes well known blacks, have athletes and actors at the top of the list.

Malcolm then gets personal with information that was once again left out of the "mainstream" history books (far too many of the quality publishing companies are run by Owen's white ethic pals) which emphasize glorification of integration, the civil rights movement in general and Dr. Martin Luther King, Jr., in particular:

> I would like to just mention just one other thing else quickly, and that is the method that the white man uses, how the white man uses these "big guns," or Negro leaders, against the black revolution. They are not a part of the Negro revolution. They are used against the Negro revolution.

Moreover,

> When Martin Luther King failed to desegregate Albany, Georgia, the civil-rights struggle in America reached its low point. King

> became bankrupt almost, as a leader. Plus, even financially, the
> Southern Christian Leadership Conference was in financial
> trouble; plus it was in trouble, period, with the people when they
> failed to desegregate Albany, Georgia. Other Negro civil-rights
> leaders of so-called national stature became fallen idols …

If they were so credible, why couldn't they (meaning the civil rights leaders) get financed by the masses? Where was Jesse Owens while all this was taking place? In *Blackthink* he claims that he was familiar with King and how much he "loved" him. Many of them were already ripping off black church, taking up collections and spending the money on themselves, suits, hotel rooms and personal needs. The civil rights leadership lost their juice because their strategy was ass backwards, it was shallow, and the white man found them a joke as they sought to get the white system to give up its profits in the name of morality. Nowhere in American history has the white man done that. Jesse Owens should have taken notes.

Malcolm is also correct in his use of the term "fallen idol." What is an idol? An idol can defined in many different ways. For instance, it can be, "a greatly loved or admired person." In black political circles it seems to fit the following definition: "a picture or object that is worshipped as a god a representation or symbol of an object of worship." That's why black people continually fall for the okey-doke and keep re-electing these charlatans who bring nothing back to the community and do nothing to improve their lives. More profoundly, however is the following definition which I believe is the most appropriate when it comes to the white man, negro leaders and ministers. An idol is, "a false god, an object of extreme devotion." This is why I believe Jesse Owens idolized white people in general and was so "devoted" to their way of life, regardless of how much he was being mistreated by it.

Anyway, Dr. King and the civil right "leadership" had to figure out a way to right their positions. And that's just what they did. But first they were attacked by the masses of people and some other negroes (not Owens, of course) who were expecting these "leaders" to make some major inroads. As Malcolm reported it,

> As they became fallen idols, began to lose their prestige and
> influence, local Negro leaders began to stir up the masses. In
> Cambridge, Maryland, Gloria Richardson; in Danville, Virginia,
> and other parts of the country, local leaders began to stir up our
> people at the grassroots level. This was never done by these
> Negroes, whom you recognize, of national stature. They controlled
> you, but they never incited you or excited you. They controlled
> you; they contained you; they kept you on the plantation.

As a political scientist we learn about the claim that, "all politics is local." Black people found that out fast. And that's why groups like the NAACP and the Urban League are utterly worthless. Before a local chapter can do anything they have to "get permission" from the national chapter which can take weeks or months. Meanwhile, the national chapter is busy begging for money from white-run businesses, chasing after white bitches, corporations and foundations. The local NAACPs know what the issues are and are willing to take action – but they are all too often held up and held back. And even when they take action it is usually of the "too little, too late" variety.

So while you all (along with Jesse Owens) were kissing the asses of the civil rights "leaders," they were behind closed doors running game and trying to get paid. As Malcolm X explained it,

> This happened; I've got it in documented evidence in the newspaper. Roy started attacking King, and King started attacking Roy, and Farmer started attacking both of them. And as these Negroes of national stature began to attack each other, they began to lose their control of the Negro masses.

I don't know what newspaper Malcolm was talking about, but it couldn't have been the *Muhammad Speaks* because even though he founded it, he had been banned from it. He believed what he read and maybe it was true and maybe it was the system once again using the media, as they often did, to dupe the masses of American people. But having studied King I know what kind of scoundrel he was when Coretta wasn't around, and I know how much he liked to live the good life. And Innis' asinine rants and sophistic antics were indeed a matter of public record.

The good ol' standby threat of "Marching in Washington" was always in the repertoire of the civil rights leaders, and it was one thing that truly scared white folks. (Oh, by the way – was Jesse Owens present? I think not). All those black people in one place, standing in the nation's capital for all the world to see. It was simply too much to have to go through again, having already experienced it just a year earlier. But check out what Malcolm said:

> And Negroes was [sic] out there in the streets. They was [sic] talking about [how] we was [sic] going to march on Washington. By the way, right at that time Birmingham had exploded, and the Negroes in Birmingham -- remember, they also exploded. They began to stab the crackers in the back and bust them up 'side their head -- yes, they did. That's when Kennedy sent in the troops, down in Birmingham. So, and right after that, Kennedy got on the television and said "this is a moral issue." That's when he said he was going to put out a civil-rights bill …

So black people took to the streets and as has always been the case, this prompted action. Just read the history – even here in hick-ass Omaha. The only time that black people get some of their demands met is when they threaten physical violence or actually engage in some. Those moral appeals, prayer vigils, marching protests – that's bullshit. Look at how fast Kennedy got to moving once black people started lighting up some cops. Not only did they scare the administration, but the administration scared the majority of white folks in the South. Denial of rights has been a long-time essential cog in the white supremacist machine. And this is the kind of direct action, laced with a little violence, that Jesse Owens refers to as "blackthink."

Black people, on their own and doing what was going to get results, started acting against the system without the "leadership" of King and those other negroes. Malcolm explains it, thusly:

> And when he mentioned civil-rights bill and the Southern crackers started talking about [how] they were going to boycott or filibuster it, then the Negroes started talking -- about what? We're going to march on Washington, march on the Senate, march on the White House, march on the Congress, and tie it up, bring it to a halt; don't let the government proceed. They even said they was [sic] going out to the airport and lay down on the runway and don't let no airplanes land. I'm telling you what they said. That was revolution. That was revolution. That was the black revolution.

The masses of people knew what was needed and they knew what it would take to teach white people a collective lesson. They had the plans and the energy. It was up to the civil rights "leaders" to quell that action, to slow it all down and to "take over" black initiative. Black people were scaring the powers that be and couldn't find a puppet that could reach them. Malcolm explains it:

> It was the grass roots out there in the street. [It] scared the white man to death, scared the white power structure in Washington, D. C. to death; I was there. When they found out that this black steamroller was going to come down on the capital, they called in Wilkins; they called in Randolph; they called in these national Negro leaders that you respect and told them, "Call it off." Kennedy said, "Look, you all letting this thing go too far."

This would have been the second March, would it not? If Malcolm is referring to the one that was held a year earlier, well it is clear that it was an historical event, featuring movie stars and a host of black artists and leaders. But at any rate, it is clear that the white man didn't want the fanfare. And the key to what

Malcolm is sharing is how the white man believed that he could buy off negro leadership (and why not? Hadn't he done it before?). And he gave them marching orders but they were no longer in control. So the white man threw money at these so-called "Christian" leaders. Here's what happened:

> And Old Tom said, "Boss, I can't stop it, because I didn't start it." I'm telling you what they said. They said, "I'm not even in it, much less at the head of it." They said, "These Negroes are doing things on their own. They're running ahead of us." And that old shrewd fox, he said, "Well If you all aren't in it, I'll put you in it. I'll put you at the head of it. I'll endorse it. I'll welcome it. I'll help it. I'll join it."

And that's when the worm turned. White boys were able to buy off the people who, to this day, are mentioned in the history books as "civil rights leaders." There is no mention of the bribes or of the meeting that Malcolm X is about to describe. This goes directly to the "negationism" that I have continually charged these white people with. Their history is so heinous, racist and brutal, they now have to do all they can to "revise" it; from their roles in wars and murders of innocent civilians (read: Mi Lai massacre) to their flagrant use of terms like "jap," "nigger" and "darkey" in their movies, they are revising and editing everything that would show their true nature.

And this is another example. Again, Malcolm:

> A matter of hours went by. They had a meeting at the Carlyle Hotel in New York City. The Carlyle Hotel is owned by the Kennedy family; that's the hotel Kennedy spent the night at, two nights ago; [it] belongs to his family. A philanthropic society headed by a white man named Stephen Currier called all the top civil-rights leaders together at the Carlyle Hotel. And he told them that, "By you all fighting each other, you are destroying the civil-rights movement. And since you're fighting over money from white liberals, let us set up what is known as the Council for United Civil Rights Leadership. Let's form this council, and all the civil-rights organizations will belong to it, and we'll use it for fund-raising purposes."

Despite their collective ignorance and police dog-like commitment to their country, can you nevertheless imagine how such information would have altered the thinking of white school-aged children? Seeing the depths that their nation would stoop to just to stop black people from having civil rights? So this was an imperative because if the white man doesn't do anything else, he certainly is committed to long-term thinking. Unlike black people, the white powers that be have learned that "short-term pleasure yields long-term pain."

And so the Council was formed and the civil rights leadership sold out the black community. Continuing:

> Let me show you how tricky the white man is. And as soon as they got it formed, they elected Whitney Young as the chairman, and who [do] you think became the co-chairman? Stephen Currier, the white man, a millionaire. Powell was talking about it down at the Cobo [Hall] today. This is what he was talking about. Powell knows it happened. Randolph knows it happened. Wilkins knows it happened. King knows it happened. Everyone of that so-called Big Six -- they know what happened.

And so the die was cast:

> Once they formed it, with the white man over it, he promised them and gave them $800,000 to split up between the Big Six; and told them that after the march was over they'd give them $700,000 more. A million and a half dollars -- split up between leaders that you've been following, going to jail for, crying crocodile tears for. And they're nothing but Frank James and Jesse James and the what-do-you-call-'em brothers.

So now you have it. This is what is taking place while black people are fighting tooth and nail in the South and crying "black power" in the north. And as Jesse Owens stood pat in both instances. Talking and writing about all that civil rights bullshit and praising King even while King was stabbing him – and black people in general – in the back. The so-called "leaders" were not really leaders at all: they were the willing thralls of the same system that is allowing cops to sic dogs on black women and children and gun down black men in the streets. And the same can be said for today: black leaders get paid to look the other way while white folks commit atrocity after atrocity and then, if caught, simply say "ooops, I did it again" and then it's on to the next planning session to plot black setbacks.

More on the Committee:

> [As] soon as they got the setup organized, the white man made available to them top public relations experts; opened the news media across the country at their disposal; and then they begin [sic] to project these Big Six as the leaders of the march. Originally, they weren't even in the march. You was [sic] talking this march talk on Hastings Street -- Is Hastings Street still here? -- on Hasting Street. You was [sic] talking the march talk on Lenox Avenue, and out on -- What you call it? -- Fillmore Street, and Central Avenue,

and 32nd Street and 63rd Street. That's where the march talk was
being talked.

Again, you can see the role that the media plays in maintaining the white
supremacist structure. As I've written elsewhere, the media is the voice of the
status quo. That is why Jesse Owens' book, containing the sub-title, "My Life as a
Black Man and White Man" was originally released in 1968 and then again in
1970. In the case of the major media, however, it is the lust for advertising revenue
and ratings means that you can find very little support for truly worthwhile causes.
In those days it was even worse than it is now – at least today there is the social
media dominated by young people. It's not that they give a shit about black people,
it's that they despise their parents and the system that they're about to inherit. But
remember: the enemy of my enemy is my friend.

So the "Big Six," as Malcolm called them, got paid and as we now know,
went down in history as heroes of the civil rights movement. Martin Luther King
Jr. as the "prince of peace (whose praises Jesse Owens sang the praises of);"
CORE as a champion organization behind the somewhat mentally disturbed Roy
Innis; A. Philip Randolph as a champion of the working people; Joseph Lowery, an
old man who put in work but overstayed his welcome – and several others. All of
them got paid. Where is this basic fact in the American history books? For that
matter, where is it in the African-American history books or in Karenga's magnus
opus, *Introduction to Black Studies*? Nowhere to be found.

He is talking about the historical march in 1963, and it goes down in history
as a "game-changer" in American history. But look at what was taking place
behind closed doors:

> But the white man put the Big Six [at the] head of it; made them
> the march. They became the march. They took it over. And the
> first move they made after they took it over, they invited Walter
> Reuther, a white man; they invited a priest, a rabbi, and an old
> white preacher. Yes, an old white preacher. The same white
> element that put Kennedy in power -- labor, the Catholics, the
> Jews, and liberal Protestants; [the] same clique that put Kennedy in
> power, joined the march on Washington.

And that's how they watered it down. What was a black movement – a
predecessor to the Million Man March as far as I'm concerned – ended up being
one big happy group of "Americans." And as the history books continue to get
revised and "updated" (read: whitenized), the march will end being the white
man's idea. Just as he takes credit for everything else, the humane changes that put
an end to segregation by race will end up going into his history books as something
that he instituted. King and others will just be mentioned as comic relief.

What was once black became white. Here's the analogy that Malcolm used:

> It's just like when you've got some coffee that's too black, which
> means it's too strong. What you do? You integrate it with cream;
> you make it weak. If you pour too much cream in, you won't even
> know you ever had coffee. It used to be hot, it becomes cool. It
> used to be strong, it becomes weak. It used to wake you up, now
> it'll put you to sleep. This is what they did with the march on
> Washington. They joined it. They didn't integrate it; they infiltrated
> it. They joined it, became a part of it, took it over. And as they
> took it over, it lost its militancy …

The March on Washington is remembered as being anything but militant. It has been, as Malcolm said, "watered down." It has been diluted. Just like they would do to the Black Panther Party and other black movements in years to come (including the Nation of Islam) they simply infiltrated these movements and used divide and conquer tactics to destroy the Black Power movement, opting instead to deal with the more passive, controllable and less threatening civil rights movement. The publication of Blackthink during this time period was one such attempt at divide and conquer – to turn black people into Uncle Toms like Owens.

As Malcolm put it,

> They ceased to be angry. They ceased to be hot. They ceased to be
> uncompromising. Why, it even ceased to be a march. It became a
> picnic, a circus. Nothing but a circus, with clowns and all. You had
> one right here in Detroit -- I saw it on television -- with clowns
> leading it, white clowns and black clowns. I know you don't like
> what I'm saying, but I'm going to tell you anyway …

And tell us he did. But he didn't throw rocks and hide his hand. Malcolm made it clear that he could back up his allegations with facts. Check it out:

> 'Cause I can prove what I'm saying. If you think I'm telling you
> wrong, you bring me Martin Luther King and A. Philip Randolph
> and James Farmer and those other three, and see if they'll deny it
> over a microphone.

And none of them ever showed up to refute what Malcolm said. And the media never confronted any of those "Big Six" and asked them about Malcolm's allegations. In my view this proves that it took place and that the people that you all continue to worship and praise as having done so much for so many did it, but did it just the way that whitey wanted them to – and they got paid for doing it. Just like Jesse Owens. Malcolm called it like it was and saw it for what it was:

> No, it was a sellout. It was a takeover. When James Baldwin came
> in from Paris, they wouldn't let him talk, 'cause they couldn't make
> him go by the script. Burt Lancaster read the speech that Baldwin
> was supposed to make; they wouldn't let Baldwin get up there,
> 'cause they know Baldwin's liable to say anything. They controlled
> it so tight -- they told those Negroes what time to hit town, how to
> come, where to stop, what signs to carry, what song to sing, what
> speech they could make, and what speech they couldn't make; and
> then told them to get out town by sundown …

So the system controlled the march and the "leaders" of it. And if it wasn't for Malcolm X, we wouldn't even know about it. That means that once again, the white man would have duped, deceived and dogged us. The question is how much more shit is there taking place behind our backs that we don't and may never know about? Your own Bible teaches that, "My people are destroyed for lack of knowledge: because you have rejected knowledge." And can it be any clearer that black people in this country are marching down the road of destruction because we don't study, we don't read, we won't research issues and we tend to believe everything this white man tells us in the name of "the news"?

Now, back to Jesse Owens' book and his opening chapter:

> Not that the white fellows weren't a nice bunch of guys for the
> most part. The majority weren't prejudiced. They were just like
> almost every other unprejudiced nice guy since the beginning of
> time, I guess. Their niceness didn't include making sure you got to
> take your shower, too. (p. 13).

How can Owens assume to know whether or not a white man is prejudiced or not? How could he tell? White people have been masters at masquerading their true feelings for centuries. Owens sees and believes what he wants to see and believe and when it comes to white people, that means seeing the very best in them, whether it exists or not. He writes some things that smack of sarcasm, but you know what they say about sarcasm? *Sarcasm is the body's natural defense against stupidity.*

Continuing on:

> Finally, the first auto, the one with Coach Larry Snyder driving,
> stopped beside a roadside eater. The other cars pulled in behind,
> and the white fellows began carelessly ambling out in the way
> athletes move and hurrying in to get their breakfasts. Hungry, we
> waited in our car until Larry got through talking to the woman
> behind the counter inside … When it was over he walked out more

> slowly than he'd walked in, took a few steps toward our car and
> simply shook his head … We were used to it. We'd never eaten
> with the white athletes in three years at college, let alone on the
> road much …" (pp. 13-14).

Some of the white boys sneaked some food out to the black men because they had made extra orders so they could do so. That was really nice. But so fuckin' what? We have to understand that racism is cumulative and that means that there are to be no exceptions to the "we don't feed no niggers" rules. So Owens' white teammates acted one way, but the man who owned the place, who prepared the food, had a different take. So check out what happens:

> "I don't want money to feed no *niggers!*" he bellowed. Then
> suddenly his arms were inside the car too, jerking at the plates of
> food. "You give me those!" He lunged, his hands grabbing the
> plates from us … Dave wouldn't let go of his and the man flailed
> out in insane anger, arching halfway into the auto and hitting down
> on the plate again and again with his big fist until not a thing was
> left on it. Dave dropped the plate then and was out of the car in
> almost a single motion. I was right behind him, catching him
> before he got to the man and holding on with all my strength." NO,
> Dave, no!" I whispered … "O.K.," he said bitterly. "What's one
> more time?" (pp. 14-15 – emphasis original).

Owens remembers this incident (if it really happened) almost word for word, right? He outlines the size of the man's fist, the racial statements that were made and the fact that he had to hold Dave back. And even in all that, Owens remained an Uncle Tom. This incident taught him nothing. In fact, Dave's query of "what's one more time?" is the story of Jesse Owens' life! So what if the white man treats you like shit today, deny you yesterday and have nothing but hate for you tomorrow? What's one more time? And unfortunately, there are too many black people with this fucked up philosophy walking round here today. And we need to do something about it the way we did back in the '60s and '70s. Instead of asking, "What's one more time?" our mantra was, "I bet you won't pull that shit again, muthafucka," and we proceeded to kick ass.

Owens adds that,

> For an instant I wavered. For a second or two, just like every other
> time that it happened, I wanted to let go the way I did when I was
> running or jumping, really let go, stride into that restaurant and
> pull that s.o.b. from behind his o-so-safe little counter and hammer
> him with all the anger that was in each one of us. But I didn't …
> (p. 15).

Just the fact that Owens admit that this kind of maltreatment had happened before, and he took it, shows what kind of coon he really is. All this talk about what he "wanted" to do is bullshit: if he really wanted to do it, he would have done it. He admits that he didn't do it, and that is what he should be judged by. He knew that he was being insulted and that he should do something about it because if he didn't, that racist white man would believe that he could mistreat any other black people who came into that situation. But Jesse, like the true sellout that he was, just stood pat, tucked his tail between his legs, and shuffled off into the sunset.

Even in that, check out Jesse's interpretation of the situation:

> I believe we beat that man that afternoon. I for one went out there
> and ran my balls off, ran out all the frustration and anger and fear
> that was inside me. And afterward, that man from that crumby
> little restaurant in Indiana walked up to me and did call me *mister*.
> By asking for my autograph (p. 16).

Nigga, please! How can you believe you beat somebody? Either you did or you didn't. If you have allowed white people to run over you your entire life and this is just another example of it, all I ask is "Jesse: where is thy victory"? he has to lie about the fact that the same man from the diner came up to him and called him "mister." Yeah – Mr. NIGGER probably! But you know that shit didn't happen. This is one of those all-American kumbaya stories that are told to make it appear as if racists eventually learn their lesson and all of a sudden start loving niggas.

He wants us to believe that this peckerwood asked him for his autograph. Why didn't Jesse trade the autograph for a plate of food? Why didn't Jesse use that request as a teaching moment to tell him, "Sir you treated me and my black mates like dogs earlier and now you want an autograph. I cannot comply because that would be like agreeing with what you did. So please – get the FUCK out of my face." You know, something along those lines.

Instead, here is what Jesse got out of all this:

> And maybe his attitude was different, too. Possibly he wasn't
> actively prejudiced anymore and beneath it all felt that skin color
> really didn't make any difference. Beneath it all, that is … I feel
> we beat that man that afternoon, and most other afternoons. But if
> anyone asks me to say it was a total victory, I can't tell them that.
> It wasn't. Life doesn't add up that way (p. 16).

Stupid muthafucka. How would he know how life adds up – he's never lived it! He's a coon that is, like the "negro," "a set of reactions to white people." He doesn't understand thing one about race relations or racism. He's like those

Christian assholes who go around trying to get you to change your life and haven't a clue about the history or nature of the Bible or its leading proponents. They repeat what they've heard, like some retarded parrots. This is the best way to sum up Jesse Owens, and he admits as much in the following paragraph:

> I've been a Negro in America for fifty-seven years, and I want to tell you it can be pure hell at times and can shake anyone's sureness. Often it's worse if you were the world's fastest human … *God, why couldn't I have been born like THEM?* (p. 17- emphasis original).

He admits he's been a "negro" and he chose that term at a time when it was clear to anyone who was black that "Black" was the preferable term. A "negro" is a special kind of black: a "tom" for the most part. Karenga (1967) once wrote that, "The negro was made and manufactured in America," and Jesse Owens is but one example of this kind of thinking.

Again, let me borrow from Bro. Malcolm X (1964):

> And if you came to the house Negro and said, "Let's run away, let's escape, let's separate," the house Negro would look at you and say, "Man, you crazy. What you mean, separate? Where is there a better house than this? Where can I wear better clothes than this? Where can I eat better food than this?" That was that house Negro. In those days he was called a "house nigger." And that's what we call him today, because we've still got some house niggers running around here …(Malcolm X, 1964).

And in 1968, such a person was Jesse Owens – confused and on the border of being psychologically shattered. For one thing he was a one-way integrationist, akin to his role model Martin Luther King, Jr. Check out his reaction the day King got shot down:

> I was in New York, walking back to my hotel. It was a cool dusk. All at once people began grouping on the streets. I kept walking, but snatches of their talk slowed me. Then I heard it. Martin Luther King, Jr. had been shot. He was dead … I think it was a French poet who said that a great man's dying is an imitation of the end of the world. Martin's death seemed that to me (pp. 18-19).

Martin Luther King, Jr. has just been shot down and everybody in the streets knew a white man was involved in it somehow, and this black bastard is quoting French poets! What was King going to do for a tom like Owens? Later in the book you can see that they talked from time to time and that is nothing more than a classic case of the blind leading the blind. King loved white bitches and fucked them behind Coretta's back – as the FBI documented. He was a typical minister, talking out of both sides of his mouth. And as Malcolm X proved, King – along with others - accepted a payoff from white boys to co-opt the civil rights movement. King had a lot of followers, but that was because Christianity taught them to be nonviolent. But again, as a cultural nationalist from the '60s once wrote, "The only thing that nonviolence proved was how savage whites were."

Moving on:

> And I could only hope that nightmare *was* part fantasy. Because whether you agreed or disagreed with Martin Luther King, Jr., whether you were a black militant or a Wallaceite or any of the fifty things in between, you sensed, even if you tried to hide it from yourself, that this was a genuinely *good* man. You could have seen the films of him with his children in Memphis, you might only have heard him speak a few times, or you may even have had the privilege of knowing him personally. But you knew it (p. 21 – emphasis original).

That is such bullshit. The people who believed in King's philosophy automatically assumed that he was a good man. They didn't see what he was doing behind closed doors. If they did they would realize that King was just like any other minister: full of shit. He had been groomed by other Uncle Toms and in fact, just before he came to prominence he was engaged to marry a white girl. That's right. His mentor talked him out of it, promising him that they had big plans for him and they went out and "found" him a girl. Of course she had to be high yellow and that's what brought Coretta Scott to the fore. This is what you find out when you study people and don't sit around busting a nut over the headlines in the newspapers and claiming that they were such "genuinely good" people.

Instead, black people then – as now – fall for the ministerial okey-doke. They keep believing in their ministers and their preachers, even when they know that most of these niggas (not King) are former thieves, former con artists, f former rapists, former murderers and former jailbirds. The pulpit is the refuge of the scoundrel. And they use that gift of gab to talk congregation members, mostly black women, out of their money and in many cases, out of their panties. But as has been the long tradition of our people, we continue to fall prey to these pimps in the pulpit. Check it out:

> Martin was that absolute goodness. I remember the first time Ruth ever heard him in person. He was speaking at the 49th Street Church near our apartment on Chicago's South Side. "He's like an

... angel, Jesse," she told me afterward. He's not a man. He's an *angel.*" I knew what she meant ... (p. 21-emphasis original).

Owens makes King out to sound like Jesus, and nothing could have been further from the truth. This fact in itself shows that the remaining parts of this book, all emanating from Owens' warped mind, are going to be equally distorted. He is a hero worshipper of black people who are passive and tommish, like himself. He admired people who are white man's niggers like Joe Louis, Willie Mays and people of that ilk. Anyone who wants to help black people or who stands up to the white man is labeled a "blackthink" and is therefore painted, throughout this book, as an enemy of black people.

The next chapter, a portrait of Owens' father, gives us some insight onto why Owens was so afraid of – and in love with – white folks.

Chapter 2: Henry Owens' Torture

This chapter outlines some of the trials and tribulations that Jesse's father, Henry, endured as he worked to raise a family during some seriously racist times. Again, with a background and with experiences like the ones he saw his father endure, you would think that Owens would have been more racially astute than he obviously turned out to be. But such was not the case. He shares with us the pains of Henry Owens and as an historian I can tell you that they are a reflection of the pains that hundreds of thousands of black men encountered as they worked to try to survive in a racist and hostile society.

The article begins with a quote from a 1960s television western called "The Big Valley." "The Big Valley" was an American western television series which ran on ABC from September 15, 1965, to May 19, 1969, starring Barbara Stanwyck, as the widow of a wealthy 19th century California rancher and Richard Long, Lee Majors, Peter Breck and Linda Evans as her family. The quote he selected was, "Suffering? Do you know what suffering is? Suffering is seeing your mother and father sold on the auction block!"

It is doubtful if any of the white Barkley family members -- undoubtedly the descendants of land grabbers and Indian killers -- made this statement. It was probably being uttered by someone who, at the time, was a member of an enslaved group. So why not credit that person? Why credit a western, one about a white family with a lot of land that they stole from Native Americans (read: "Bonanza," "High Chaparral") and then imply, through your omissions of these facts, that the quote can be attributable to this wealthy family that is run by a blonde matriarch (played by Barbara Stanwyck) who, in reality, was a lesbian?

At any rate, the chapter titled, "Henry Owens' Torture" begins:

> No one called me nigger until I was seven. That was
> because an Alabama sharecropper's child in the First World
> War years almost never saw the white man who owned his
> every breath. Owned … You won't find Oakville, Alabama,
> on the map today. Eight miles from Decatur, in the northern
> strip of the state, it was more an invention of the white
> landowners than a geographical place. Whatever had the
> smack of civilization to it was in Decatur (p. 24).

They got by the best way they could, with their father hunting rabbits and his parents planting a garden. But as he makes clear,

> But those few rabbits and vegetables didn't go very far with nine
> mouths to feed. So you always ended up at the owners' store for
> food, just as you made to go there for tools. My father never paid
> any money at the grocery. The owner's man just entered our debt
> on a sheet of paper with #1 at the top – we were the first of eight
> families who worked his spread of two hundred and fifty acres –
> and in December of every year, the white man totaled up what you
> owed against the worth of your crop to find out how much you
> were ahead (p. 25).

Now comes the clincher:

> But you never came out ahead. It always happened that those
> "Cheap" tools and supplies you bought cost more than the nearly
> quarter of a million square feet they hoped you to plant, just as the
> weekly potatoes and beans and con bread (you only bought meat
> two times a year, on the holidays) always came out to more than
> the six thousand pounds of cotton you enabled the owner to send
> North (p. 25).

Do you know what this sounds like to me? It sounds like the same *modus operandi* that Jews used against black people who had migrated North (as well as those who lived in the South) when they would open their "corner grocery stores."

Senator Ernie Chambers often tells the story of the time when he was seven or eight years old. He and his father walked into the store and his father asked the Jewish merchant how much an apple cost. The merchant said, "Two cents – two for a nickel." Ernie, always a bright kid but nevertheless respectful of his father remained silent, but knew that the merchant was ripping his father off.

In like manner, the sharecropping that Mr. Owens endured was par for the course, and should be broken down where possible because far too often Jews stand by while the race issue is framed as "black and white" when, more specifically, a great deal of the onus of those "white folks" should be placed at the door of Jews.

Evidence of this fact is in abundance:

> Southern Jewish politicians were at the forefront of the disenfranchisement of Blacks. The removal of northern troops from the South after the infamous "1877 Compromise" and the subsequent establishment of Jim Crow Black Codes made it virtually illegal for Blacks to participate in the cotton-based agri-business bonanza generated from the forced labor of the Black ex-slaves. The new system they set up was called "sharecropping." However, this system was not new to the European Jews that set it up. They had a model from their secretive holy book called the Talmud and it was similar to the Old Testament system that Joseph set up for Pharaoh (Muhammad, 2010).

Why wouldn't Owens, whose book deals with various aspects of race and ethnicity, specifically state that the white folks that were exploiting his father were Jews? I'll tell you why: because his friends were Jews as was his publisher. The white boy who helped him write the book was probably a Jew and even if he wasn't, he knew enough to know that they'd never get the book published if Jesse provided written evidence of how Jews exploited his father as they had done so many other black people.

What follows is a description of what Jews did to so many black men, of which Harry Owens (Jesse's father) was but one case:

> The new sharecropping system went like this: Cotton was the only cash crop that the Jewish merchants would accept as collateral from Black farmers in exchange for the staples he needed from the merchant to feed his family until the crop was harvested six months later. The Black farmers would then have to give that crop back to the merchants who loaned them the money at whatever interest and additional charges that these merchants saw fit, so that by the end of the harvest season the Black farmer wound up owing more money than at the beginning of the season

The key is the use of that word "interest." Also known as "usury," it is a fee that Jews used to acquire money from those they loaned money to. They have used this tactic all over the world and were one of the major reasons that Hitler despised them so much. They simply ripped people off and would get away with it in the name of "good business." To this very day, they continue to exploit poor communities although their Arab brethren have replaced them in black communities in major cities, especially in Detroit and Milwaukee. Again, I am saying that people like Jesse Owens don't have the guts to say, and why? Because they fear Jewish reprisals: terminations from jobs, alienation from financial interests, accusations of "anti-Semitism" all over the media.

Later Jesse talks about how the family got fed up and moved North. That was par for the course for most black "sharecroppers." Again, Muhammad teaches that,

> Cotton and sharecropping broke the spirit of this agrarian class and drove their children to the cities, leaving their land behind to be confiscated by the children of their former slave masters. This cruel plan destroyed the natural inclination of Black people to be industrious and productive members of a communal agrarian village and destroyed the economic fiber of the Black community. As "King Cotton" made Jewish merchants the kings of finance, the sharecropping system of production drained the economic wealth of Black people in America.

And this is the real reasoning behind what Henry Owens, Jesse's father, ended up having to do. And remember these words: "As "King Cotton" made Jewish merchants the kings of finance, the sharecropping system of production drained the economic wealth of Black people in America." I will address other ways that Jews and other white folks exploited Owens and other blacks later in this book.

This exploitation was inter-generational. Jesse Owens recalls it thusly:

> A few negroes had left and gone North. But Henry Owens was over forty years old, an age not made by half a dozen negro sharecroppers in Morgan County. It was late to pull up roots. And like most other sharecroppers he was the son of the son of a slave. His own grandfather had told him the stories of being legally shut out, stories of death that came in the night, sometimes at the hands of the white man and sometimes through simple starvation … (p. 26).

The abuse of black men by white plantation owners and farmers is an issue that is far too often ignored in the history books. And the role that Jews played as a part of that relationship is kept quiet because they are the ones who are writing the history and making the textbook publishing decision. Owens' father went through hell and you would think that would have prompted Jesse to use his fame to make the issue known and to be more involved in fighting for the rights of farmers. But did he? No. He was too busy kissing the white asses around him and spent much of his time looking for more asses to kiss.

The problem with the black farmer, including his farmer, is an issue that today's young people should study and learn from. Again, Owens:

> So, deep down in that invisible place where a man decides what to do, my father felt that we could have it even worse than we did in Oakville. He wasn't going to dare take a chance on that. The whole world would have to jerk out of orbit for him to pack us up and leave (p. 26).

His father had a right to believe that even the tribulations of today are better than the uncertainties of the future. He was directly being hit by racist activity and had a family to feed. Owens experienced similar racism but like the gutless asshole that he was, he chose "flight" over "fight." His father ran only as a last resort; Jesse's whole life was about running in more ways than just on the track field; he was a "runner" whenever and wherever things got too hot. It was much easier to blame militant black people than to point his finger at his racist white buddies.

But even the caution of a man like Henry Owens has to have its limits. As Jesse recalls it,

> In theory, of course, my folks had a fifty-fifty deal with Jon Clannon, but fifty percent of nothing amounts to nothing. So we lived in fear of him and of his power, and the fear was justified … We'd had a particularly good crop that year. Even with exorbitant grocery bills every week, it had still gotten us out of debt. That threatened John Cannon's hold over us, I guess, and he wanted to do something about it right away;. Hat he proposed to do was to revise his deal with my father. Sixty-forty, instead of fifty-fifty. Retroactive (p. 28).

Now Jesse knew about all this. He claims to have loved and respected his father. And yet none of this abuse of his father stopped him from turning into one of the biggest sellouts of all time. You would think he would despise white people but the reverse was true: he loved white folks more than he loved himself. Even with these white people ripping off his entire family and changing his life to the point where they had to pack up and leave, that didn't stop Jesse from suffering from a severe case of "anglophilia." But the story is not yet over:

> "And what about my family?" my father had shot back, finally beginning to lose forty two years of control. "We work hard. I

> want my sons to amount to more than I have!" "Your sons will
> never amount to anything – just be grateful if they *survive!*" the
> man had shouted back. That last statement had stuck in my father's
> craw. He struggled to spit it out for the next two days, but it only
> lodged deeper. That Sunday after church he told us that we were
> leaving Oakville for Cleveland (pp. 28-29 – emphasis original).

Now a white man says this about your sons, to the point where your father has decided to pack the family up and leave. His father never forgot those words – "Your sons will never amount to anything – just be grateful if they *survive!*" Those were fighting words for most people under most conditions, but in those days times were a little different. But at least the elder Owens had the balls to take action against such an insult:

> But we got the hell out. As I said, for my father Cleveland wasn't
> much different from Oakville. Yet for me it was like another
> planet. It gave me a chance. And one chance is all you need, no
> matter what the black thinkers say (p. 29).

The "blackthinkers" never put down having or looking for a chance. What in the fuck is this Uncle Tom talking about? All that is negative he attributes to the more militant black people – and then he turns around and pretends to be some kind of authority on race relations. He sounds just like some white liberal who, like so many of them, want to act as if they have a monopoly on the truth. At the same time he only shows disdain for black militant leadership:

> It's no accident that the Rap Browns and Stokely Carmichaels
> sometimes sound like the Clannons. Because *blackthink* – pro-
> Negro, anti-white, bigotry – is what makes the new negro and
> white extremists of today tick, and it's not much different from
> John Clannon's *whitethink.* Irrationality and violence, above all,
> are at blackthink's gut (p. 29 – emphasis original).

Owens needs his ass kicked for writing and then publishing such bullshit. To begin with he coined the term "blackthink," and he uses it in the most insulting ways possible. It is almost as if he is saying that if you think black first, then something must be wrong with you. It is as if he believes that if you think integration and loving the white man, you will be far better off. Jesse Owens is a sellout, plain and simple.

He then claims that blackthink is "pro-Negro, anti-white bigotry." Is it? Or is it just discovering and then announcing the truth about race relations in this country, holding up a mirror to the white man so he can see the reality of his heinous history? There is nothing "irrational" about thinking black; Karenga once wrote that, "Thinking black is thinking collective minded." And that is what scares people like Jesse Owens and his white masters: black people were uniting behind race, history and similarity of condition and not just around bullshit religious principles, banging tambourines and competing for who has the biggest house and the newest car.

Jesse has flashes where he appears to know better than the Uncle Tomfoolery that he doles out in his book. For instance, where he shares the following story:

> I recall hearing about the white mob in Georgia that lynched a bunch of Negroes because someone there had murdered the white owner . They never knew if that someone was a colored man or not. They didn't care. When in doubt about anything murder a Negro – or a bunch of negroes – was their creed. Only this time one of the men they hung had a wife who was eight months pregnant and who just couldn't stand to see her husband taken away. She clawed at the shoes of the white men as they dragged him to the tree, she screamed to the next county when they put the rope around his neck. So they strung her up, too. Only they didn't tighten the knot enough to kill her, just to dangle her above the fire they'd made so she's slowly burn to death> Before she lost consciousness, her ready-to-be-born baby dropped into the flames. That wasn't the worst of it. As the baby fell into the fire, the white men ran to their homes to call their wives and their children. To watch it roast. (p. 30).

Not only was Owens recollecting the trials and tribulations of his own father, not only did he start his book off with a tale about being turned down for meals as an athlete because of his race, but now we have this story, one that took place more often than the history books would lead you to believe. These white people were savages, which is why their movies and popular culture are so quick to point the finger at Native Americans, Blacks and Latinos and label US as the savages. But here's my point.

Owens knows all this shit is happening and he knows it happens regularly. He knows that at the basis of such treatment is racism, not "blackthink," which he tends to blame for everything. The black people snatched off the street and lynched were low-key negroes just like him. And yet knowing all this, having seen what he's seen and heard the types of stories just shared, this ass kissing sonofabitch just kept right on kissing whitey's ass, just kept on kowtowing – just kept on selling out the race that was the victim of white racism, while aligning himself with the victimizer.

So where does he point his disjointed black finger? At black folks. Peruse the following:

> The difference is that today's black extremist is born with a platinum spoon in his mouth compared to what his great-grandparents had to go through. You wonder at times how any one of them then survived mentally, let alone physically. Historian Lura Beam put it better than I can: "The slave lived subject to the fear, shock and pressure that unhinge people now and send them to mental hospitals" (p. 32).

Two points here.

First of all take note that Owens has to find a white woman (Lura Beam) – whose claim to fame is a book that she wrote about Maine – to quote about the black condition? This is a characteristic of a true Uncle Tom: when in doubt, run to the white man (or woman) for confirmation and affirmation.

The second point lies in Owens' claim that, "today's black extremist is born with a platinum spoon in his mouth compared to what his great-grandparents had to go through." What kind of comparison is that? No black man is born with a platinum spoon in his mouth no matter how wealthy or famous he may be. Just the fact that he's a black man in a white racist society is going to have him walking on the same pins and needles as old man Henry Owens did. And furthermore, Jesse is comparing people born in enslavement to people who were supposedly "free" but were still being harassed, dominated, directed, oppressed and killed by white people. What kind of comparison is that? Jesse wants to find progress where there is none so that his pal the white man can feel good about himself.

And what also makes Jesse a race traitor is the fact that he knows better and consciously chooses to lick the white man's ass. For instance, he writes:

> So if the white man who owned you "loved" you, it wasn't even in the way that he loved those hounds of his that were always ready to corner you. When a dog died, there might have been a few days of sadness on the plantation. When a slave died, the usually feeling was anger – anger that less work might be done that day. It was up to the other slave to make up for it, unless *they* wanted to be beaten or starved (p. 33).

Who said the white man loved the black man that he oppressed? You can't love someone who you consider a sub-human? You can't love someone who you envy, hate and fear. You can't love someone who you can lynch at the drop of a hat. So if the thesis of a statement is ass backwards, everything that stems from that incorrect thesis is equally distorted. Just like Owens' mindset.

He compares the love that the white man has for his dog with the ill feelings he showed for the enslaved. That was an unfair comparison. The dog was allowed to sleep in the house and oftentimes ate at the table with the master. The enslaved person could not do this: we got scraps and made the best of them. The dog was not castrated, lynched, raped or burned. The enslaved individual, male and female, actually was. Again, Owens' belief system is totally off-kilter.

And it extends to an understanding (or lack thereof) of his own hard-working father:

> So if Henry Owens was verbally abused, grossly over-worked and sadistically treated by the system into which he was thrown, at least he could pray when he wanted and be sure his wife was his alone to love. Leaving this for the North was taking a chance on the unknown, and the unknown could only be worse. That's why it took an earthquake to pry Negroes like us loose from the cotton fields (p. 33).

What kind of concessions are these? Praying and having a woman that is all yours are essentials for any human being. So why does Owens act as if this father is fortunate to have these things to do? The fact is, pray in one hand and shit in the other and see which one fills up the fastest. That's how I feel about that kind of bullshit. But as for having a woman, how would Jesse know? Black women were being raped behind closed doors and dare not tell the husband for fear that he would get killed kicking that white man's ass (by mobs, never by the individual white man). Secrets are being held to this day about black women being raped by these white boys – some of them being impregnating and putting the child on the husband. This is what should be written about instead of attributing to Abraham Lincoln, some kind of bullshit belief that he "freed the slaves."

The chapter concludes as follows:

> I've tried to make something of my life, but when I put it against what Henry Owens did, it doesn't seem like much, considering the opportunity I had. And when I put what most of today's blackthinkers, with their opportunities, have accomplished against what Henry Owens accomplished, it comes out zero (p. 34).

The reason that when he puts what he's done up against what his father did, there was no damn comparison. Even with all my degrees, national awards and the like, I would never compare myself with my father, who didn't even graduate from high school. He was a real man who raised eleven kids, ten of his own, and never once abandoned my mother. He worked hard doing hard core labor at a Naval Weapons Station (loading bombs) and then came home and built one home from the ground up and helped to improve another one once we moved to California. Those were real men back in those days, and they faced hard core racism. And I'm sure that the racism that Henry Owens had to deal with was far worse than that experienced by my father.

But my point is simply this: "it is what we do in our daily lives that define and demonstrate our real views and values." Jesse Owens won four gold medals and made a white racist nation look good. Whether or not he actually made Hitler look bad is a matter of subjective reporting by white boys and Jews who hated the Nazis. But what did he do with the rest of his life? He kissed white ass and wrote books trying to degrade and denounce what would come to be known as "the Black Power Movement." In other words, he took the side of the very people that had given his father so many Excedrin-sized headaches.

And therefore the "torture" that Henry Owens endured, while he may not have recognized it, also had a lot to do with the fact that one of his sons, Jesse, would grow up to be one of the biggest Uncle Toms in history.

Chapter 3: But Equality is Here

This chapter provides some examples of what Owens views as "negro progress" and as I dissect each, you will be able to see the thought processes of a true sellout. The chapter also shows how far a sellout will go even when talking about all the "negro opportunity" there was.

To begin with, to talk of "equality" is an elusive goal. The white man suffers from a God complex and has a system of white supremacy. The key to the survival of both is to make sure that no other being on earth is EVER deemed an "equal," not even his own woman. Look how he's treated her and devised a system of sex role socialization that demeans her and limits her human potential. And if he'll do it to the woman that is a key to providing him with more racist kids, then you should know what he will do to people of color, who he both envies and hates.

With that having been said, the chapter begins with a quote from the Chicago Urban League. In recent years I have written a number of articles on the black experience in this country and in the early days, the National Urban League put in good work assisting black people from the North to settle into southern cities. But over the past several decades, they have outlived their usefulness, beginning when their President, Vernon Jordan, got shot in the ass back in May of 1980 on his way to "have lunch" with some white woman while at a conference in Fort Wayne, Indiana. From there it has degenerated, funded mostly by white corporations and doing very little that the masses of black people would deem "relevant."

The quote from the Chicago Urban League, which I always viewed as one of the more progressive branches, is, "If a Negro kid wants to go to college, he can – and usually to the one he wants to go to." The issue is not whether or not the kid is going to get into a college. The issues are the quality of the college, what kinds of changes the kid will be put through once he arrives on campus, what kind of racism he's going to encounter in the community where the college is located and exactly what he is going to do when and if he manages to graduate.

Furthermore, this chapter is packed with a plethora of bullshit assumptions that Owens attempts to pawn off as facts. As I dissect this section of the book, you will get an idea of what I mean.

The beginning of the lies and distortions of reality begin on page 35 where Owens makes the following claim:

> … Believe it or not, most black men today can start just about equal with the white. We may not begin with as well-off a set of parents, and we may have to fight harder to make that equality work. But we *can* make it work. Because now we have the one all-important gift of *opportunity.*

Such a hypocrite. He begins claiming that "most black men" (how did he arrive at such a percentage?) can start off "just about equal" with the white. Wait a minute: what is "almost equal"? Either you're equal or you're not. And what decides what gives a black man that "almost equal" status? Who determines it? Does the black man think, "Well, I don't want to be completely equal to the white boy, I'll just take some partial status"? None of this shit makes sense, does it?

Then jess claims that we may not start off with parents who are as well off as the white mans. And who determines that? Why do black parents lack resources when compared to white parents? Owens adds that, "we may have to work harder to make that equality work." How do you make equality work? Isn't it a natural state? Doesn't his Bible and the Constitution of the United States make claims about the equality of mankind? So why do black men have to work harder in order to make something that is god-ordained and legally mandated "work"?

Despite these contrarieties he nevertheless claims that "we CAN make it work." How is that? Because Jesse Owens says so? Did HE make it work? If it was working, why did he run and jump in Berlin and then come back to America and have to run against race horses in order to eke out a living? But wait: this asshole, despite the plethora of mistakes already pointed out, has the solution. According to Owens, equality can work because "we have the one all-important gift of opportunity."

What he is really saying is that the white man is going to give black people equality. I know this because he refers to opportunity as a "gift." And what are gifts? They are GIVEN to you by someone else. So if we start off equal with the white boy as Owens claims, why would we need a gift of opportunity in order to achieve what Owens claims we already had?

In an attempt to support the previous asinine statements he's made, he then offers up the following:

> Most whites and Negroes have been brainwashed to believe that black men and women, with a few exceptions such as athletes, entertainers or postmen, don't have much chance in America. It's a lie. If the negro doesn't succeed in today's America, it is because he has chosen to fail. Yes, there are exceptions. But there are exceptions for whites, too (p. 35).

> Radio and TV are mirrors of our culture and all-important means of communication. More obviously than anything else, they show how immensely the race situation has changed. I'm not merely talking about the Negro-generated and Negro-performed music disc jockeys play, or the talk shows that can't get their fill of Negro spokesmen or Negro problems. I'm talking about the people who spin the records and flip the switches and gather the news and run the stations. And own them. There are many white –owned radio stations in which negroes figure prominently, but there also is a mushrooming phenomenon today called *Negro radio* (p. 36 – emphasis original).

After sharing that he had his own jazz show on radio in the early '50s at a white station and then ended up with one on a black station, he then moves on to another area where he knows very little about the facts. But that's alright: his conjecture, wild theories and general bullshit will suffice for the purposes that he has. Check it out:

> Television tells much the same story. When I'm in a hotel room, I try to write, maybe a speech for the next night, possibly this book. So I don't watch a lot of TV directly, but I often have it on for company. What do I see? Negro detectives and negro secretaries to white detectives, negro deans of colleges and Negro confederate soldiers. Negro nurse and Negro doctors. Negroes using aspirin and negroes buying boats, Negroes – well you name it. And the chestnut about blacks being big on TV because it's part of the entertainment world just doesn't apply *These programs reflect our society* (pp. 36-37 – emphasis original).

Appearance is not essence. Sure there are a lot of black people on television today, but look at how most appear: as singers, dancers, clowns and comic relief. On the flip side there are the appearances on dramatic shows as drug dealers, pimps, thugs and gang members. As long as the white man (read: Jew) is in control of what goes on and remains on television, black people and other people of color will always receive short shrift. Numbers are not enough; there are more appearances now, but at what level of life?

And yet Owens, who has shown that he doesn't know much beyond the track and field area, continues to pawn his opinion off as if it is an educated one or that his words have relevance. He claims in regard to the black presence on television that, "And the chestnut about blacks being big on TV because it's part of the entertainment world just doesn't apply These programs reflect our society." They sure do: niggas ain't shit in the real world and they ain't shit on television! The ones on television act more like white folks than do the ones in the ghetto, but both sets of "negroes" are powerless in a nation where power is valued above else. And that is the way television has always treated black people.

Even today in 2016, the white major news talk shows have their version of black "control." Eugene Robinson (oftentimes a panelist on NBCs "Meet the Press") and Clarence Page (PBS's "The McLaughlin Report"), both top-notch written journalists, can't talk worth a shit once the camera is on. Both have an incredible stuttering problem, but this is who the white man chooses. Juan Williams, as big a tom as he is, remains the laughing stock of Fox Sunday and only gets to answer the "nigga questions" – the questions that have to do with race. And even then, he's usually interrupted by Chris Wallace the show's host.

And these are the serious shows. The rest are that super hero/situation comedy type bullshit and black people don't get any justice because the same people who were in control of television in the 1930s are the same ones in control today. But the self-proclaimed sociology Jesse Owens has more (unsolicited) analysis to offer:

> Negro radio and Negroes on TV are only the top thousandth of the iceberg of our geometrically growing black economic power and opportunity in America. This year black men and women will spend fifty billion dollars in the United States. Someone is doing something besides looting stores or standing outside university administration buildings. Not that I'm saying these kids who march outside the offices of college presents are wrong. But I will say one thing: in 1937, it was a different story. Not only didn't a young Negro have time for university sit-ins – he was lucky if he could sit in the classrooms (p. 37).

Jesse Owens is a dyed-in-the wool asshole, and the previous quote supports this allegation.

For instance, in 1977 while attending Diablo Valley College in Pleasant Hill, California, I reviewed a book by D. Parke Gibson called *The $30 Billion Negro*, which had been written eight years earlier in 1969. By 1968 or thereabouts, when Owens was writing *Blackthink,* that number had swelled to $50 million. And by 2013, it was more than a trillion; or at least that's what Baker (2013) claimed in an article that appeared in the November issue of *Black Enterprise* magazine:

> There are 43 million African Americans in the United States, 13.7 percent of the total population, the second largest racial minority in the country. The median age is 32 and 47 percent are under 35 years of age. The Nielsen Company study entitled "African-American Consumers: Still Vital, Still Growing," which was commissioned by the National Newspaper Publishers Association, shows the underrepresented potential and spending power of the African American community. The report's findings, which will be presented at the June conference of the National Association of Black Accountants Conference in Nashville, Tennessee, found that the African American population is an economic force to be reckoned with, with a projected buying power of $1.1 trillion by 2015.(Baker, 2013)

You may ask, "what does this have to do with Owens, his numbers and his conclusion regarding "negro progress"? Recall a poem that old white men would pass around and pass down to fellow race members: "A naught is a naught, and a figure is a figure; all for the white man and none for the nigger." All the millions, billions or trillions in the world don't omit a key fact: the level of the economy where we are most visible is the tertiary level – that means that we are consumers. The primary level is the planting and developing side; the secondly level is where what is planted or developed is taken out of the ground and manufactured. The third level – where black people are supposedly spending all this money – is where we consume what white folks produce and develop. We spend money. So fuckin' what?

Remember earlier when this Uncle Tom was talking about the blacks on radio and television and then equated that with progress? Well later in this chapter, pay close attention to the way that this internationally acclaimed track star, a man who brought fame and notoriety to the United States right in Hitler's face, was treated by his white buddies:

> Then two white promoters came to my apartment one night. They
> had an idea, negro baseball, and they needed a "name" to publicize
> it. Naturally there were no well-known colored baseball players
> because none had been allowed in the major leagues so they had to
> go outside of baseball. I was a natural choice … (p. 39).

Wait a minute before we continue, let's deal with this previous excerpt.

This is the same way that black people are "approached" today just before a television program or movie is made that needs a dark face. They want to promote something and appeal to a black audience. In the area of sports, the major sports are dominated by black people, both from America and from the world of Hispanics. An article in Sports Illustrated dealt with the growing "Hispanic presence" in pro baseball, but here's what I saw: almost all of those "Hispanics" had dark skin! They were from Cuba and various parts of South America. So peckerwoods, get it straight. Ethnicity is one thing (where you're born, your language, what kind of food you like, your religion), but melanin (skin color) is the key: and the brown gene dominates for sure!

Then Owens adds:

> The idea really grabbed me at first. I thought they wanted me to
> play or at least be manager of one of the two teams they planned to
> have touring the country playing against each other. But that
> wasn't quite what they had in mind … They wanted me to run a
> hundred years against a thoroughbred racehorse before the game
> each night … "Nothing doing," I told them in a temper. "You think
> about it," one of them said shrewdly, "We'll be back on Sunday."
> … But when they returned on Sunday … I heard myself say, "I've
> decided to do it." So I sold myself into a new kind of slavery (pp.
> 39-40).

He admits he sold himself into what he calls "a new kind of slavery." Yeah – it's called "self-enslavement"! This nigga is such a coon, such a jerkoff, that he agreed to allow himself to be humiliated in this way. These are white men coming up with such an idea, and they didn't stop with Owens in the 1930s. They've also arranged similar deals with the likes of Olympian Michael Johnson and world record 100 yard dash holder Usain Bolt. Black men running against horses. And who gets the money? The white man gets it, that's who. But more importantly than the money is the image of control that such competitions show to the world, and these kinds of events are videotaped and preserved.

Despite the fact that he's admitted to being "beasitified" (my term), he nevertheless has the gall to state the following:

> Negroes are *people*. Many of them, most of them, are vitally
> interested in the race problem. They spend a god deal of their time
> trying to deal with it or things relating to it. But they eat and sleep
> and work and love and play and worry, too. And if they don't do
> these things, they won't be any damned good with the race crisis or
> any other crisis in this world (p. 43 – emphasis original).

Such a statement implies that Owens believes that most people don't think black people are human beings. He certainly hasn't been treated like one, and neither was his father, Henry. And yet, despite this "animalization," he still begs the white man for acceptance, tolerance and "opportunity." He still begs the white man to see him as someone who is "worthy." This is a sinfully degrading message to be sending to young black men and women in a published book that also serves to give white people who read it an illusory sense of superiority.

His lack of understanding (and common sense) continues to manifest itself no page after page. For instance, he writes:

> Yet reverse bigotry is all around us today. In most intellectual
> circles and many middle-class ones, black is "in." What one writer
> called "the black gold rush" is on. "Instant negroes" has become a
> familiar term in business and education. The treasury department
> threatens to withdraw its money from banks that haven't hired
> negroes, but where are they going to get negro bankers? Extremists
> demand that Negro history be taught only by black teachers. *What*
> black teachers? (p. 43 – emphasis original).

How can there be "reverse bigotry"? Where was the white boy who co-wrote this book with Owens? Was he as stupid as Jesse? Bigotry is bigotry, and to use the term "reverse bigotry" implies that the only time that bigotry is working effectively is when it's aimed at black people!

As for the "black gold rush," that was just the response to the black power movement and the lack of creativity of white people. They see something new and bold and they try to promote it, market it and steal it. Many of these white people start wearing Afros, starting donning dashikis and bubas, they wanted to learn Swahili and white scholars started writing books about black people. Black wouldn't have been so widely publicized had it not been for white curiosity and fear. "Instant negroes" would not have been in vogue had not whites needed "negroes" to appear because black people had always been around other black people. So to protect their own feelings of guilt and ignorance, white folks invited a few black people over or sponsored a few black organizations – the same thing they continue to do to this very day.

The demands for black history are met with arguments from blacks and whites and Jesse Owens, the quintessential "negro," seems to take both sides when he asks, "Extremists demand that Negro history be taught only by black teachers. *What* black teachers?" Black history should be taught and, having come up during the heyday of the black power movement, I also believed that black people should not only teach black history but black studies in general. According to my logic at that time, white people already had teaching jobs and had used them to debase and lie about Africa and about black people. Using my logic at that time, I didn't want a peckerwood anywhere near a black studies or black history teaching position.

That was then and this is now. I have taught black studies and black history at several major universities, and I have a degree in it. Based on what I've seen in these departments, with few exceptions, white people could not possibly do a WORSE job in front of the classroom than some of these clowns. And that applies to this very day. So that takes care of that issue.

As for the dearth of black teachers, the same issue at a different level exists today. I don't think someone with background inAmerican History can teach Black History unless they understand the black experience. In this context, there are not enough white or black teachers around to do a good job. In the case of Black Studies, these so-called black scholars today have doctorates in sociology, psychology, communications and every field BUT Black Studies. Then they see a teaching position and apply for it, showing that they took one or two black studies classes back in the day. And they get the job. So what is being done is that these black people are getting on the job training; the conscious students in the class are teaching THEM the grassroots shit that they should have known when they signed the teaching contact. And that is the issue of the "lack of teachers" today.

But Owens doesn't know what he's talking about and his white buddy who helped him write the book is apparently as mentally bankrupt as he is. For instance, it is written in the book that,

> But if there aren't enough teachers or bankers yet, there're enough men and women and children simply wrapped in brown to *produce reverse social discrimination* in most strata of our society. "Have you had your Negro for the week?" is a line in the act of one night club comic I know. Or: "You bring the punch, Alice; you bring the extra card tables, Barbara; you bring the canapes, Cheryl; and I'll bring the Negroes." (p. 43 – emphasis original).

Wrapped in brown? What's wrong with this muthafucka? If black people were simply "wrapped in brown" I'm pretty sure that many of them, being the types of Uncle Toms that Owens is, would have simply removed the wrapping! Reverse social discrimination? That is an institutional issue and who controls the institutions? Therefore it's straight out "social discrimination" and there is no need to put the word "reverse" in it. Again, this implies that the only time that this discrimination is functioning correctly is when it is aimed at people of color! How ludicrous!

And his poor attempt at humor sounds like that Dean Martin/Jerry Lewis-type bullshit. You bring the Negroes? Several years after *Blackthink* was published, the writer Thomas Wolfe wrote an article and a book with a theme not dissimilar from the bullshit that Owens is spewing. First came a 1970 article in *New York magazine* called "Those Radical Chic Evenings" which was about a party that Leonard Bernstein (a Jew) held for the Black Panther Party and after that came a book by Wolfe called, *Radical Chic & Mau-Mauing the Flak Catchers,* which dealt with people of color and their response to San Francisco's poverty programs. Both the article and the book addressed what Wolfe saw as the conflict between black rage and white guilt.

This is akin to what Owens is talking about. He thinks that being black is some kind of vogue joke. I recall a scene from one of the episodes of "Julia" a TV show about a black single parent nurse working for some Jew liberal doctor. In one scene they're on the phone and since she talks like a peckerwood she felt it necessary to tell him, "Dr. Chegley – you do realize that I'm a negro." He responds, "Is that what you really are or are you just trying to do what's in vogue?" See what I mean? White people and sick negroes like Jesse Owens think and joke alike. They don't take race seriously until black people start kicking their ass, burning down their cities and cursing them out.

The chapter on "equality" being here has not proven that to be the case at all. And to add one more insult to the injury that is Jesse Owens' nerve to speak out on race issues, is the closing paragraph of the chapter:

> The deep, disturbing truth … is that bigotry in reverse is still
> bigotry, still stems from the same myth of Negro inferiority and
> still ends up making the black man or woman a thing or an issue or
> a project or a problem at the expense of not making him or her a
> *person* … Still, reverse bigotry is dwarfed by the true catastrophe
> of today – that the Negro is in danger of being maliciously,
> tragically brainwashed (p. 44 – emphasis original).

Owens simply doesn't get it. With white racism, discrimination and bigotry raining down on his black ass 24 hours a day, he feels it necessary to coin a concept of "reverse bigotry" and act as if the problem is with black people. But even a broken clock is right twice a day, and without knowing it, Owens indicts himself in the closing sentence of the chapter where he writes, " … the Negro is in danger of being maliciously, tragically brainwashed."

The reason for the brainwashing is 400 years of enslavement. After slavery supposedly ended there was no "de-briefing" so what you had were people like Owens' daddy running around sharecropping (read; still trusting white folks) and getting ripped off, still pretty much for free. Then today, you got "negroes" like Clarence Thomas, Ward Connerly, Dr. Ben Carson, Condoleezza Rice and other sellouts proving that the brainwashing continues to infect and affect black people, many of whom are given or appointed to powerful positions so that they can infect others with this "America is for everyone" bullshit. From swearing under oath and the national anthem to a belief that "the system is the solution," the brainwashing continues at an unabated rate.

In simpler terms, Jesse Owens is only one of tens of millions of casualties of this long-term indoctrination process.

<u>Chapter 4: Negroes Have Human Hangups</u>

This chapter's title raised some concerns because it implies that black people are not human beings. Throughout the book, in fact, Owens continues to hammer home the fact that black people can breathe, can think and so on. He sounds as if he cares more about what white people think than what he knows to be the case. This is vintage uncle tom thinking. This is what Malcolm X was talking about in the following excerpt from his 1964 speech, "Message to the Grass Roots" when he was describing the "house nigger":

> If the master's house caught on fire, the house Negro would fight
> harder to put the blaze out than the master would. If the master got
> sick, the house Negro would say, "What's the matter, boss, we
> sick?" We sick! He identified himself with his master more than
> his master identified with himself … (Malcolm X, 1964).

So much does Owens want the white man's love and attention he feels that he has to explain his humanity to them. So the title of the chapter, "Negroes Have Human Hang-ups" sounds more like an ape talking to a trainer than it does a human being speaking intelligently to another one.

A second concern is how the chapter begins. Owens begins his chapters with various quotes, they are usually from white people or equally confused "negroes." In this case he begins with a list of organizations with their purpose and numbers from a book by yet another white man Irving J. Sloan, called The American Negro. And the organizations are taken from a section cited as Entries under "Negro Organizations."

While groups like the NAACP , National Urban League, Black Panther Party and others go unnamed, he lists the American Teachers Association and the fact that it has 37,000 members; Alpha Kappa Mu Honor Society with 6,680 members; Alpha Kappa Alpha Sorority (40,000 members); Ancient and Accepted Scottish Rite Masons (20,000 members), Ancient Egyptian Arabic Order Nobles of the Mystic Shrine with 24,000 members; and Alpha Phi Alpha Fraternity (8,000 members).

What is the purpose of this listing? Are all of these members black? I doubt it? Of what function are these Masonic groups? The sorority and fraternity are black as far as membership, but certainly have white values since they consider themselves "black Greeks." Owens is an Uncle Tom and as a result, he would only tend to acknowledge organizations and agencies that he deems "good for the white man to know about." And these are but a few (many more have been added since 1968, trust me).

As human case studies Owens tends to offer up first names of people and then explain their behavior in order to make the point he is trying to make at that time. There is no evidence that these people exist. And he mentions only the first name as if he is trying to protect their identity. Why? After all, the white man is his pal and he trusts whitey, does he not? Why not give someone a little extra publicity by putting it in his Uncle Tom primer of a book, where his pale buddies could see?

Personally, I think he's lying. You can be the judge for yourself as he discusses a guy named "Pete":

> Pete is a Negro who talks with a smile, and always reasonably.
> He's so reasonable, in fact, that both negro and white friends have
> called him "the one black man who's been left untouched by
> prejudice" (pp. 45-46).

He just described the perfect Uncle Tom. In other words, he described himself. But Pete, who supposedly actually exists, is more than just the skin-and-grin coon that was described above:

> A forty-three-year-old college graduate with an excellent job on a
> large metropolitan magazine, Pete smiles when people tell him
> how "amazing" his lack of anger is. But inside he seethes. For
> inside is a staggering mountain of hostility, and, every few months,
> it boils over and Pete's attractive wife goes to her job wearing too
> much makeup which doesn't quite hide the bruises on her face (p.
> 46).

Owens is a lying muthafucka. How could he have so much personal information on this guy? And if Pete had any kind of hostility in him, why didn't he use it to kick Jesse up in HIS ass? Why is he taking it out on the woman? And why do people like Owens think that someone saying how "amazing" it is to be lacking in anger is a good thing? How would they know if this guy was angry or not? In fact, just making that statement directly to Pete's face is a fuckin' insult. White people have a tendency to do that shit: because they think so little of black people they feel that whatever they say, as long as it's coming from them, is going to be deemed to be a compliment.

Owens' bold-faced lie continues:

> Pete is angry. Pete is violent inside. Maybe even sick. But not because he's a Negro. Because he' a man – with a man's problems. Pete and Corinne, you see, have never, not once in fifteen years of marriage, been really able to make it in bed together. And it's destroying them both (p. 46).

So fuckin' what? Pete can't get a boner, so he's pissed off. What does that got to do with the price of eggs? There are black men with erectile dysfunction, which is a direct negation of the societal stereotype of the black man who walks around with a perpetual hard-on. But it happens. But if Owens is willing to go into such detail about this imaginary guy's sex problems, why can't he also delve into the white man's historical envy of the black man's sexual conquests of white women? Why doesn't he write about white women who chase black men down, whether the men are rich or poor? I think you know why.

Back to Owens and his (fake) case study:

> Pete's problem is his skin color, that his impotency comes from the supposed psychological emasculation of the Negro male by the white race. Because part and parcel of that emasculation myth is the phony legend of Negro sexual superiority. The black man, the story goes, made up for his suppression in the only place that he could: bed. He has thus come to be a supreme sexual animal, a tireless and incomparable lover (p. 48).

All of this is based on supposition, conjecture and bullshit. Owens takes one stereotype and tries to offset it with another. And he is not qualified to even have an opinion in either case. He's just an asshole saying what he knows the white man wants to hear and what the black man won't read. His white co-writer is getting a chance to throw in his little racial viewpoints as well, with Jesse, as has been his lifelong tendency, right there to take the heat.

But Jesse the sexologist, is on a roll. Check out the following:

> That, of course, is crap. Some white women may respond more to
> negro men because black lovers are taboo, and Negro men
> generally may be more culturally uninhibited than WASPS and
> Jews and Britons (though less than Italians and Frenchmen and
> Berkeley students), but that doesn't change the Negro into
> Superlover. Every black man when he gets into bed with a woman
> has the same problems that *men* have, tempered by his own
> individual personality and values. Like Pete (p. 48 – emphasis
> original).

Pure foolishness. The chapter is called "Negroes Have Human Hangups" but all that he wants to talk about are black people's failings. We have human hang-ups that white people envy and that we take for granted: dancing, singing, our spirituality, our athleticism, our survival code and so on. But Jesse wants to interject as much "whiteness" into his explanations of the black condition as he can, because in his view, black cats bring bad luck, angel's food cake is white and devil's food cake is black. The bad guys wear black hats and the good guys wear white hats. He is as brainwashed as most negroes during that time but he brings another variable to the table: stupidity.

The chapter continues:

> Pete had what is known today as a "Jewish mother." She's pretty
> prevalent among negroes, too. And among most other families. A
> hundred years ago it might have been different. But today a whole
> new generation of Nero males has grown up who were raised in
> middle-class homes by a mother who sometimes doted on the first
> son to the point where he couldn't cut it later in a mature male-
> female relationship. I realize that this also contradicts the phony
> myth of the typical Negro family as hopelessly fragmented, with
> the mother either an unwed welfare or "widow" to a man who has
> left her long ago (pp. 48-49).

Jewish mothers? Does that mean that they're strict and dominating? Well let me tell you something else about Jewish women: out of the women who marry and date black men, a disproportionately high percentage of them are Jewish women. If the Jewish male is such a great provider, why are the women looking for black dicks to suck? Maybe the Jewish mother is so strict because she's so sexually frustrated from not getting fucked regularly enough. Ever thing of *that?*

Owens writes,

> Pete has everything to live for and he knows it. He's intelligent,
> educated, makes good money, and, like a geometrically increasing

> number of Negroes, has never really bothered emotionally, socially
> or professionally by the color of his skin (p. 50).

Jesse Owens doesn't have a single god-damned statistic, graph, map, chart or data base to back up all this shit he is pawning off as fact. Pete has no more to live for than any other black man in a white racist society. There are plenty of intelligent, educated black men who are now in the morgue because some racist ass cop decided that the black man looked too good or the black man was with a white bitch or the black man was at the wrong place at the wrong time.

How does Owens arrive at the claim that there are a "geometrically increasing number of Negroes" who are doing anything, let alone those not being bothered by the color of their skin? This is a damn lie. And what he probably means is "exponentially increasing," not "geometrically increasing." Dumb fuck. In his quest to prove a point that all is well with race relations he is not only willing to lie but he's also willing to put himself out there was one of the major perpetrators of racial stereotypes.

But it is not enough to defend the white man and the system that oppresses black people. You also have to degrade and debase black people who dare to stand up to that system. And again, that is where Jesse "the oreo" Owens comes in:

> It's the Harry Edwardses who have sold themselves (and are
> threatening to sell America) on this myth, just as some southern
> landowners sold us another myth a hundred and fifty years ago.
> How can a small group of writers and political activists have such
> a staggering influence? That's what's so dangerous about
> blackthink and why it's so important to expose it. A midget can
> paralyze a giant by putting one finger in the right spot on his neck.
> The course of history has often been guided by the few who knew
> its pressure points. The chances are much less of this happening in
> a free country, but its' still possible (p. 60).

To answer this asshole's question about why "a small group of writers and political activists" can have such "staggering influence," let me offer up the following response.

First of all, it's not a small group. It was made up of a large number of black people who began to see through the bullshit. It started with the Underground Railroad and has evolved through Marcus Garvey, W.E.B. DuBois, Malcolm X and so many others – all people that Owens never even bothered to mention in his bullshit book.

Secondly, the basis for any "staggering influence" that black writers and activists may have had is because what was being said was based in actual facts and the truth, not the manipulated manifestations of reality that were engineered by cavity creeps like Jesse Owens and his white co-writer.

Third and finally is the claim that, "The course of history has often been guided by the few who knew its pressure points. The chances are much less of this happening in a free country, but its' still possible." These words were published in 1968. It is now 2016, some 48 years later. That's almost half a century. And in this day we can see that this "free country" is getting its ass kicked, domestically and internationally, by people who not only know the pressure points, but who are also responding to the age old atrocities that this country has inflicted upon people of color –and white women – the world over. The chances have increased "exponentially" since the time when Jesse Owens was considered "relevant."

But what is Owens' interpretation? Like the bombastic and racist Donald Trump of 2016, the bootlicker of 1968 views the situation as follows:

> The sad fact is that a hypersensitive and naïve public, an often out-of-touch "moderate"'" leadership and a sometimes headline-hungry press have played perfectly into the hands of the blackthinkers (p. 60).

Owens sounds just like a white man. He thinks like a white man. And he is frustrated because he cannot actually be one. This is the deep-rooted problem in this whole issue. He hates whomever and whatever the white man hates, and he craves whatever the white man craves. Remember reader: this is a muthafucka that ran a race against race horses for money. And if that's not enough to show what a fuckin' robot he is, just re-read the titled of the chapters in this book. And remember the sub-title: "My Life As A Black Man and White Man." Having read the book, I think the sub-title should be, "My Life As a White Man – Period."

In a statement that is part history and part stool pigeon (snitch), the coonish collaborator offers the following insights:

> Carlos and Smith did give the black-power salute, of course. But even their thoughts at the Olympics weren't consumed by the race situation. First, they had to worry about winning. If they didn't get up there on the medalists' pedestal, they weren't going to be giving any salutes at all. And Tommy smith's feat in winning the two hundred meters took monolithic concentration on that event and nothing else. It was even more amazing because that afternoon he pulled a muscle in his groin, one of the more painful injuries a sprinter can have. In the beginning, it didn't seem as though he'd be running the finals at all a few hours later. But a white physician from Oklahoma named Cooper worked on him, and Tommy ran. And broke not only the Olympic record but the world mark (p. 63).

Only a true "nigger" would take the accomplishments of a black man and give credit to a white physician. But at least Owens is consistent: he did the same thing in his own case as you will later scene: he literally credits the Nazi Luz Long with his (Owens') success and victory in the broad jump! Now do you see why I have nominated Jesse Owens as the biggest Uncle Tom in the history of the universe?

His insights on Carlos and Smith continue:

> Tommy is a high-class boy, and I think that much of what he did at the Games were influenced by John Carlos and by Tommy's wife, who is really extreme on the subject of black power. And speaking of wives, there wouldn't have been any demonstration at all if the Consultant's committee hadn't found places for the wives to live. Carlos had brought his wife Kim, and she was living unauthorized in a segment of the athletes' quarters. The Olympic Committee was about to remove her and I think if she had been sent home, her husband would have gone with her … (p. 63).

This makes the second or third time that he has referred to Smith as "boy." Smith was a grown man. When I interviewed John Carlos back in November of 2011 during his presentation at the Pan-African Connection in Dallas, Texas, he didn't have much positive to say about Tommy, either. He made it sound like Tommy didn't want to talk much about the black power salute and that once back in America, he was more concerned about finding a job than anything else. If Tommy's wife was a conscious sistah, she wouldn't have necessarily objected because she wanted to eat too. But is this really something to put in a book for everyone to read unless – you are trying to embarrass the black power movement through divide and conquer?

That makes two white gestures by Owens: referring to Smith as "boy" and the attempt to divide and conquer the two black men who stood strong on the podium that night in 1968. Owens further offers that,

> Without John, I wonder if Tommy Smith would have given any Nazi salutes. But I met with them and then with the Olympic Committee, and the next day Mrs. Carlos had a place of her own to stay in, with the Committee paying for it (p. 63).

A "Nazi salute"? That would mean that the millions of black people who identified with what Smith and Carlos did would have to be "Nazi sympathizers"? And it would mean that the black power salute, which became a key trademark of the black power movement, would be a derivative of Hitler. Jesse Owens needs his ass kicked for such a statement. The black power salute was no more a Nazi salute than and Pledge of Allegiance is an Oath to the Ku Klux Klan.

Nevertheless, Owens claims he met with Smith and Carlos and he doesn't explain why. But he was there to represent white interests of this there is no doubt. He was there as a snitch for the white man, as a "boy" that whitey could count on to inform on what took place, and as someone who would represent whitey's views. See for yourself:

> Finally, I got fed up. "You know, Carlos," I yelled, "you talk about Whitey this and Whitey that. Everything's 'get Whitey out of my hair!' But when it comes to the most private kind of meeting of all, here you are with good old Whitey! He goes everywhere you go. Man, *I* can get along without him. How come *you* can't?" (p. 63-- emphasis original).

First of all I don 't believe that cowardly sonofabitch Owens said anything like that. I am pretty sure, having met John Carlos – who is still an imposing figure when I talked with him in 2011 – would have kicked Owens' ass all over that room. I think Owens sat on his ass and kept his mouth shut. But let's stretch reality a bit and assume that Owens did grow a pair and confront John Carlos the way he claims he did.

What would be his purpose? Why would he make it sound as if Carlos was some kind of Uncle Tom because a white man was there for publicity purposes? Why would he make the claim that he (Owens) could get along without the white man when he knows that is a fuckin' lie? Owens needed white people the same way that a young child needs its parents. Jesse Owens was dependent on white people because white folks were his role models. He loved them more than he loved himself and he's proven that time and time again with his own words.

Owens placed that lie in the book to convince white readers that they need not fear because he (Owens) had their back and white interests would be represented in this sea of black militant thought and action. The chapter, "Negroes Have Human Hangups" surely is a testament to Owens' working to convince white people that black people are, indeed, human beings! And in addition to that, he wants to convince the reader that white people are trying their *garsh-darndest* to do everything they can for those people (meaning black folks).

Need an example? Check out the following passage:

> Well, a negro kid *can* make it here, *especially* here. It's no accident that there's a higher percentage of colored major league baseball players than in the population at large. Or that almost half the pro basketball players are black. It isn't because that's the only place they'll let us in, either. No one let Einstein into mathematics

> because he was Jewish or white. And it isn't because we've got
> "rhythm," either. It's because we're *making* it (p. pp. 63-64-
> emphasis original)

Even his own words paint him as an asshole. After blabbering about how a "negro kid" can make it here (meaning America) the first examples out of his mouth are athletics, specifically pro baseball and basketball. Then he adds that these aren't the only places where we can make it. But he doesn't mention any others. He then skips over what could have been added as evidence and goes straight to the Jews and talks about Einstein and mathematics. And if any of these areas – baseball, basketball or mathematics – are indicators of having "made it,' it would be mathematics. As the age-old adage teaches us, "It is the strong who rule the weak but in turn, it is the wise who rule the strong."

In the world of Jesse Owens, black people were "making it." And just how is that Mr. Owens? The position of the races – black and white – are basically in the same position as they were when Henry Owens was sharecropping and when Henry Owens' father was working under a slave system. Where is the evidence of "making it" asshole? If black people were "making it," why was he staging races against thoroughbred horses for white entertainment and profit?

The fact is, Owens feels that it is his duty to prove that integration was working and was the solution to all problems. Even though he couldn't provide much evidence of black people "making it," his strategy is probably that if you say it often enough, and offer up vague, undocumented statements, sooner or later the gullible American public will accept his bullshit as facts.

For instance, relying on the white man's studies and reports, the buffoon of the broad jump writes:

> The Lou Harris study following Martin's murder proved it. *Even then*, at the negro's moment of greatest disillusion in this century, less than one black in nine favored any kind of separatism. Less than one in twenty opposed desegregation. From scholarly studies such as the analysis by Johns Hopkins University's James Coleman and the Kerner Commission surveys to what you can see with your own eyes by looking around you once you turn off the rantings of a few soap boxing blackthinkers, the facts are plain. Well in excess of ninety-five percent of all negroes are no more militant than I am (p. 67).

First of all, the 1960s were not "the negro's moment of greatest disillusionment in this country. That would mean that this decade would trump enslavement, sharecropping, lynching periods and so on. Just because Jesse Owens says it doesn't make it so; actually as we can see, when Owens says it, we can pretty much conclude that it's a damnable lie.

Furthermore, he claims that the Harris study concluded that less than one black in nine favored any kind of separatism. I'm a social scientist among other things. Here's what I know: black people don't trust white people calling them up on the phone asking them political questions. And if that is the case today, then you can imagine how it was in the 1960s when black people were far more racially conscious. Therefore, the survey was skewed to put it mildly.

Third, what would you expect black people to say, whether they meant it or not? They're not going to tell some anonymous peckerwood voice on the phone that they want racial separatism! All that fighting for integration that their tommish leader Martin Luther King Jr. was advocating and you think that Lou Harris is going to get answers that show black people are collectively willing to separate? Use your fuckin' heads, folks.

Fourth, Owens then adds what he believes is the coup de grace when he makes the white-endorsing claim that, "From scholarly studies such as the analysis by Johns Hopkins University's James Coleman and the Kerner Commission surveys to what you can see with your own eyes by looking around you once you turn off the rantings of a few soap boxing blackthinkers, the facts are plain. Well in excess of ninety-five percent of all negroes are no more militant than I am."

The fact of the matter is those "scholarly studies" were biased. Their job, like that of Owens, was to assuage the American conscience and to quell any beliefs that a race war was pending. Therefore their conclusions were drawn before any surveys ever took place. They had to prove to the white majority that the white man was still in control and that niggas were no threat to the status quo.

Fifth, notice that while the biased "scholarly studies" that Owens cites are described with respect, what do black people get? He refers to what we have to say as "rantings of a few soap box blackthinkers." Really? How about novels like Baldwin's *The Fire Next Time* (1963) or Harper Lee's *To Kill a Mockingbird*? What about his pal King's book, *Where Do We Go From Here: Chaos or Community?* (1967)? How about *The Autobiography of Malcolm X* (1965) or the findings of America headed for separatism ("two societies, one black, one white – separate and unequal") by his pals at the Kerner Commission. Oh, and by the way, the full title of that "scholarly report" was The Kerner Commission on Civil Disorders. So the entire nation was brimming with works that pointed out racism and promoted "black power." My question is: what planet was Owens visiting when all this was taking place on planet Earth?

That is why when Owens makes the claim that, "Well in excess of ninety-five percent of all negroes are no more militant than I am," he is insulting millions of black people who were shouting, "Say it Loud, I'm Black and I'm Proud" and making pro-black groups like the Last Poets, the Watts Prophets, Sly and the Family Stone and others major successes in and around black communities. If Owens wants to admit that he's a sellout, that's his business. But he is committing an act of race treachery by attempting to make it appear to his readers that most black people were as mentally fucked up as he was.

But the lies are not enough. Next come the outright insults:

> In fact, to most of them the Harry Edwardses and Jim Formans are like some newspaper caricatures, the other side of the image that Stepin Fetchit used to play in films, As one of my sons-in-law said to me not long ago, "Where has Rap Brown *been*, man?" Except that it's not funny (p. 67-emphasis original).

Since when does Jesse Owens speak for all black people? Where does he get the *cojones* to write as if he's some kind of authority? Not even the conservative Dr. King would have the nerve to do that. But here is Owens acting as if he can sit as judge of black men who are confronting a racist system and trying to defend and develop black communities – two things Owens has *never* bothered to commit himself to.

Caricatures? Stepin Fetchit? First of all, Lincoln Perry (Stepin Fetchit) was a good brother in real life and contributed to black causes and was a good friend with Muhammad Ali. Secondly, how can this super-tom talk about someone else when his own daily actions clearly show that he's a race traitor through and through. In fact, he was a modern day Stepin Fetchit in real life!

Quoting other toms in his quest to undermine black initiative, Owens closes out his chapter on "negro hang-ups" by proving that he is undoubtedly suffering from the biggest hang up of all: *reality denial*. He writes,

> Dr. Raymond Mack of Northwestern University's Center for Urban Affairs carries this a step further. He thinks that even negro rioting among the extremists may be going out of the picture. Why? Because the negro is so well off and getting more well off with each new day. Yes, the Negro has problems – sometimes terrible problems. But they are almost always *human* problems now, and who in the hell doesn't have those? (pp. 67-68-emphasis original)

Riots going out of the picture? As long as this system continues to abuse black people in the ghetto, allow cops to gun us down and pass racist legislation, the black people in this country are always going to do something about it. In the days of Owens there were real riots; today there are those bullshit prayer vigils and protests with signs, but they still scare the shit out of the white man and his negro lackeys. I think that the riots in Augusta, Georgia (1970), Houston (1974), Miami (1980), Tampa (1989), Crown Heights (1991), Los Angeles (1995), Cincinnati (2001), Toledo (2005), Santa Cruz (2010), Baltimore (2015) and let us not forget the 2014 race-oriented riots of August of 2014.

Owens and his pal who made the riot prediction were both as wrong as wrong can be. If white people want to play Nazi, black folks in America ain't gonna play Jews. White people know that, which is why their police departments have been transformed into paramilitary units to patrol the ghetto and act the part of an army of occupation. They fear us, and well they should. We continue to represent, as Malcolm X once called it, "the hate that hate produced."

And yet another "negro hangup" is on the part of any "negro" who doesn't understand what I've just pointed out to you in this chapter.

Chapter 5: Anatomy of a Militant

How would this collaborationist know what it takes to make a "militant"? So far his analyses have been wrong, when not ass-backwards. And yet there is a chapter in the book *Blackthink* that is devoted to the subject and therefore, worthy of critical race analysis.

The chapter begins:

> In one sense, every Negro must be a militant if he has any
> manhood at all. But blackthink-bred Negro militancy and
> revolution are simply the biggest of black herrings. But it isn't
> enough to say that speeches by the Stokelys are what set off these
> huge hoaxes. Who really creates them? Why? What does it mean
> to this country? The answer lies in the anatomy of a black
> extremist, at the very gut of blackthink (p. 69).

Again, this man is attempting to sound like an authority on a subject that he knows nothing about. Even in the previous paragraph he contradicts himself and comes off sounding like a total jackass. Let me explain.

To begin with he says that every black person has to be a militant if they have any manhood at all. He didn't say "should be" but "must be." That means that in his view, in order to be a man you have to be militant. If this is the case, then why does he not practice some himself? Why is he such an Uncle Tom? I'll tell you why: because he has his own definition of, his own brand of "militancy." To him, being militant means going along to get along; it means kowtowing and not making waves; it means agreeing to run races against thoroughbred horses in exchange for money. In simple terms, Owens' view of militancy is what anyone else would refer to as "accommodationism."

Secondly, what is a "black herring"? It's a play on words. The term "red herring" usually refers to something that misleads or distracts from a relevant or important issue. According to one source, a red herring "may be either a logical fallacy or a literary device that leads readers or audiences towards a false conclusion." So when Owens writes that blackthink is a "black herring," he means that it is bullshit, it is fake and it is not real or genuine. Idiots shouldn't engage in plays on words when they can barely understand the basics of the language.

He says that the speeches given by militant bruthas are a hoax. And what is a hoax? A hoax is defined as, "a humorous or malicious deception:" So the black people speaking out against racism and who are promoting a "pro-black" agenda are trying to dupe black people and white people alike? This is what Owens wants his readers to believe? By promoting bullshit like this Owens is setting people up to get their asses kicked. Black men and women died standing up to this system and here comes this Uncle Tom talking about it's all a façade.

So now the sprint-happy sellout is going to spend the rest of this chapter "explaining" to us what he calls, "the anatomy of a black extremist, at the very gut of blackthink." This should be good for a few laughs.

He starts off with a caveat: he writes,

> For I'm not condemning every extremist. I can't agree with every single thing that Billy did, yet I feel there's got to be a place for the strongest kind of dissent in our society. More important, there's got to be a place – an important place – for dissenters like the Bills in particular (p. 73).

Thus far in this book, this black muthafucka has done nothing else BUT 'condemn every extremist.' He has called black people Nazis and he has degraded just about everyone and anyone who is not an accommodationist on the level of Martin Luther King Jr.

Then, sounding like some kind of white segregationist who wants black people put in concentration camps he writes, "there's got to be a place – an important place – for dissenters like the Bills in particular."

Owens sounds just like the white man who constantly talks about black people "knowing their place." No, not their role, but their "place." Owens has been so well-trained by his white masters that he believes that this is what black people should be concentrating on doing. And do you think a man who thinks like this is the type of man who is going to tell us anything genuine about "The anatomy of a militant"? His goal is to lock up black people who think progressively and to lambaste them; his goal is to put down any signs of black resistance to white racism and to transform us all into ass licking accommodationists. Like him.

Drawing from personal experience, he tosses in an ego trip or two in the following paragraph:

> While in East Technical High School, I broke the record I the hundred-yard dash, running it in 9.4 seconds. I'd been coming close, but until I actually did it no one noticed me much. Once it happened, though, the whole world seemed to be at my door. Reporters wanted interviews, and even long-distance calls came to the school for me. But then the real stuff began to happen. Colleges started sending letters. Some of them even sent people. Everyone wanted me to go to his university. At *his* cost. Many f them were willing to have me live in high style, in fact. One school offered me not only my own six-room apartment off the campus and a new car, but "use" of two beautiful women whenever I wanted. Colored, of course (pp. 74-75).

Even when he boasts about himself he cannot help but snitch or "blow the whistle" on others. Doesn't he know that the accusation that a college offered him two black girls for his own use is a serious allegation? Doesn't he realize that if his book was of relevance, that statement could be subpoenaed by the NCAA and penalties levied, that he could be FORCED to testify? But this Uncle Tom knows what he's doing: he's making it look as if the white man wanted him so badly that he (Owens) could have had anything he wanted – much like the black athletes of today. His claim to fame was that he could run really fast. That's it. They didn't know if he could cut the mustard in college classes or not nor did they care – they'd have other people doing his work for him – just like today. The white man's tactics and priorities have not changed when it comes to the treatment of black people and it's because of the success they've had with brainless buffoons like Jesse Owens.

Next comes another of his (imaginary) case studies. This one's name is "Ted":

> Ted doesn't actually have any philosophy, new or old. He changes his views on issues as fast as a different extremist leaders can lay a hand on his shoulder and blow in his ear. He's in the majority as far as today's militants are concerned but, majority or not, he's still a hanger-on. And the reason he's going along for the ride is that it's the *easy* way. One vacation he said it to his brother in a rare moment of honesty. "Check," he confided, "I'm just doing all this to cop out on the homework. And sometimes I hate myself for it" (p. 79 – emphasis original).

Now how would Owens knows who's in the majority and who is in the minority when it comes to people who think a certain way? Did he conduct a survey? Did he ask around? Has he done any research at all? Of course not. And do you know why? Because he doesn't know how. He's like those old-school southern bitches who sit on the porch and exchange gossip and rumors and then spread it all over the community until it becomes fact. It's all about conjecture, homespun metaphysical assumptions and wild theories. But that's okay: he's accomplishing his goal, which is to work toward making the white man look flawless while throwing stones and making fun of black people.,

The concept of "copping out on homework" is something all college students do, athletes or not. How do you think I've made hundreds of thousands of dollars in non-taxable income over the decades writing papers for these losers? And speaking of losers, Owens never got a college degree from Ohio State until many years later they "gave" him an honorary degree, which really doesn't mean shit. In his book he never talks about studying, doing homework, having exams or any of that. And he is remembered, after the Olympics, for holding jobs as a gas station attendant, a sports promoter (racing horses) and owner of his own dry cleaning business.

Now tell me: *who copped out?*

Continuing with Ted:

> Yet when Ted goes back to school, his self-hate will turn itself
> outward, against teaches who've spent a lifetime in intellectual
> pursuits, against fellow students who only want an education,
> against a society that is pretty rotten in places but for which he
> really has nothing better to substitute (p. 79).

This is how he views black students on these racist white campuses? He absolves the classroom teachers for their role in the perpetuation of racism. He absolves them for the ordering of textbooks that are filled with lies written by their predecessors. Owens admits that society is "pretty rotten in places" and says that Ted has nothing better to substitute. And guess what? Neither does Owens. If he is willing to admit that there is rot, then can there be any doubt that he has been infected and influenced by it?

His hatred for his own people has clearly been established. But in case there was any doubt, read how he describes black militant speakers and his response to what they had to say:

> Not long ago I was speaking at a big college in the New York area.
> Afterward, I walked across the campus to where a fairly well-
> known black militant was also giving a speech. He was ranting and

> raving and had the audience on their feet ranting and raving much
> of the time. For a minute, I was actually afraid they were going to
> march out of that hall and tear down the school. But the speaker
> knew just how to quiet them whenever things got to the pressure
> point. His words would go soft and honey-dipped, he'd stop still
> and s few seconds later the audience would be like a group of
> statues … (p. 80).

Yeah – speaking at "a big college in the New York area." You name names when it comes to black people who you can slander, but when it comes to the white man, you protect his institutions unless you're using the name to make the system look flawless.

So he speaks at a big college. What was the topic? Why was this college dropout even speaking? His story is one of leaving school for sports and never returning for his degree. Don't we have enough niggas like that? Owens is no role model for black kids – he's an embarrassment. He goes to hear a speaker and can't even be open minded enough to appreciate the reaction to the audience, obviously comprised of people who WANTED to be there. Instead, he criticizes the people for having a reaction akin to that which you might find at any black church on Sundays. What he describes in terms of the speaker's control of the audience is not much different than what those bullshit artist ministers do to black people "in the name of God" every Sunday.

But it is Owens' intention to make the people who believe a certain way to appear to be hypnotized or mesmerized. It is his intention to make the speaker sound like nothing short of a demagogue. It is his intention to undermine black, progressive thinking people and replace it with his brand of ass-kissing and Uncle Tomfoolery. Then, check out what happens:

> … I could only take it for about fifteen minutes, then went outside
> for a breath of air. Just as soon as I loosened my tie, a young man
> came through the doors and walked over to me. "You're Jesse
> Owens, aren't you?" I nodded. "Slumming?" "I like to hear all
> sides," I said (p. 80).

He could only "take it for about 15 minutes." Owens couldn't bear to hear a speaker that was lambasting his white master. When you dogged out white folks, you dogged out Owens because, after all by his own admission, he was a white man. So when he told the young man that he wanted "to hear all sides," he was once again telling a lie. He couldn't deal with anything that was not singing the praises of America and his white role models. As Jack Nicholson shouted to Tom Cruise in the movie, "A Few Good Men," "You can't handle the truth"!!!

Then come the lies that Owens occasionally sprinkles in to make black people appear to be con artists:

> … None of this is news to me. Not one white man in a hundred thousand can retire at forty. But a number of Negroes today are finding a way through blackthink. Some of them will even make it by thirty, in fact. Some of them *have* made it (p. 81).

How did Owens arrive at that figure of not one white man being able to retire at age 40? Did he consult AARP? Does he have any actual figures to back up his blanket lie? Of course not. There were white boys who inherited trusts and had legacies and were therefore not in a position to even have to be concerned about retiring: they never had to work in the first place! Why didn't Uncle Tom mention that little fact? And today, in the 21st century, we know of white boys who are barely out of their 20s who are millionaires and billionaires. So again, Jesse will lie in an attempt to take the white man's side of any argument.

He then implies that thinking black and public speaking about the black condition is some kind of con game that can make black people rich. When black people started getting paid for speeches, it was the white man who needed them to do it to calm down those college campuses and to bring those campuses in line with the "free speech" that they claimed to believe in. Furthermore, when black people speak on major issues, they usually don't speak locally; they talk generic bullshit and oftentimes only glance over issues of racism. The so-called "black leaders" who make the real money – Rev. Jesse Jackson, Maulana Karenga, Tavis Smiley and those of that ilk – are usually invited in during some cultural holiday like Kwanzaa, Black History Month or Martin Luther King's birthday.

What blacks have "made it"? As was cited earlier, people like Sammy Davis Jr., Billie Holiday, "Little" Richard, Muddy Waters, Chuck Berry died broke – but their Jewish agents and attorneys didn't. But that's not all. What about the black celebrities who went broke and are still alive: Gary Doudant, T-Boz of the group TLC, Dionne Warwick, Sinbad, Evander Holyfield and Michael Vick, to name but a few? They had white agents, managers, real estate specialists and others who helped them blow those millions of dollars after they "made it" and when the money was gone, Owens' white buddies were nowhere to be found.

Owens' onslaught nevertheless continues:

> Still, even if an important group of the militant leaders are opportunists or idealists who sold out, I'm not trying to make devils out of them. I don't see any real difference in selling ideas you don't' believe or in selling refrigerators or deodorants you don't dig. I guess racing against scared horses isn't much different,

> either. It's something most of us do. It's also something we should
> grow out of (p. 81).

The insinuation here is that black people speak out to get money but when all is said and done, they don't really believe it. In other words, Owens believes that black people who speak out against racism and the discrimination against the system are just bullshittin' the masses. Now don't get me wrong, there are people who do this on a regular basis, but it was not the black militant speakers that the sellout Owens is describing. This group is in every community in America with a sizable black population. That groups is known as "ministers." Some call them "preachers." I call them "pimps in the pulpit" and "hallelujah hucksters."

Owens says that such behavior, if it exists, is something we should grow out of. Did he grow out of it? No. He remained an Uncle Tom until the bitter end. Did he grow out of kissing all that ass? No. He continued to be the white man's favorite Uncle Tom, a title that he accepted awards and monetary favors for. So what he is describing and attributing to the "blackthinks" (as he calls them) is actually the kind of behavior and the types of motives that he, Jesse Owens, is really guilty of!

Jesse Owens seems to hate anything that promotes blackness:

> … Yet just as important is the blackthink that has become a profit-
> thing to many, many more people than those few who expect to be
> millionaires – from the printers who publish the pamphlets to the
> politicians who use blackthink to get votes … (p. 82).

First of all the printers. Who in the FUCK do you think printed up all those "No niggers allowed," "We don't serve coons," "no negroes or dogs" signs that were all over the United States back in the day? Who do you think is responsible for all that hate literature circulated by the Ku Klux Klan, the White Citizens Council and other groups? That shit wasn't donated: white people scraped up donations and paid professional printers for that shit. And they still do it to that day. For that matter, these racist major newspapers whose views are pawned off as facts – where are *their* checks and balances? They are protected by the First Amendment, that's what.

And as for using propaganda to gain votes, that's what politics is all about, asshole! The Black Panther Party newspaper (*The Black Panther Intercommunal News Service*) had as much a right to be distributed as any other, but Jews and other white boys would continue to try to sabotage the national distribution, including closing down the truck lanes and keeping the paper off of presses. Did you know that? *The Muhammad Speaks* continues to get the word out in its current form as *The Final Call*, and is a quality newspaper. People have the right to print what the fuck they want. The white man controls all the major newspapers and I don't see much sympathy for black people in most of those newspapers. Do you?

So on Jesse's planet, not only are the "blackthinkers" con artists who print and speak lies about good ol' whitey, but they are also provocateurs who intentionally want to fan the flames of racial hatred. And now we come to other black ne'er-do-wells: the rioters and the looters. According to Owens,

> …To the looters. Do you really think that the rioters who grab the television sets and the vacuum cleaners from shattered store windows during riots are black revolutionaries? The revolutionaries are almost always cool calculators who plan the thing, set it off and know every expert technique to keep it going. But the rioters themselves? They want the television sets and vacuum cleaners. Militancy is the excuse that lets them take these things. Some of them would've broken in anyway and stolen those goods, but others would've looked longingly at them day after day and only wanted to do it (p. 82).

Poverty is what creates revolutionaries, especially in "the land of plenty." Watching these sick peckerwoods spend $60,000 for a chair or flaunting their wealth and their homes on television – that's what creates revolutionaries. The people who loot are attacking the system and trying to get something knowing full well that the stores that are located in their area are fully insured. That's what no one ever wants to talk about. When those assholes who own the stores and the businesses get their windows bashed in or merchandise stolen, they re-build, lie to their insurance companies, get their money back and get on about the business of capitalist exploitation. If Owens would take his head out of his ass, he'd know that.

Militancy is no excuse. Toms like Owens were looting just as much as anyone else, although he would like you to think otherwise. He admits as much when he says of the looters that, "Some of them would've broken in anyway and stolen those goods, but others would've looked longingly at them day after day and only wanted to do it." And that is my point: people who are constantly being bombarded with the message that "if you try you can make it," and yet thanks to on-going racism and discrimination they keep getting passed over. Like Owens did: and when he was approached, he ended up working menial jobs, racing thoroughbreds and not even close to earning the kind of money that white boys with inferior talent were earning. This is why people riot and loot – asshole!

Continuing:

> So from the lowest looter to the highest sounding race profiteer,
> black think for money isn't pretty. To its dollar-hungry pitchmen,
> it's like a kid's chemistry set in which someone has mistakenly

supplied the chemicals in full potency. Yet even the blackthink
profit-prophets don't chill my bones like another kind of militant,
the one who *has* to do what he's doing not because he believes in it
and is honestly turned on like the Billys or even because he doesn't
believe in anything and is drifting aimlessly like the teds But
because he's sick (p. 82 – emphasis original).

So as far as Owens is concerned, no one who has black skin can do a damn thing that is right. No one who is black has the right to stand up to a government or to a race of people that have abused black men, women and children for centuries. No one who dares to point out society's inequities is nothing more than someone who wants something for nothing. Jesse Owens makes George Wallace sound like a member of Black Lives Matter. Owens is an abomination and an insult to black humanity.

Then he talks about someone named Lonnie (another unnamed case study) and uses this supposedly real person as a way to flip black militants into a somewhat different arena:

Then he met an older man who introduced him to homosexuality.
By doing what the man waned he could stop living in underground
parking lots. But the man gave him more than room and board.
Even though it was in a perverted fashion, this was the first person
to care about Lonnie since his older sister. So the boy came to
depend on it. By the time he was fifteen, Lonnie was a full-fledged
homosexual … (p. 83).

Introduced him to homosexuality? I know this book was published in 1968, but such warped thinking! He was introduced to homosexuality, that means that he either took it up the ass or was sucking dick – or a combination of one or both of the above. At any rate, he was doing what he did in underground parking lots. Now comes the conjecture, where Owens refers to homosexual interaction as a perversion and assumes that this was the first person to care about Lonnie since his older sister.

Really? And just how would Jesse know all this intimate information and the details? Was Jesse a rump roaster or a fudge packer behind closed doors? How would he know that the boy came to "depend" on such attention? Was Jesse there? Was he a jolly jabber? Did the boy confide in him and if so, why would he tell Jesse such intimate information?

When Owens claims and concludes that by the time Lonnie was 15 he was "a full fledged homosexual," this stupid statement is yet another indicator of Owens' naiveté. If a person is gay, he was that way at birth. That is my belief. You can't be partially gay or "bi-sexual" as these dumb ass millennials claim. Either you like pussy or you like nuts banging upside your head – it's one or the other. And furthermore, what the fuck does this have to do with the topic of the chapter, which is supposed to be, "Anatomy of a Militant"?

Now Owens divulges his *real* intentions and interests in Lonnie's "case":

> But one thing he isn't. He is not motivated by what Negro psychologist Kenneth B. Clark calls "a genuine Negro fear of moving outside the 'pathetically protective' walls of segregation.' Because Lonnie isn't Negro. He is white. His parents are white. There isn't any more negro blood in his body than there is in George Wallace's. Still he attracts negroes – both to his cause and to his bed. Because he knows what the most downtrodden Negro feels and has felt. If any black-power advocate ever tells you that a white man can't understand what it's like to experience what some negroes have in America, don't believe him. Lonnie knows (pp. 84-85).

So now black people are gays in disguise? Black militants are faggots? Is this what Owens is implying? Maybe he's speaking for himself. After all, he's the one who got out there in front of thousands of people and ran around a track in modified bikini draws and some spikes! He's the one who showered with other men for a great deal of his life. And he's the one who hung out, oftentimes behind closed doors, with white boys. What is Owens' conclusion? Read it for yourself:

> Put them together. Now you see it like it truly is. Now you know who's copping out where really fighting whitethink is concerned. The militants are most often the *real* Uncle Toms (p. 85).

So Owens was committed to flipping the script and pointing the finger at black militants. This whole chapter, which is supposed to share the "anatomy of a militant" did nothing more than insult black people, absolve white people of their racist ways and institutions, and then insinuate that black militants were taking it up the ass behind closed doors.

Now do you see why I have dubbed Jesse Owens the biggest Uncle Tom who ever lived? And he's not even done yet. The next chapter places even more doom and gloom on black militant progress and activity in a title that tells you that this is where the Olympic Oreo cookie is headed. The chapter is called, "Blackthink Won't Win."

Chapter 6: Blackthink Won't Win

When the title reads, "Blackthink Won't Win," this is not a statement of fact; it is a prediction, an actual HOPE that is being shouted by Owens. He doesn't want black people with dignity to "win" anything. In this chapter he makes reference to but doesn't mention the courage of people like Nat King Cole, but he spends pages kissing the asses of toms like Willie Mays and Joe Louis.

As you will see in this chapter in particular, this Uncle Tom's obsession with "white is right" has no equal. He begins this chapter from a novel by Roderick Thorp (white) called Dionysus. I located a review of the novel from a quality book analyst site, Kirkus Reviews, and it provides us with a number of reasons why, of all the quotes he could have used and of all the novels Jesse Owens could be reading, he chose this one.

Here is the review:

> Though a long shot from *The Detective*, Mr. Thorp's new novel still has a few of the former's ingredients-length and a little forbidden sex. Otherwise it's the very introspective study of Paul Zindel who returns home after five years of worldly exposure as a jazz musician. Paul had been a high school hero as well as phenomenon (the only Negro), and his cut-off was even more complete since his father was the pastor in the white community church. His stepmother too is a whitey although his half-sister Peggy can hardly pass. At loose ends, Paul is trying to find out where it's at, where he's at. At least he can sympathize with the dilemmas of 18-year-old Peggy with her white boyfriend and their disapproving father. Their togetherness becomes too together and they have an affair which tends to mess up an already mixed up household. But then Paul meets Ellen, an older English woman; Peggy becomes pregnant (hopefully her non-fraternal boyfriend) and they both end up castigating their father who had been quite a swinger in his day. Conversations drone on interminably; the black/white syndrome is, of course, measured in slow cadence; the reader is left in a state of gray paralysis (Kirkus Review, 1969).

So Owens quotes from a book permeated with interracial relationships and sex – and since a white man wrote it, there are most likely also an abundance of stereotypes. On the cover of the novel, which was published in 1969, is a picture of a black youth sitting down and a white woman, nude from the waist up, standing behind him. Of what fuckin' relevance is this book? It falls on the selection of the quote on page 86 that Owens chose to lead off the chapter which, again, is titled "Blackthink Won't Win." Here's the quote Owens chose to lead it off:

> " … I was full of hate, just full, and not only for the white man, but for every living thing. No one can go on like that."

--Roderick Thorp in Dionysus

First of all, the quote was IN the book written by Thorp, not by Thorp himself. Secondly, to imply that Thorp said it takes away the relevance of the quote, which obviously comes from a mis-guided black man. And this brings me to point number three.

Throughout *Blackthink,* the treacherous Owens continues to imply that black people, especially black men, are pathological. He wants the reader to think that black people who don't take shit from the white man (the way he did) or to oppose white racism are somehow mis-guided. And the quote he selected from the novel is aimed at supporting those beliefs. To Owens, all of this racial stuff is about hatred by both blacks and whites. And that black people are every bit as guilty of hating their former slave master as the slave masters descendants are for daring blacks to have the gall to refuse to take that shit any more.

Even the name of the chapter shows Owens' intent and ideology: when he offers that "Blackthink won't win," he is saying that black people who protest and resist will always lose. He is saying that standing up to and confronting your oppressor is an act of futility. Owens despises black consciousness and awareness, gives it a nickname ("blackthink") and then spends an entire book downgrading it. In this chapter we see how big an Uncle Tom Jesse Owens is, how he stands up for the Jews (who probably manipulated the final edition of the book), and how silly and sick he is on the issue of reparations.

I believe that the thesis of this section of the book can be found on page 87 where the bootlicker in cleats:

> One thing I want to accomplish in this book is to still the fear, of
> both whites and negroes, that if and when the extremists try
> anything really wild, there'll be millions upon millions of black
> bronze faces steaming out of the woodwork of our cities to join in.
> For blackthink has destroyed the confidence of the white and
> Negro in each other and next to this, the destruction of property is
> almost unimportant (pp. 87-88).

What a sick fuck. He is writing a book with a white man to "still the fear" that black people won't flood the cities. No, not "stream out of the woodwork" as he put it (implying that we are termites or roaches), but to get into those streets. Black people weren't afraid of that taking place – only his pals, the white folks. So his job was to protect them by "exposing" black people and labeling us in the same way that white people had done over the centuries.

Back to the chapter's beginning, where Owens offers the following quote, intentionally kept anonymous, to start off the chapter: "The great demonstration strengthens the individual … the man who is exposed to serious oppression needs that strengthening … justification of using the most brutal weapons always depends on the presence of a fanatical belief in the necessity of the victor, of a revolutionary new order … The most striking success will always be on whenever the new view is taught to all people, and if necessary, is forced upon them …" (p. 86).

And what was the purpose of this particular quote? Owens tells us in the following passage:

> The credo of a leading black revolutionary? Bits of speeches by black militants? There are two answers to those questions. The first is *yes*, in a sense. For, give or take an adjective or a comma, almost all of the black extremists of today have made statements nearly identical to the one you have just read. But the second answer is *no*, the quotation did not come from any American militant. It was written by Adolf Hitler in Mein Kampf (p. 86).

So to further defame and castigate black militants, Owens uses a quote from a sick fuck like Hitler, equating black people once again with being Nazis. He does this throughout the book, from the thinking and the protest glove fists to quotes from Hitler. At the same time he kisses the asses of, kowtows to and generally hopes to assimilate into the culture of, the white folks who during the time his book was published, were acting very much like Hitler in the guise of Richard Nixon, the law and order campaign, the myth of black capitalism and a host of social atrocities.

The comparison between black people's resistance and right wing racism continues as Owens opines,

> Suppressing the personal identity of the individual into some group, the end justifying the means, force instead of freedom. These are what make every despot and potential despot tick, whether it be a Hitler, a George Lincoln Rockwell, a KKK'er or a black militant (pp. 86-87).

The terms that Owens mentions are variables that go into the role of someone who wants to bring about serious social change. You need not be a despot, a dictator to believe in the end justifying the means or groupthink when you are standing against a demonic and oppressive system. When Owens writes "force versus freedom," he shows how stupid he is: freedom is a goal and force is what is used to obtain that goal – they are not opposite entities but in many cases, overlapping realities. Look at how this nation was taken over and how the British were vanquished.

And again, he wants us to think that a black militant and a member of the Ku Klux Klan or a racist like George Lincoln Rockwell can be compared. The former is fighting for civil and human rights against a system that has denied them; the later forces are the right wing versions of the people who are the deniers of those rights! Wake up, Owens, wake up!

But the bootlicking Owens feels more comfortable blaming racism and systemic race hatred on black people, just as he does in the following passage:

> Blackthink gives the obvious white bigot a platform he never had before. The quiet white racist is supplied with an unspoken "proof" of his own prejudices. The average white, who really isn't too involved in race except where it touches him, becomes irritated with it all. But most important, the essentially unprejudiced white, the genuine liberal who has spent part of his life battling for the Negro in one way or another, is crushed. After all these years, he's suddenly "Whitey"; he's on the outside looking in. And if he looks in too long, he might wind up in the hospital (p. 88).

How could thinking black give a white racist a platform? The object of talking and thinking black is to deny peckerwoods the platforms they've long held! Is Owens on crack or what? Then he claims that "The quiet white racist is supplied with an unspoken "proof" of his own prejudices." If you are a white racist you can afford to be quiet verbally because actions speak louder than words. By being white, you are in cahoots (by race) with a society that oppresses people of color. Do you think animals trapped in a zoo distinguish between black and white people who pass by and gawk at them? Of course not. All they know is that these human muthafuckas have taken us from our natural habitat and put us in these cages. The "quiet racist" is one of those spectators who wants to go to the zoo but doesn't want to take responsibility for the trapped animals within the cages.

Owens is again wrong when he writes that, "The average white, who really isn't too involved in race except where it touches him, becomes irritated with it all." That's my point: the average white boy is involved up to his teeth in race issues, but he wants to avoid that fact! He or she wants to pretend as if they're not prejudice; after all, they "pay money to go see the Harlem Globetrotters"! That kind of shit. They're all involved in race, especially the ones who try to act as if they aren't. They capitalize on it, market it, make money off of it, create entire communities because of it and have fun exploiting it.

Since white skin is obviously Owens' standard, he continues to take their side when he writes that, "But most important, the essentially unprejudiced white, the genuine liberal who has spent part of his life battling for the Negro in one way or another, is crushed." "Battling for the Negro"? Who died and made those white muthafuckas our saviors? They don't fight for black people; they fight for their own people to work with them in hopes of trying to keep black people from kicking off in that ass! In Owens' viewpoint, white people can simply do no wrong and it is the black man and woman who are the real problem. Is it any wonder that Owens found it easy to get this bullshit book published?

Of course who owns the publishing houses? Jews, that's who. And that's why the book is intermittently sprinkled with concerns about and on-going defense of, the Jews. For instance, on page 88 Owens posits the following:

> The most diseased example of this is the wave of anti-Semitism
> among militant backs today. To me, it's just a final demonstration
> of the sickness of blackthink – one more parallel between
> blackthink and Nazism. I mean, why the Jews? They're a minority
> just like us, and a minority who went through hell even longer …

The Jews don't need Owens speaking for them – although they won't turn it down. They have been using black people as "lightning rods" and "buffer zones" for centuries in this country. Most (if not all) of the civil rights groups in this country are funded by Jews and have Jews on their boards of directors. The stadiums and arenas that black people perform in at the professional level are all owned by Jews. When you point out the negative images that Jewish-run Hollywood puts out about blacks, or if you say ANYTHING about Jews without their permission, they brand you an "anti-Semite."

The along come Uncle Toms like Jesse Owens who has to stand up and defend the most powerful ethnic group in America. Jews control the political arena, they dominate the economy and their people commit crimes that rip off the American people for billions (read "Billions") of dollars and they become famous for it. The Jews have a long history of bilking entire countries, which is why they get run out of everywhere they go. Hitler outlined this in his book *Mein Kampf.* While he was a loon, even a broken clock can be right twice a day. In the words of Chancellor Williams in his book *The Destruction of Black Civilizations*, "it is doubtful if even a devil can write a book that is totally without truth."

More bullshit from Jesse Jackson, the one-man Jewish Defense League, continues:

> And *that's* why the militants hate them. Because the Jews did go
> through it all, and survived. Blackthinkers don't hate the Jews
> because they own some slum buildings (a lot of Protestants do, too,
> and many more Negroes – as I'll go into later), or because a lot of
> Jews have colored maids, or because the Jews have been the
> leaders in the "tokenism" civil rights movement of the fifties and
> sixties. The blackthinkers are anti-Semitic because so many Jews

did what the militants don't want to do. They've overcome. That
doesn't sit well when you've copped out yourself (p. 88 –
emphasis original).

So he links up this "anti-Semitism" and equates Jews with being as
oppressed as black people. He thinks that black concerns about Jews has to do with
the fact that Jews own "some slum buildings." No, it goes much deeper than that:
these assholes are making decisions about the urban shape of the cities and they
have input into the segregation of black people. Remember: the first "ghettos" had
nothing to do with black people, but were the places and areas where the Jews
were forced to live while over in Europe.

And one last point before moving on. Super Tom makes the comment that,
"The blackthinkers are anti-Semitic because so many Jews did what the militants
don't want to do. They've overcome." If Jews have "overcome" it has been for the
scams they've run on people no matter where they've gone. The key to that scam is
their ability to loan out money at high ass interest (usury fees), and that Bible-
related bullshit that a lot of people buy into where the Jews are supposedly "God's
chosen people." But the key point is that if Jews have "overcome," they did it by
stepping on other people. And in America, they had a perfectly concentrated and
vulnerable population to exploit: black folks. I'm sure Jesse Owens is aware of
this.

But it seems that Owens' real fear is made clear on page 89 when he posits,

> Yet the mental self-destruction, the anti-Semitism, even the Jim
> Crowism and the actual damage to life and property, none of it
> scares me as much as one thing that blackthink is doing to this
> country. *It is conditioning us to use violence to solve our problems*
> (p. 89 – emphasis original).

All the shit that this bootlicker is naming is stuff created by white folks, and
the Jews were right there with them. When there's segregation, it's the Jew that
sets up the corner grocery store, sells the black man and woman those outlandish
clothes that we like so much. It's the Jew who is buying pussy from black women
when he can get away with it. So this shit about damage is relative: we might burn
down some shit and loot, but it's the Jew that inflicts the economic and
psychological damage to ghetto residents.

And then comes the ultimate lie. Owens claims that black people are
"conditioning" other black people "to use violence to solve our problems."
What???! This country was conceived in violence! It is the European who brought
violence over here, used it against his British brothers, and then created a nation
over here that used violence to obliterate the Native American brothers and sisters,

and chase the Mexicans out. What's wrong with Owens' concept of historical accuracy?

This sick Uncle Tom, striving so hard to be accepted by his white masters, continues his tirade:

> And the bitterest irony of all is the way that blackthink would chain the negro while touting freedom to him. "They're coming over to our way of thinking," Black Muslim Cassius Clay said of the non-Muslim Negro extremists a couple of years ago. And they are. Militants are asking not for a better education, for example, but for black education, with black teachers and black dormitories, Jim Crow schools, in other words. From "Black Easter" to the "New Republic of Black Africa," it's the same principle. Segregation. Sure, the window dressing is nicer now, but it's still going back to where we were. (p. 89).

There are so many flaws in the previous passage that if I didn't take time here to correct them I would be as fucked up as Owens is. So let the teaching moment begin.

In the first place, how does thinking black "chain" black people to anything? This is white boy thinking. When you think and promote your own race and pride in it, that is a feeling of liberation. The adage teaches us that if we don't know who we are, then we can't know who our opposition is, and that is what's wrong with Owens. By his own choice, the name of his book (which he co-wrote with a white man) is "My Life As a Black Man and White Man." Since he couldn't change colors, that means that MENTALLY, he lived both lives. And he continued to "think white" during a time when black pride was at its zenith. That's why he's so damn confused.

Secondly, he wants to quote Muhammad Ali, but this is 1968; Ali changed his name from Cassius Clay in 1964 – after he beat the ass of another Uncle Tom by the name of Sonny Liston. That means that Clay was no longer, but was Ali for four years *before* Owens published his book. Why won't Owens call Ali by his name? Ali beat the shit out of Floyd Patterson when Patterson announced he would call Ali "Clay" just before their fight. Ali beat the shit out of Patterson who, by the way, was another Uncle Tom of Owens' ilk.

Third, why does Owens refer to Ali as a "Black Muslim," a term that was rejected by Ali and other members of the Nation of Islam at that time, a name intentionally used by the media to scare the hell out of gullible white folks. And again, when you think white you see things the way white folks see them, and that is what Jesse Owens did throughout the entire book that he titled, *Blackthink*.

Fourth, the claim that militants are asking for "black education" and not "education." This was a logical outgrowth of black consciousness. Once it was discovered that the white man's textbooks and his "educational system" were rife with racism and lies, the call for "black education" was simply a call for the truth. I don't really recall anyone referring to it as "black education," but when Owens tells a lie, he wants it to stick, so he makes it as extreme as possible. Not even the so-called "black colleges" can be said to be teaching black education, because their curriculum is as white as any white college in America.

Fuckup number five can be found in the Owens claim that the call for blackness ranges from "Black Easter" to the "New Republic of Black Africa." First of all it is not "New Republic of Black Africa." The proper name for the organization was "The Republic of New Africa" and it was founded in 1968 on three black nationalist principles: first, separate (not segregated) land base in the south for black people to live; secondly, reparations of several billion dollars because of slavery and third, the decision by black people to decide whether or not they wanted to remain U.S. citizens.

The second component of the claim by Owens regarding "Black Easter" is bullshit but, like the Republic of New Afrika, the term does have a link to 1968, the same year that Blackthink was published. But it's not what Owens tries to imply it to be. *Black Easter* was a novel by James Blish, a white man. It won an award for being the best fantasy novel, a story about an arms dealer who hires a magician who deals in what the white man calls "black magic" to unleash all the Demons of Hell on earth for a single day. It was first published in 1968. The sequel is *The Day After Judgment.*(Wikipedia, 2016).

So what was Owens talking about? He mentions a "black easter" as if it were the black version of the Christian holiday. He mentions the RNA but gets the name ass backwards. All of this took place in 1968, the same year that his bullshit book was published. Where were his fact checkers? Where was his editor? What was the white boy who co-wrote *Blackthink* doing while these major mistakes, including calling Muhammad Ali out of his name, were being made?

Sixth and finally, Owens thinks that the call for black holidays and organizations are somehow evidence of "segregation." How could this be? Perhaps it might be separation (as the case with the Republic of New Afrika), but that means that both sides agree with it. Segregation is imposed by one side (white folks) on another side and forced on them. Black people therefore cannot be segregationists.

The chapter titled "Blackthink Won't Win" tends to show that Owens is the one who is losing: losing the battle for sanity and truth! His asinine assumptions continue:

Sometimes they'll talk with you. But in the background is the gun and the knife, the riot and the revolution. It's no *discussion* when one debater holds a pistol in his hand and says, "If we don 't do I this way, we'll do it *this* way … I have confidence that we're going to lick this thing, that the overwhelming majority in America and the new generations coming up will whip both white bigots and blackthinkers alike … " (p. 90).

Owens sounds just like a white man, a racist cop, or some cracker at the bar spreading his bullshit to his fellow drunks. When he writes that "in the background is the gun and the knife, the riot and the revolution," he is paving the way for black people to get hurt. He is generating fear of black people who have a different point of view. He is showing what a true asshole he is!

And what is he really describing? He is describing the very tactics that white people have used against those whom they have oppressed for centuries: proselytization at gunpoint or, back in the days, at sword point. The white man uses threats and coercion to convert black people to his way of thinking. He uses the threat of economics, he uses material coercion against black families (turning off utilities, eviction, etc.), he uses political coercion with lies about not voting being some kind of betrayal and so on. And then there is his military forcing "democracy" down the throats of the world.

Like the true milquetoast that he is, Owens writes, "I have confidence that we're going to lick this thing, that the overwhelming majority in America and the new generations coming up will whip both white bigots and blackthinkers alike." Who is "we"? Of course its him and his white buddies. And again, he equates black thinking people (progressives) with white bigots. He should know that bigot is in and of itself a negative term. So he thinks negatively of white racists and of black progressives. To think black is to be a problem. That is Jesse Owens' thinking. And remember all the shit Jesse had seen, had been through and had admitted to. And he STILL hates himself and other blacks as well.

So not only is he a self-hater but he's also a coward. Read carefully the following clip:

… But if I have one fear for my country, it's that we're becoming more and more used to seeing violence "solve" problems and are getting closer and closer to thinking that some kind of revolution is inevitable. Blackthink isn't one hundred percent bad. It was born partly out of Negro pride, and o of its effects has been a white awakening. But even if the militants were right about every single thing they advocate, the means they're using and threatening to use to win their ends would make it all worthless (p. 90).

"His" country? He has no stake in it. He won four gold medals overseas and when he got back to American shores, he was treated like shit. Like millions of other black men who went away to war or elsewhere, once you come to America you see that you were treated better by people far away than the peckerwood on American shores who claims to be so "fair."

He writes that, "Blackthink is one hundred percent bad." Is there really anything or anyone who is totally bad? A pedophile? A rapist? A murderer? Godzilla? Jesse Owens? I can think of no living entity that deserves to be written off as being one hundred percent bad. But look at what Jesse does: he writes off a thought pattern by black people who are only standing up against their oppressor. He is a self-hater and a race hater. And that's why white folks love what he has to say. And that's why they published his book.

From time to time throughout the book, Owens mentions some other Uncle Toms, usually from the world of sports, that he associates with. From Willie Mays to Joe Louis, they too seem dense when it comes to race relations. In regard to the latter athletes, at the time the heavyweight champion of the world, here is how Jesse describes their "connection":

> Joe and I had been lucky to come along at a time when the imagination of the American public at large was ready to be captured by negro athletes. Because of this, we had unique roles to play in our culture, and it welded us together as friends. Our lives crossed only several times a year, but we understood each other from the beginning (p. 91).

Owens says that Louis and he had "unique roles to play in our culture." Yeah: the role of "coon." There were a lot of them and to this day, as Malcolm X stated elsewhere in my book, "we still got a lot of house niggers running around here."

And while on the subject of Joe Louis, there are some other areas in the book where "the Brown Bomber's" name comes up. For instance, Owens shares the following snippet:

> But there were other people who helped me, too. Joe Louis was one, He became the first Negro to win the Associated Press Athletes of the Year Award, in 1935, and I followed in 1936. Not another Negro won it until Willie Mays in the middle fifties, and, until Jackie Robinson came along in 1947, Joe and I had to carry a major load as far as the Negro image was concerned. Of course, there were black men in other fields of endeavor, more than anyone suspects, but sports and show business and politics are what gets the attention in this country … (pp. 101-102)

All three of the black men Owens named – himself, Mays and Louis – were toms. All three were the kinds of "negroes" that the white man teased, made fun of and held up in a way that they would be remembered as little more than just some "negroes with athletic skills." Toward the end Mays tried to get involved in a little civil rights bullshit, but Frank Robinson and Hank Aaron were far more involved than he was, which is why they received less fame in terms of helping black people. Joe Louis – a straight up Uncle Tom and the antics he went through as a big nigger are almost as brutally embarrassing as those of Owens. He was known as "the Brown Bomber" – but when it came to caring about black people, I see him as just another "bronze bum."

Let me interject some similarities between Joe Louis and Jesse Owens at this juncture.

Just as Jesse would end up kissing the ass of Luz Long following the 1936 Olympics, Louis would do the same thing with a German Nazi peckerwood named Max Schmeling. Back in the day I recall my father following those fights and he and his pals would often debate the greatness of Louis, My research in recent years uncovered the fact that not only was Schmeling a Nazi, but he actually kicked Joe's ass out in the 12th round in the first fight – just like Long broke Jesse's record during warm-ups in the Olympics. But in the second fight, Louis knocked Schmeling out in the first round – just like Jesse defeated Long when it really counted during the Olympics.

In addition, some background is relevant here:

> … Although the two champions met to create a pugilistic spectacle remarkable on its own terms, the two fights came to embody the broader political and social conflict of the times. As the most significant African American athlete of his age and the most significant African-American boxer since Jack Johnson, Louis was a focal point for African American pride in the 1930s. Moreover, as a contest between representatives of the United States and Nazi Germany during the 1930s, the fights came to symbolize the struggle between democracy and fascism. Louis' performance in the bouts therefore elevated him to the status of the first true African American national hero in the United States (Wikipedia, 2016).

Both men, Lewis and Owens, had been a focus of African American ("Negro") pride because of what they were able to do – for the white man. The white man played up both of their accomplishments because by defeating individual white men they had also struck a blow against Hitler's Nazi/Aryan white supremacy doctrine. But what black people should remember and as I continue to work to drive home is the fact that both nations – German and America – were bastions of white supremacy as far as black people were concerned. The only difference was that America's symbol was a cross and the Nazi's was a swastika – also known as "the twisted cross."

And take notice at the previous historical piece offered by Wikipedia. Even when historians try to do their best their racism comes to the fore. The web-based encyclopedia states that, "Louis' performance in the bouts therefore elevated him to the status of the first true African American national hero in the United States." The first? After over 200 years of slavery? After all the black people who died in the wars for these peckerwoods? After the work that Harriet Tubman did working to liberate black people? So again you can see who the "black heroes" are in the minds of white people: *niggas who silently serve them.*

With that having been documented and made clear by me, let's go back to Owens' personal flashback:

> There were lots of Negro performers in show business, naturally, but none of them really broke the color line until Nat Cole got a regular TV show in 1957. As for politics, the Negro was lucky to get to vote, let alone run for office in the thirties and forties. So it was mainly Joe and I. And I thanked the Lord for Joe. Not that I didn't try to live up to the honors I'd been fortunate enough to gain. But big Joe didn't have to try. He was a beautiful, natural man (p. 102).

First of all the professional name used by the man known as "Nat Cole" was and remains "Nat King Cole." He was born Nathaniel Adams Coles, but that's not really germane. What IS germane is that once again Owens leaves out the parts of a black man's life that shows how racism fucked his life up. But I won't leave it out.

Sure, Nat was the first brutha with a regular TV show in 1957. But what the bootlicking Owens failed t mention (intentionally) was that Nat King Cole chose the cancelling of his show than to continue on the air worrying about sponsorship. Here's some brief background on what Owens left out:

> When Nat King Cole became the first major black entertainer to host a television show, advertisers stayed away—but not Rheingold; Rheingold was the New York regional sponsor for Cole's show. As early as 1965, Rheingold aired television ads featuring African American, Puerto Rican and Asian actors, to appeal to its racially diverse customer base. The company's headquarters was in the Bushwick section of Brooklyn. Rheingold was the official beer of the New York Mets, and its advertisements

featured John Wayne, Jackie Robinson, Sarah Vaughan and the Marx Brothers. They also sponsored The Jackie Robinson Show which aired on 660 WRCA radio in New York City on Sunday evenings between 6:30 and 7 PM during the late 1950s and early 1960s.[7] (Wikipedia, 2016).

Now the reason that I interject this is not to sing the praises of Rheingold beer because they merely exploited what was popular and obviously were targeting black people in much the same way that PowerMaster, Private Stock, St. Ides, King Cobra and Steel Reserve are marketed to black people to this very day. You don't find these beers in suburban stores, but they're all over the inner city markets, oftentimes placed in huge tubs and left right near the front counter where young people have to walk past them to purchase groceries. But that's another story for another time.

This is about Rheingold and its sponsorship of the Nat King Cole Show and the fact that Jesse Owens had to know about what I am sharing with you. Nat was the bomb and even white people had to admit it. But Nat stood his ground. When he moved into a white neighborhood and some white folks burned a cross on his lawn, the neighborhood association told him that they didn't want any "undesirables" in the neighborhood. Nat told them, and it was quoted in the newspapers, "Neither do I And if I see anybody undesirable coming in here, I'll be the first to complain."

So now you see why Owens avoided this part of the story. Nat King Cole was the opposite of the kind of Uncle Tom that Jesse Owens was. The only blacks that Owens had time for and therefore felt were worthy of mention were toms like himself. But let me add one more thing about Nat before moving on:

On November 5, 1956, The Nat King Cole Show debuted on NBC. The variety program was the first of its kind hosted by an African-American, which created controversy at the time … in order to help the show save money—The Nat King Cole Show was ultimately done in by lack of a national sponsorship. Companies such as Rheingold Beer assumed regional sponsorship of the show, but a national sponsor never appeared. The last episode of The Nat King Cole Show aired December 17, 1957. Cole had survived for over a year, and it was he, not NBC, who ultimately decided to pull the plug on the show. Commenting on the lack of sponsorship his show received, Cole quipped shortly after its demise, "Madison Avenue is afraid of the dark." (Wikipedia, 2016).

In simple terms it was Owens' white buddies that did Nat King Cole's show in. The same white man whose ass Owens is kissing while singing the praises of bootlickers like Joe Louis and others I've named. Moving on with this chapter where Owens tells us, "Blackthink Won't Win":

> Coming after my encounter with Hitler in Berlin, Joe's dramatic
> first round KO of the Nazi heavyweight really drove home the
> point. But above all, Joe Louis drove home another point. If he was
> a great fighter, he was a great human being. It came out of his very
> pores. To watch him walk was to sense it … Joe himself never
> argued race and wouldn't have had the words to do it if he'd tried.
> He did a lot of silly things after he was heavyweight champion,
> just as yours truly did. He tried to come back with a roll of fat
> around his middle bigger than a truck tire, he got into big tax
> trouble with Uncle Sam, the lowered himself to refereeing
> wrestling matches and almost put one of his ribs through his heart
> doing it (p. 102).

To begin with, Owens needs to stop buying into that white propaganda about him having "confronted" or "encountered" Hitler. Hitler didn't want to have anything to do with that black muthafucka and Owens admits as much. How did he encounter anyone other than Luz Long, the broad jumper who he (Owens) credits with helping him win that particular medal? How did he encounter anything even remotely related to Naziism other than the fact that he was in that stadium?

He was a coward and an accommodationist – just like Joe Louis was If a tom says someone is great, that person must also be another tom. In the previous excerpt you can see where Owens says, "Joe himself never argued race and wouldn't have had the words to do it if he'd tried." That means when race issues came up in discussions, Louis had nothing to say. That means if someone called him a nigger, he had nothing to say. And just like the white man had Jesse Running against horses after winning four gold medals, the white man did something similar to Louis: so broke was he that he had to referee those fake-ass wrestling matches. And though fat as fuck, he (Joe Louis) had the gall to try to make a comeback. Just like Willie Mays tried to do and a host of other washed up negroes who got addicted to the white-backed fame, the money, the white bitches and the houses. These coons give a whole new meaning to, "keep on keepin' on."

Owens will have nothing to do with black people who can think for themselves. On page 96 he shares the following incident and analysis:

> A short time ago I was watching one of the many discussions by
> negroes about negroes on TV. The subject was the black ghetto. I
> wouldn't say the panel was well-balanced. All were militants, and
> it really seemed that the only question was who could outdo who in
> heaping blame and bitterness on whites.

There is a difference between "heaping the blame on whites" and confronting white people with the fact that they are fucked up and you are going to do something about it. It is this latter reality that sellouts like Jesse Owens fears the most.

At any rate, when one of the bruthas mentioned how black men are dogged out by whites and how black women are forced to be whores (Jesse claims that the black speaker said, "He has to make whores out of our women!"), Jesse's view is as skewed as that particular brutha who spoke out. Here is what the clueless turncoat analyzed the situation:

> Barbara is no exception. Every whore and pimp and criminal I've ever known or know of has been someone who took the easy way … But not as a way of life. And the final difference between all the millions of Negro women, married and single, who act like women and other handful who are whores is the differences between every person from the beginning of time who didn't weaken and those who did … *no one forces anyone to be a prostitute* (p. 97 – emphasis original).

That is such bullshit because in America, everybody – male and female, black and white and in between – is a fuckin' prostitute! This country is about making money and duping people into selling their bodies and having the nerve to call it "work." The biggest pimp is not even the government (although it gets its cut of the proceeds). The biggest pimps are the few people at the top playing games and watching people jump through hoops. As the Last Poets taught in their poem, "E Pluribus Unum,

> So the power's in the hands of the ruling classes/
> Playing God with the fate of all the masses/
> And the people don't get any/
> In the land of the plenty/
> Because E Pluribus Unum means "one out of many."

So black women are whores and Jesse doesn't like it? Why did he sell his own ass and sign a contract where he would run a race against thoroughbred horses? Wasn't the contract put together by people who were "pimping" him?

Moving on:

> Today's extremists aren't stupid. Usually, they're well educated, articulate and highly intelligent. But I'm glad none of my daughters married one. Because no I.Q. is high enough to break through a mind filled with hate. I've talked to extremist after extremist in the past six or seven years, first trying to understand

them and later trying to get them to understand themselves. In
every case, I've come to see how their militancy is in an almost
exact proportion to their lust for revenge and, beneath that, to their
own hidden feelings of self-disgust about themselves (p. 97).

So if you're intelligent and you talk negatively and truthfully about the
system that is oppressing you, that means that you are spewing hate as far as
Owens is concerned. And that is why he wouldn't want any of his daughters
marrying a brutha like that. Because he knows that in order for that to happen, the
daughter would have to agree with her husband and she would see her father as the
sellout that he was.

Jesse Owens is a sellout. Why else would he have discussions with black
people whose views he doesn't agree with in order to "understand themselves."
No, that's not why he's having the discussions. His job is to attempt to bullshit
these folks into thinking that they are wrong about the white man, that the white
man is our pal and there's just been a big misunderstanding – on OUR part! That is
what Uncle Toms do. The black man who thinks in black terms is Jesse Owens'
enemy and note his conclusion about such people: "I've come to see how their
militancy is in an almost exact proportion to their lust for revenge and, beneath
that, to their own hidden feelings of self-disgust about themselves." Translation: if
you can't stand whitey then it's because you hate yourself. What a crock of shit.

And what would a chapter about blackthink not being able to win would be
complete without knock against reparations – compensation for being enslaved for
over 300 years with no pay? You can rely on Judas to offer up an example and
another case study:

> One fanatic revolutionary didn't even argue the point with me
> about whether or not he wanted revenge. *"They ... owe.. us,"* was
> all he whispered. I was so struck by this frank hate, I couldn't say
> anything for a minute. Then I told him, "Yeah, they owe us.
> You're goddamn right they owe us. But it's a debt we'll never
> collect on. So why don't you kick the habit?" (p. 98 – emphasis
> original).

If Owens concedes that a debt is owed, then why act like a little bitch and
say, "fuck it, there ain't nothing we can do"? Do his white pals have this attitude
when bill collection time comes around? Fuck no. If you don't want to pay they
sue you, file a lien against your shit or have you take to court. You can even go to
jail for owing THOSE muthafuckas. But even a tom like Owens who concedes that
there should be reparations doesn't have the heart, brains or balls to confront HIS
debtors.

He tells the young brutha to "kick the habit" of expecting payback from whitey. Why doesn't HE kick the habit and stop tomming? Why doesn't he get that white money off of HIS back and start acting like a black man? Why does he have to use a peckerwood to author a book with the peckerwood's name being as prominent in the byline as the subtitle of the book? These are things that Jesse Owens should have worried about because in the end, it was Jesse Owens who was the one who was fucked up in the head or as the Latino bruthas and sistahs would say, *loco en la cabeza* (crazy in the head).

The chapter on why "Blackthink Won't Win" unceremoniously concludes with yet another insult aimed at the militant black person:

> He didn't. And he *will* collect. In psychological self-destruction. And in the crippling of a rational rights movement that wants to make sure no new debts are incurred. And even in a possible revolution, but not by militant blacks … I'm saying that blackthink is a vicious, unfair, destructive philosophy and that the massive majority of the people in this country – white people and black – will never let it flourish even if it means treating looters and rioters like the robbers and arsonists they are. Yeah, they owe us. But we're beginning to owe them, too (p. 98- emphasis original).

So not only won't blackthink "win," but this slave-minded bastard has come to the conclusion that blacks are going to end up owing white folks. Owe white people? Are you crazy, muthafucka? We already made a 400 year of unpaid contributions of free slave labor for which we have no received a fuckin' dime! How much more work to this asshole expect us to put "involuntarily donate"?

He lets us know in this chapter what he thinks of any black people who understand race relations and see the white man for what he is. He writes, and I quote, "blackthink is a vicious, unfair, destructive philosophy and that the massive majority of the people in this country – white people and black – will never let it flourish even if it means treating looters and rioters like the robbers and arsonists they are."

The only way blackthink – the truth about race relations – wouldn't or couldn't win would be if simpleton-ass niggas like Jesse Owens were leading the way. Fortunately for us, they are not.

Chapter 7: I Know Because I've Been There

This chapter is a pity party, plain and simple. And this bootlicker continues to refer to the Horatio Alger story, which I call the Horatio Alger *myth*. For those of you who never cracked a book, the Horatio Alger story can be summed up the way it is by Wikipedia: "The "Horatio Alger myth" is the "classic" American success story and character arc, the trajectory from "rags to riches". It comes from the novels of Horatio Alger, Jr., which were wildly popular after the Civil War in the United States."

When you're black, you don't need to be attributing any modicum of success you've had to some bullshit myth. Even those who do gain some semblance of success do it based on the white man's criteria. Horatio Alger was a peckerwood who succeeded, got paid and then gave his money to his fellow whites when the bills came due. How can you compare this formula with a nigga who gets a chance to earn money doing something, but then turns around and ALSO gives the money to a white bill collector? Horatio Alger my ass!

And yet here is ultimate accommodationist, Jesse Owens, attributing as much as he possibly can to any white man he can think of. His view of black people is most similar to the way the white man has viewed black people over the years. For instance, he writes,

> I'm not going to bend your ear with all kinds of tales of
> government trucks driving into your neighborhood and handing out
> powdered milk so that the newest baby in the family might
> possibly live. If you're over forty, you remember it well enough. If
> you're twenty, it wouldn't mean anything to you anyway (p. 100).

So it is under the umbrella of this stereotype-laden "niggas-is-all-po" veneer that Owens opens up about Horatio Alger:

> First of all, no one would ever even be able to mistake my life for
> Horatio Alger yarn if it weren't for some people who kept
> rescuing me when I was going under for the third time. I've said
> what my parents did. A lot is expected of parents, but my family
> went far beyond what was expected of anyone … No, my family
> went beyond the call of duty. That's why I couldn't go on to Ohio
> State until my father had a real job. I appreciate what they did even
> more now than I did then. I only wish they were alive for me to tell
> them how much more . (p. 100).

When Owens admits that he was figuratively "going down for the third time," why didn't he share how much of that was of his own doing? How much of it was because of discrimination or white racism? He is more than willing to attribute "being rescued" to white people as he does all that is of a positive bent, but what about those problems he encountered. No, he is no Horatio Alger: he is a Gunga Din.

This asshole tries to talk about how appreciative he was and is regarding the roles that his parents played. That is what parents are supposed to do. But let me tell you this: if I were Jesse Owens' father and I watched all that ass licking he did and how he continued to love the very white people who had worked to destroy my life and who at one time told me that my children would be "lucky to survive," I would have kicked Jesse all up in his ass. If his parents were alive they would see what he has done and if they read Blackthink, I don't think they would be very happy about the "picture of impoverishment" that he painted of his Pops.

Moving right along:

> But even with everything my parents tried to do, it wouldn't have been enough for a "success" story without Charles Riley. When he first asked me to go out for the track team in fifth grade, it wasn't because he saw any potential champion in me. It was because he saw a potential corpse. My legs and the rest of me were so thin I looked like a malnutrition case (pp. 100-101).

This bootlicker puts a white man above his own parents. Not only that but now he had reduced his parents roles to what they "tried" to do. See what I mean? When you're an Uncle Tom of Jesse Owens' caliber, there simply is no bottom, no limit to what you will go through to show the world that you are, indeed, whitey's willing thrall!

I am a former athlete – a basketball player of some caliber, playing against real competition in the California Bay Area. I didn't only practice and do drills, but I watched those peckerwood coaches. I watched the basketball coach I played for, I watched the ones who coached the junior varsity and freshman squads, and during off season I watched the football and track coaches. I also watched those racist muthafuckas who called themselves wrestling coaches.

With all my observation-oriented analysis, I saw white men exploiting black people. They didn't give a shit about us. They were doing it because they got paid a little extra on their paychecks, got some fame from the community, and had access to budgets that they spent on their bullshit gear and very little on us. Owens was another victim but evidently he is giving this Riley character more credit than he deserves. But then again, we're talking about Jesse Owens: a nigga who would have been happy if the white man had walked over and *shit* on him!

See for yourself:

> In the same way, if you ever asked Charles Riley for advice, he'd never answer directly. Instead, he'd tell you a little story and let you figure out the moral for yourself … We never talked about white and colored. There was no reason to. He taught *that* by example. (p. 101 – emphasis original).

You dumb muthafucka! He didn't answer the question directly because he didn't KNOW the answer! When have you ever seen a white man pass up the chance to sound like an "expert" on something? He used those "little stories" to buy time, to bullshit and to basically tell you to get the fuck out of his face. I bet if his kid would have asked him that question Riley wouldn't have resorted to some fuckin' tale or fable as an explanation! The fact is, Owens saw more in Riley than Riley evidently saw in himself. What he "taught by example" was that no black kid was worthy of a direct or definitive answer to a question of ANY kind.

Owens continues to babble:

> There were other people like Martin who contributed to my "Horatio Alger story," too: Bill "Bojangles" Robinson, who offered me a job touring the country with him when I was at low ebb; Ralph Metcalfe, the phi Beta Kappa become president pro tem of the Chicago City Council who acted like a big brother to me at Ohio State even though we had a fierce competition on the cinders; Larry Snyder, my coach at college, another white man who proved to me again that prejudice is a matter of choice, not coloring (p. 107).

If it's not a white man it's some other Uncle Tom. I don't know much about Ralph Metcalfe, but I know that he was on the same track team as Jesse, was a sprinter like Jesse and as a result, he knew Jesse. If Metcalfe knew Jesse then he had to know that Jesse was a tom. But rather than waste time trying to take Jesse's head out of the white man's ass, Metcalfe went to Chicago and went into politics where he served as a member of the U.S. House of Representatives from Illinois' 1st District from January of 1971-October of 1978.

More specifically,

> Ralph Harold Metcalfe, Sr. was an American track and field sprinter and politician. He jointly held the world record in the 100-meter dash and placed second in that event in two Olympics, first to Eddie Tolan and then to Jesse Owens at the 1936 Olympics in Berlin, Germany. Metcalfe won four Olympic medals and was regarded as the world's fastest human in 1934 and 1935. He later went into politics and in the city of Chicago and served in the United States Congress for four terms in the 1970s as a Democrat from Illinois.(Wikipedia, 2016).

So Metcalfe was probably a good brutha. And the fact is he may have been better than Jesse. The late great tennis pro Arthur Ashe, who stood up for black causes during his day, said, "Nowadays, experts think back to Owens and Metcalfe and wonder which of the two was better on closer inspection. Owens won the AAU 100-meter title only once; Metcalfe won it three times. Owens failed to win the AAU 200-meter title; Metcalfe won it five times in a row. Owens won the Intercollegiate 100-yard dash twice; Metcalfe three times. And again in the Intercollegiate 220-yard dash, Owens won it twice to three times for Metcalfe. What does all this prove? Maybe nothing but the results are surprising when compared with the relative publicity they received" (Ashe, 1998: p. 26).

Chicago's got some pretty astute black folks, even the very poor ones. Metcalfe has schools and streets named after him. So in answer to Ashe's concern about why the publicity went to Jesse, the answer is clear to me: Jesse was an ass kisser and Metcalfe wasn't. Metcalfe went to a black city and made a name for himself and Jesse just kept on tomming and skinning and grinning and taking whatever he could get.

He probably only mentioned Metcalfe because the name would be conspicuously absent had he omitted it – his white co-writer probably strongly suggested that Jesse at least give the man who was faster than he was, some minor acknowledgement. And minimal it was.

But Owens' obsession with white people, his uncle tomfoolery, are not limited only to the American white man. He shares the time that a white man from South Africa saves his life. Here's what he wrote:

> He was a specialist, but he wanted to call in another specialist, the man he thought was the best neurosurgeon in the country, Dr. Bill Tobias. Dr. Tobias shocked me a little when he first walked into my room the net day. He was so young, and he talked with a British accent. It turned out he was from South Africa … "I want you to operate as soon as you can. And once you're in there, I want you to do everything – I mean everything – that has to be done to make me myself again. I want you to take chances if you have to, even if it means I might not ever get up off that table" (p. 115).

The sign of a full-fledged Uncle Tom is when he is willing to put his own life on the line to bail out a peckerwood that he just met. Now if we are to believe the previous passage, a white boy comes into the room which in turn, makes Jesse somewhat "shocked." But it wasn't because he was white: it was because he was young and had a British accent. Any other black person would have been even more apprehensive after finding out that this muthafucka was from South Africa which, at the time, had an apartheid system in place that was akin to the Jim Crow system in America. But knowing all this, Jesse ignores these "racial warning signs" and what does he do?

Like the true laboratory rat that he wishes he was good enough to be, Owens immediately submits to the white boy! He immediately calls for the operation and then gives that peckerwood literal carte blanche to "do everything that has to be done." But that's not enough. Owens adds that, "I want you to take chances if you have to, even if it means I might not ever get up off that table."

One can never tell when Owens is telling the truth or lying. But he knows what he is and there is no doubt in my mind that he was a big enough ass licker to tell a white man to "take chances" with his (Owens') life. In fact, he WANTS him to do it even at the risk of death. Now can you see why I have dogged out Jesse Owens for being a super-tom? Now do you see why this coon rates high on my list of "biggest ass kissers of all time"?

Next, he describes the operation and its outcome:

> On May 18, 1965, thirty-six-year old Dr. Eli Tobias put me under
> anesthetic for the first time in my life and performed the most
> delicate kind of surgery on my spine. Two days later I was
> standing straight as a javelin, and nine days after that I was playing
> golf and making plans for the future again. That summer I won the
> championship of my country club against players half my age,
> breaking par in a grueling thirty-six-hole playoff. The trophy I got
> stands next t my Olympic medals. I owe that trophy, and a lot
> more, to a white African named Eli Tobias (p. 116).

Just like he could credit a Nazi, Luz Long, for "helping him" to win that gold medal in the broad jump, now he gives another Nazi – Eli Tobias – the ultimate compliment. Yes, South Africans were akin to the Nazis based on the way that they treated black people in that country. Blacks were placed on "Bantustans" just like Nazis in Germany put Jews in "ghettos." Jesse just loved white skin, period. It didn't matter if it was a racist redneck from Alabama, a Nazi from Germany or a Dutch Boer from South Africa, Jesse Owens was a straight-up anglophile – *he loved white folks more than he loved himself.*

As the chapter bore out, it seems that much like Joe Louis, Jesse Owens also had tax problems. A great number of black people who earn money do. And I think it is because of poor planning, and that includes the decision, all too often, to hire the white man – specifically Jews – to do our books for us. I link tax issues to accounting problems and look at all the black "celebrities" who died broke. As Muhammad (2012) wrote,

> Some of our greatest icons, such as Sammy Davis Jr., Billie
> Holiday, "Little" Richard, Chuck Berry (and the list goes on) lived
> rich, yet died broke while Jewish managers, accountants, attorneys,
> business advisors, and others fed their families for years off of

their largess. Few entertainers in the history of Black America
have been able to say that their assets and true net worth were are
prominent as their talent and popularity.

All of the above were pretty much bootlickers in different ways. None of them really gave a shit about the politics of race. A few married white bitches. And they still got fucked (literally and financially). Jesse Owens got away with a fine, or, as he describes it, the judge said the following:

> "So I am going to fine you. You are hereby fined $750 for each of
> the four years, a total of $3,000. I am not going to place you on
> probation, because you do not need probation. You will pay your
> responsibility without having to have a probation club over your
> head. They have plenty to do to straighten out people rather than to
> spend their time with *you*. I am convinced if you have the money,
> you will pay …. That is the judgment of this court" (p. 120 –
> emphasis original).

The moral of this story is that all that Uncle Tomming and ass-kissing apparently paid off, or so most people would think. But just you remember what Jesse did for this nation, the message he sent to Hitler and those Nazi peckerwoods, and how he now ends up thanking the court for not sending him to jail. And how does this Uncle Tom concludes this chapter that he titled, "I Know Because I've Been There"? like so:

> As of right now, I've been to twenty countries in the last four
> years, and I've planned double that for the next four. Yet even if
> something should happen to me, even if I checked out tomorrow
> and never got to see my idea grow into what it can be, I can't
> complain. But I sure don't know who Horatio Alger is. Because
> the battles that count aren't the ones for gold medals. The struggles
> within yourself – the invisible, inevitable battles inside all of us –
> that's where it's at. *Life* is the *real* Olympics (p. 121 – emphasis
> original).

Say what???? The Olympics were contrived and controlled by white people. The Olympics has people from all over the world running, jumping and competing for cheap ass medals that are probably worth $85 in a pawn shop (that's what Lisa Leslie said during a May 21, 2016 interview with Byron Allen on "American Athlete"). Despite the so-called "fame," it's how you market yourself after you win a medal that is most important. Life is the real Olympics, Jesse? The only difference is that in life, the competition is rigged so that the ultimate lesson learned is the white man looking at you and saying, "I win, you lose."

Chapter 8: Showcase the Good

When some Uncle Tom is suggesting that you "showcase the good" or that the "good be showcased," the immediate question that comes to my mind is "showcase it to WHOM?" And then, "Showcase the good for WHAT purpose?" It is clear after what I have shared with you in regard to this pencil-necked sellout by the name of Jesse Owens is that he's suggesting that black people show the white man what he wants to see so that we can curry favor with him and get him to "be nice" to us. But Owens goes further: he paints a negative picture of progressive thinking black people and seems to imply that since these are black people who want to do battle with the white man and his racist system, they (black people) should be harshly dealt with.

In a word, the white man can take the writings of Owens and use them to indict any black teenager, any black male, that the cops come across because the picture that Owens paints of black people, even back in 1968, is a picture chock full of stereotypes and racist assumptions. Not only that, if the white people and out-of-touch negroes who read Owens' book are to believe it, black people, as a whole, are nothing short of a "menace to society." Owens' *ersatz* "consciousness" is for show and is disingenuous to say the least.

For instance, he opens up this chapter asking to "Showcase the Good" by literally showcasing the bad:

> It's Friday night in Detroit. A gang of half a dozen colored teen-
> agers are roaming the streets, looking for trouble. A year ago,
> maybe less, they'd gone out on those streets at night only as petty
> thieves or pranksters. Yet somewhere in the months that followed,
> they turned into criminals. Pills made them looser, booze made
> them bolder. Eventually they traded dime-store pilfering for armed
> robbery and assault. Of course, that's no big event in most negro
> neighborhoods … (p. 122)

This racist fairy tale – fodder for trigger-happy cops – is just what the white people wanted to read in 1968 as they clamored for more "law and order" which translates to mean "control those niggas!"

And it gets worse. This fabricating bastard continues his stereotype-laden rant:

> What these four fifteen-year-olds and two fourteen-year olds will
> do tonight is an "event" in any neighborhood, though. They'll get
> wild on speed, enter apartment and make a man watch while they

> rape his wife and eleven-year-old daughter. Then they'll take all
> the money in the house and beat everyone senseless to erase the
> memories for them …. (p. 122).

This muthafucka must have just watched the movie "Death Wish" or else he's just read "A Clockwork Orange." What is the purpose of this shit? What does Owens hope to accomplish by documenting what he claims is the truth in a city known for being majority black and then creating the most base crimes he can think of? Has this Uncle Tom no conscience? Does he not know the consequences of putting such things in writing and selling them to the white man?

Of course he does. *He just doesn't give a shit.*

This idiot, who was no educational wonder himself (he didn't even graduate from college), then points his retarded finger at the education system and, of course, it's black people's fault:

> Yet there are no black teachers, or at least not anywhere near
> enough to handle all the negroes in New York City, to say nothing
> of the rest of the country. Most school boards have tried to hire
> every single black instructor they could find, have even bent
> requirements to let in any Negro who's even half qualified. But
> you can't change three hundred years of history in one semester.
> There just aren't that many black teachers. Yet as long as their kids
> are taught by whites, a lot of people in New York City and
> hundreds of other places will prevent kids from getting any real
> education at all and may sometimes disrupt an entire school system
> …. (p. 123).

So if there's a shortage of black people doing anything, it's not because of the white man. According to Owens' logic, white folks are doing their best to hire black people but there just are not enough of us who are "qualified." Guess what? This is the same bullshit excuse that peckerwoods in the realm of education use to this very day: not enough elementary school teachers, not enough middle school/intermediate level teachers, not enough high school teachers, not enough college instructors – who are black, that is. So because they are trying too hard, and because they don't want to be accused of having a "quota system," these good ol' white folks just do what they have to do: hire their own.

According to the apologist Owens, "Most school boards have tried to hire every single black instructor they could find, have even bent requirements to let in any Negro who's even half qualified." All I can say in response to this bold-faced lie is, "prove it, muthafucka"! Where is the data that shows that "most school boards" do anything as it relates to hiring blacks other than as security guards and janitors. Prove that they've got contacts that enable them to go out and locate black instructors. Prove that they don't shy away from the east and west coast where the progressive thinking teachers are located and opt, instead, for the Deep South where the "trained negroes" (like Owens) can be found. Prove that a peckerwood administrator would put his job on the line by hiring or "letting in" any black person "even half qualified." Jesse is a lying muthafucka and he knows it – and his white co-writer knew it as well.

Realizing that he's not an educator, a scholar of any kind or even a clear-thinking individual, he offers the following ersatz caveat:

> So I'm certainly not going to presume to give final answers. What I feel I can do is to draw on my experience to indicate some directions that might be taken with certain fundamental kinds of dilemmas. My experience hasn't been only as a Negro who's known both up and down, but as someone who's worked for local, state and federal systems – and worked to change those systems as a private citizen. So where do you start? (p. 124).

This nigga is an embarrassment to himself and to the race. And let me add that his editors and co-writer are right along with him. He sounds like a complete and utter ass. Let's break down the previous excerpt so I can show you what I mean.

First of all he says he's not going to "presume to give final answers." Well that sure in the fuck what it sounds like to me, not just in this instance but throughout the book. This asshole has been playing sociologist, race relations expert, international advisor, psychologist, historian and literature expert. What are his credentials? None. He couldn't even graduate from Ohio State. It was many years later when he finally got an "honorary degree" and it wasn't even a doctorate – it was a funky Bachelor's. So he was still being disrespected even after running and jumping for those peckerwoods.

He claims that all he "feels" that he can do is draw on his experience and provide some "directions that might be taken with certain fundamental kinds of dilemmas." If it's a dilemma, then the problem has no real solution no matter how much direction he provides. There's a big difference between a dilemma and a problem. And as for him drawing on his experience, look how far that got him. All he's described so far are his experiences as an ass kisser and accommodationist. That approach ain't gonna solve any problems: *it's an approach where you learn how to disguise, lie about and avoid problems.*

Third, exactly what *are* his "experiences"? He says, "My experience hasn't been only as a Negro who's known both up and down, but as someone who's worked for local, state and federal systems – and worked to change those systems as a private citizen." Experience as a "negro" and a dime will get you a cup of coffee. Nobody is interested in those kinds of experiences because those experiences are not marketable – not by the people HE is in love with, at least. And he has solved no problems: he admits that his experience has to do with working for somebody else. And nobody what level you work at, you still end up being a response to someone else, a taker of orders. That is the kind of experience we had during slavery!

Not that anybody asked this muthafucka what he thought, but he tells us anyway in the following paragraph:

> I think there will probably have to be a reorientation of the forces
> of law and order in this country for what I want to come about.
> Most policemen do what they're told, are only supposed to see the
> surface of things, and not be psychoanalysts or sociologists. But if
> the guidelines for law enforcement are changed – to be both
> stricter *and* more lenient, as the situation demands – police
> behavior will change and eventually there won't be the riots for the
> crime in general that there is today (p. 126 – emphasis original).

This asshole is calling for a police state! Like Nixon during that same time period, he is justifying a "law and order" culture which translates to mean that lawless white boys with badges get to shoot down niggas! Every time this country starts talking about a "war on crime," a "war on poverty," a "war on drugs," black people get dogged out. President Bill Clinton was getting his ass kissed by black people, but that big-nosed muthafucka locked up more young bruthas than anyone in recent member. The "war on drugs" made white people rich and again, black people got locked up. Through asset forfeiture black people lost millions of dollars of stuff, and that included anyone who was even *associated* with a drug dealer.

Jesse Owens talks about seeing the surface of things and he can't even do that much. He's blind when it comes to the history and tradition of racism in this country. Even though he whines about how his father got dogged out, he seems to have forgotten that little fact. His proposed "reorientation of the forces of law and order" is nothing more but increased empowerment of the same peckerwoods that were abusing Henry Owens and any other black person in this country.

Owens is a pure Uncle Tom. For instance, he continues his "proposal" as he writes,

> That has to start from high up. J. Edgar Hoover has said many
> times that the first goal of our society is law and order and that this
> distinguishes us from other countries. President Nixon says Hoover
> has his full confidence. Well, he doesn't have mine because I feel
> the first goal of our society is justice – freedom. Law is only the

> means to those ends, order only the result of using laws the right
> way to achieve the ends … (p. 126).

This nigga is quoting J. Edgar Hoover? That cross dressing peckerwood who, at the time that Owens' book was being published, was waging a campaign against the Black Panther Party, the Nation of Islam, the Republic of New Africa, the Weathermen, the Students For a Democratic Society, the US organization and any other group that was confronting America and pointing out this country's racism and contradictions for the world to see. Owens doesn't want social change or the end of oppression: he simply wants to be a part of whatever the white man has in store for black people – as long as its negative.

Just the fact that Owens trusts the white man to use laws "the right way" shows how stupid he is. The white man IS using the law the right way: the right way to maintain his system, his way of life and to keep black people in positions of peonage. That's why the majority of inmates in America are black and brown, the majority of the unemployed on a proportional basis, are black and brown, and a large percentage of those gunned down by white cops are black or brown. Do you think this is a fuckin' quirk? Of course it's not.

Only white people – and Jesse Owens (who admits he's white mentally speaking) believe that law and order is "good for everybody." As Owens puts it,

> When you start to get widespread disorder, that isn't a signal for
> stricter laws and more arrests. It's a sign that some of the laws you
> already have or some of the people enforcing them are unjust (p.
> 126).

So he admits that the system could be flawed. But does that stop him from fighting against it? Of course not. The best he can do is think that "some" of the laws might be bad or "some" of the people who are enforcing them might be unjust. What Owens has to learn is that the white man's laws are like a cancer when it comes to blacks; the purpose is to eat away at the fabric of the black community – infants, teens, black males, black women – and then make money off of the problems that you have created for them. This has been going on for decades and people like Owens turn a blind eye to it. Even with all the ass he kissed, the problems still found their way to his front door, did they not?

And yet he continues his ceaseless cacophony of emotive labeling:

> Education is another thorny problem. Partly because it will take a
> generation to get the black teachers needed. The books themselves
> are changing, though. Publisher after publisher, easily a majority
> by now, are putting Negro history into textbooks as fast as it can be
> written. Frankly, I think the trend is well underway here and that

> many federal, state and local school boards are doing a lot. Others, especially in the South, should be pressed to join them (p. 127).

Why would it take a generation to get black teachers that are needed? Why not just promote the "paraprofessionals" and "teacher aides" that white people used to use up in schools around the nation? Why does Owens think that black people are slow learners? And where are the training programs? What were those black colleges doing all this time? These are questions that show how little Owens thinks of his own people and how little he knows about the teacher education process.

He again embellishes the facts with his claim that, "Publisher after publisher, easily a majority by now, are putting Negro history into textbooks as fast as it can be written." That is a specious statement. Putting black people into textbooks is only the beginning. After all, Little Black Sambo, Black Pete and other coons were in some of the textbooks but it was degrading and based on stereotypes. Looking back to 1968 when Blackthink was published, we can see that black people are in the books and that far too many of those books were written by Jews. The issue I have with this is that Jews want to become "experts" on black people, pitting us against the American white man and in doing so, deflect attention away from what they (the Jews) have historically done to our people. That was the plan 48 years ago and that *modus operandi* is still being employed today.

Education has always been viewed as a panacea. But look at all of the educated Uncle Toms running around America today. So the type of training you get before you are "educated" by white people makes all the difference in the world. As one cultural nationalist wrote, "Education without dignity is invalid."

Moving back to Owens:

> But what must be accomplished – and what can only be accomplished by going to the root of the black/white problem – is for the Negro to become convinced that it's most important for him to get an education, regardless of who he gets it from. One of the most disturbing things about blackthink is its new anti-intellectualism, its rejection of learning simply because that has been the white man's bag. I'm no intellectual, but I'm damned sure that if the negro wants to fulfill himself, he'd better make certain he fills up on learning (p. 127).

When Owens offers up one of his jive-ass suggestions, it's always telling the black man what he ought to do; he's always talking about what "the negro" must do in order to do this or that. Why doesn't he direct some of that unsolicited advice to those peckerwoods that he seems to love so much? You know why? Because he knows that they would slam the door in his face! He knows they would slap him on his head and say, "get out of here nigger. When we want your advice, we'll beat it out of you." So he picks on the sector of the population that is powerless and that has genuine love for what he accomplished, niggerizes them with stereotypes and lies, and then tells them that they need to get an education. And then what Jesse? Does that education mean that the white man is going to drop 300 years of racist beliefs and hire the first spook who walks through the door? Hell naw!

Owens says there are three things that can be "done about it – and everything else," but I could only find two of them. This again goes directly to bad advice, bad writing and bad editing by the white co-writer Niekirk and the others who were involved who should have corrected this kind of egregious error. At any rate, here are the "tips" offered by Owens:

> First, you work *long range*. Don't expect to undo hundreds of years in a month or two. Or a year or two. Most of us agree pretty much on the of today's race crisis – the one tyrannical decision the United States made when it broke away from Britain's tyranny; to keep some human beings less than human by calling them slaves
> (p. 128)

Work with whom? He's already written off black people as a bunch of losers. He despises the militant bruthas and sistahs and the Uncle Toms surely are not about to engage in any serious planning for the race. So he's talking to and for white people and telling them what to do to "help the niggers." He's willing to mention slavery, but he again gives white people too much credit by implying that all they did was "call us" slaves. They niggerized and dehumanized us; they lynched us and segregated us; they worked us from "can't see in the morning until can't see at night." And they did it all on the basis of race. This nation's scum founders doing battle for religious rights against the British is a far cry from a 400 year process of dehumanization – which is still underway.

To Owens, everybody seems to be in the same boat, despite the tribulations of enslavement that I just named, tribulations that only black people were exposed to. There were oppressed whites, true; *but they weren't oppressed because they were white!* But let Owens tell it, it was all one big family of the dispossessed. In his words,

> For every bit of bigotry against blacks, there is prejudice against yellow skin, against Jews, sometimes even against white Protestants. For every poverty –stricken negro, you can find two poverty stricken whites. There are proportionately more negroes in trouble than whites, but a white man's empty stomach acts the same as a black man's and a white women gets just as terrified when a black intruder enters her home a a black woman does when a white man enters hers (p. 130).

My first question is where is Owens' data? What is behind statements that show that "for every bit of bigotry against blacks" there is also prejudice against other people? And who is the source of all this hate and vitriol? And don't some of these other groups also join the white man in teaming up against black people? And of what relevance is the claim that, "For every poverty –stricken negro, you can find two poverty stricken whites"? So what? They ain't po' because they're white, I'll tell you that much! So Owens seems to have taken it upon himself to convince the reader that race doesn't matter all that much and that indeed, "negroes" aren't the only ones who have it rough. Remember now: this is 1960s period, the height of the black power and civil rights movement. And yet Owens has chosen to play the role of Uncle Tom. He continues:

> Second, no matter how much bad there is, the very best way to get
> rid of it is *by exposing the good.* Don't just hack away at the roots
> of evil. They go all the way to China. Plant next to prejudice
> another tree that grows so big and high that discrimination has to
> wither and die (p. 132).

With that rather fucked up metaphor about trees out of the way, Owens then gets to babbling so much about Arthur Ashe, Willie Mays and Rod Laver (who hailed from racist South Africa) and his bullshit views on education and race relations that he forgets that he said there were three points, not just two. His editors and whoever helped him write this drivel should have caught this major mistake. But the title of the chapter was condescending enough in my view, and almost as brutally embarrassing as the closing the closing section of the chapter where he impishly writes,

> Find the good. It's all around you. Find it, showcase it, and you'll
> start believing in it. And so will most of the people who come into
> contact with you. Showcase the good. Believe in it. It's real, baby.

He talks about "finding the good" and that it's "all around you." How about the good that is WITHIN you? Don't black people have any internal characteristics that can be deemed good by this super tom? What he really means is HIS version of "the good" and that means shuffling, skinning, grinning, laughing when ain't nothin' funny and scratchin' when don't nothin' itch. A bigger ass kisser would be difficult to find.

<u>Chapter 9: Black Man, Heal Thyself</u>

Still hung up on that white man's novel, he begins Chapter 9 with yet another quote from Dionysus. The quote is, "There are many ways to call yourself a nigger." Some white man put these words in a black character's mouth, and tomming ass Jesse Owens deems it to be qualified for quoting. Bootlicking is as bootlicking does.

This is a chapter where Jesse Owens the self-appointed race relations expert takes off his dunce cap and puts on a different hat: that of urban development expert. His views on housing and demographic transition are as warped as his views on race, skin color and social stratification. Now, for the chapter analysis

Following his bullshit quote cited earlier, he then begins with what I deem a "coon version" of a white cliché where he writes, "Some of my best friends are Negroes. But not all" (p. 136). Why would a black man feel the need to say, in a book, that "some of his best friends are negroes"? I'll tell you why: because he doesn't want white people to think that he is pro-black on any level. The emphasis of the statement is not on the word "negro," it is on the word "some," meaning not "most" and not "many." And then, by adding that, "but not all," that seals it: he can now be counted on to resume his duties as Uncle Tom of the Year and white folks need not have to worry at all about this particular "house nigger."

Owens then attempts to foolishly delve into race relations on another level: that of what Dr. Frances Welsing might call "color confrontation" and what I refer to as "color coding." In his description of the light skinned/dark skinned phenomenon, check out what this asshole has to say:

> Once or twice it struck me that the three men and their wives were all rather light-skinned. Ruth and I both happen to be the same. But I didn't ie it much thought … We didn't see our other "friends" again. It was a shock when I heard the truth, but thinking back, I could see how it was. Not that this was the first time I'd ever encountered Negroes who were prejudiced against negroes because their skin was dark. It happened in my boyhood in Cleveland, it happened in my fraternity house at Ohio State, it's happened hundred and hundreds of times since (pp. 136-137).

Light-skinned versus dark-skinned black people. Really? Is this an issue that should be aired in public in front of a bunch of peckerwoods, the people who played a role in those colors existing in the first place? They raped our great-great grandmothers and as a result, a slew of mulattoes, quadroons and octoroons came to the fore. White people don't give a shit; of course they would prefer a light skinned black person walking around the office, but in their book "a nigga is a nigga," and they act accordingly. Light-skinned bruthas and sistahs like Malcolm X, Angela Davis, Elaine Brown, Huey P. Newton, Maulana Karenga, Louis

Farrakhan, Elijah Muhammad and so many others showed that what was written long ago is most accurate: "Blackness is three things: color, culture and consciousness."

Then Owens makes a point worthy of commenting on where he writes that when it came to what he called "prejudice of negroes by other negroes," "It happened in my boyhood in Cleveland, it happened in my fraternity house at Ohio State, it's happened hundred and hundreds of times since." Let me say this.

Any nigga who would join a fraternity or sorority needs his ass kicked. There is no such thing as a "black fraternity" or a "black sorority"and I don't give a shit what niggas say about it. There are people who I love very much, including my own daughter, who is a member of a so-called "black sorority." Look: if you're black, your purpose is to build black. How in the FUCK are you going to do that walking around claiming to be a "black Greek"? These niggas have lost their fuckin' minds. So when Owens talks about seeing it in the fraternity he was in, the very existence of his fraternity is an act of elitism and confusion. After all black fraternities and sororities were started for the same reason as the Black Masons, Black Elks, and other black Masonic groups: because their master, the white man, wouldn't allow them into HIS!!!

Owens shares the following point on the skin color consciousness subject:

> I remember when one of my daughters was dating a very good-looking light-skinned young fellow in college. Honor student, three sport man, all the rest. She liked him to, until he started asking about what color her grandparents were. He was thinking of marriage, you see, and wanted to make sure none of these children came out dark brown or black. They didn't get married (pp. 137-138).

Maybe not. But I'll bet he fucked her – more than once! Maybe that's why he didn't marry her – he already got the pussy and it was time to move on! Ever think about *that,* Jesse? Continuing with the rancid writings of the pseudo-intellectual:

> Historians say this started in slavery days when the plantation bosses got to like some of the mulatto children who were produced when they took the Negro women from the slave quarters for a night. Also, a light negro could pass up North and say he was Spanish or something. But I don't think you have to go back that far. Let's face it: for along time, white *has* seemed "right," and if you were black, you *did* have to get back. The hair straightening and the popularity of the Caucasian-looking Lena Horne types prove the point (p. 139 – emphasis original).

Lena Horne doesn't prove Owens' point! Lena Horne was pro-black! Jesse Owens couldn't carry Lena Hornes panty shield! She was a REAL sistah, though surrounded by Jews who wanted her and I believe she may have married one. But that's not the point: she stood by her people and supported them, far more than bootlicking Jesse Owens ever thought about doing.

Here is what Jesse Owens ought to be thinking about in this chapter which he chose to title, "Showcase the Good": He needs to do it himself. He needs to prove his thesis about all this white brotherhood that he believes to be in existence. I'll tell you what Jesse: go out in the middle of main street in Macon, Georgia and grab a white bitch and stick your tongue down her throat. That muthafucka would have been lynched so fast his head would have been spinning – literally! This muthafucka knows he's a sellout and this shit about "showcasing the good" is the grown black man's version of our mother's licking their fingers and making sure that we didn't look "ashy" when we went to school or church.

Here we are in a society where hedonism is a norm, where sexual perversions are widely accepted, where cops gun down black people, where women wear dresses that show their pussies and asses, where white men do whatever they want and get away with it, and this black muthafucka has the unmitigated GALL to talk about black people taking time to "showcase the good"?

As we say in the hood, "Nigga, please!"

Moving on with *Blackthink,* Owens babbles on:

> The blackthinkers are the worst offenders of all. Their recent craze toward Afro-dress and hair styles is just a final ironic sign that down deep the militants are more insecure about their skin color than anyone. They make too damn much of it, protest far too much about how nice it is. They're like the guy who's always talking about how great he is in bed. If something's that good, you don't' talk about it. Joe Louis never told anybody he was strong. Martin never had to say, "I'm a gentle man" (p. 139).

Again, Owens shows no mercy for those who think in militant terms; somehow we become "the worst offenders of all." This is truly white man's thinking. Owens, like so many toms of his ilk, has been totally brainwashed. His self-hate is so high and his consciousness level so low that he couldn't pour piss out of a boot if the instructions were written on the heel.

He refers to dressing in dashikis, bubas and the like, along with the Afro hair style as sign of insecurity about our skin color. That's not what it was at all. This bald-headed sonofabitch, jealous because his hair was so short that you could smell his brains, was probably jealous of all that hair that was being sprouted and the "black is beautiful" sloganizing that accompanied it. He was the one who felt insecure because he wanted so badly to be white and yet was not allowed to be. He tried to be whitey's number one nigga, but was too dumb to fit that bill when the white man had people like Martin Luther King, Joseph Lowery, Ralph Abernathy and so many others doing his work for him. And since he had no desire to be black, Owens was a marginal man; trapped in what I call "the phantom zone of bootlickers."

Owens likens the "black is beautiful" movement to a man who brags about being good in bed. He misses the point. The man who brags about being good in bed can only prove it when it comes to women. The black is beautiful movement was so pervasive even white people were trying to emulate and copy it. It was all over the world and the residue from it still lingers internationally to this day, more than half a century later. And as for King never having to say,"I'm a gentle man," the fact is that he didn't have to. The white man knew it, which is why he bribed him and then gunned him down in April of 1968. Nobody respects a sellout – not even the people who you sell out to.

More asinine assertions from Owens can be found in the following statement:

> You can give long psychological explanations as to why everyone in the ghetto is tempted to stay. The guilt of going when almost everyone you know stays behind. The fear of retaliation if you leave. A dozen other reasons. There's some truth in all of them. But there's more truth in this: just as many negroes are as prejudiced against black skin as are the worst white racists, so a staggering number of Negroes who live in the worst slums stay there *because they want to* (p. 143 – emphasis original).

There was deeper reason: because racial segregation wouldn't allow black people to move beyond a certain point. The banks call it "redlining" and "steering." If Owens would take his head out of his ass long enough, he'd know that segregation is planned and designed. Black people can want to leave an area all they want, but neighborhood associations, especially during the time period that he was in, had what were called "restrictive covenants" written into housing agreements that the person buying or renting the house would not "sell to any niggers." There are still some of these lingering around only they use slightly different language.

Then there are these neighborhood associations, akin to the ones that were featured in the movie, "A Raisin in the Sun" and on a more comedic level, "Watermelon Man." They want the communities to stay clear of black people. Earlier I cited Nat King Cole and how even he, despite all his greatness, was approached by these kinds of peckerwood groups. So these are some essential reasons that perpetuate segregation and ghettoization. The higher the population density, the greater the chance for more conflict and the more conflict there is, the more money that white cops, judges, jailers, wardens, social workers and others tend to earn.

Then Owens lies when he claims, "just as many negroes are as prejudiced against black skin as are the worst white racists, so a staggering number of Negroes who live in the worst slums stay there *because they want to.*" Black people wanted to continue breathing, continue to avoid being jailed and harassed and continue to not get attacked by white mobs. What Owens is claiming it outright bullshit.

Again, in order to avoid mentioning Jews by name Owens describes the housing like this:

> They're big houses, many built in pre-ghetto days when there
> weren't many Negros in these cities at all. Some of them were
> rather majestic homes. A few still he that look – on the outside.
> On the inside, it's something else again (p. 144).

Jews had those houses. When black people began moving North they cut those big places up into apartments and jacked up the rents and made money off of black people. And that's the way it continues today in many major cities (with Arabs replacing Jews as absentee slumlords in some cases). So again, Owens' hatred of his own people has him writing a book with a white man and placing blame and leveling subtle allegations implying that black people are stupid. Just like his white master taught him how to do. Is there any wonder why the sub-title of the book is "My Life as a Black Man and White Man"?

Continuing:

> Salesmen eat up these neighborhoods, but only on a cash-purchase
> basis. Because if you take an order and come back two weeks later
> with the merchandize, you stand a good chance of having the
> family who bought it not living there anymore. The house won't be
> empty, though. It'll be teeming with other potential customers. For
> anywhere from a half a dozen to eighteen families live in those
> houses. That in itself isn't so shocking. But what will surprise
> many people is that *Negroes* own them. Absentee Negroes (p. 144
> - emphasis original).

Again, the salesmen were Jews in many cases, as were the owners and renters of those houses. They exploited black people, and that included setting up those corner stores, extending credit and charging high interest – just as they continue to do in other parts of the world. Why do you think they get kicked out of so many countries? This is not something I'm making up. Study the Jews and you will see how they have made enemies everywhere. And now they want to hunker down in Israel, lie about being 'God's chosen people,' and act as if they are the victims even as they persecute and kill the Palestinians. But that's a subject for another book.

In this book, Owens is intentionally avoiding pointing the finger at Jews for anything other than what OTHER black people might think. He is beholden to the white man. He perpetuates stereotypes and the claims that black people own the overcrowded houses that black people were living in. Even if this were the case, the Jews still owned more and still exploited more black people. So where is that mentioned? Nowhere to be found.

Owens adds that,

> There was a time when almost all of these stores were owned by whites. But that's past history. Now the majority are black-owned. And where there are white owners, they pay a hefty percentage to some Negro to run them and make sure a big profit is turned. He turns it, too, by selling everything from appliances and TV sets to clothes and jewelry and even food at twice what he should to people who don't know much better or don't care of would have trouble going elsewhere (p. 144).

There is a difference here: the stores were OWNED by whites but they left and the stores remained owned by them – they were just MANAGED by black people. And the reason for that is because the white man (and the Jew) wanted to keep turning the profit by over-charging and didn't want that cash cow to be taken away. So they allowed some black person to "manage" the store, someone who hailed from the community that was being exploited, someone who the community would identify with, and even though the exploitation continued and the white man continued to make profits, the cash cow had a black face. Black on the outside, whiten the inside – just like Jesse "the Oreo" Owens.

Now comes the association with crime (once the white man is safely tucked out of the picture):

> Some stores sell more in the back than out in the front. Bookies are everywhere. They're black, There are Negro dope pushers by the dozens, trying to start their own people on the road to hell as young as they can get them. Sometimes they'll give the kid the first two fixes for nothing to get him hooked. When they youngster – maybe he's eighteen, maybe he's twelve – needs more, he'll rob or murder to get the money. If the addict is a girl, she'll become a prostitute, though she might not have had her first period yet (pp. 144-145).

The bookies may be black but the people who they turn the money over to are white. The people in Vegas are white. The people in the major gambling cities are white. They were then and they are today. Why isn't Owens mentioning that little fact? Then he goes back to the black dope dealers and the junkies, affirming every negative stereotype about the black community (that he doesn't live in) all the while. The black woman, of course, becomes a prostitute – a sign of how he feels about black women other than his daughters or his wife. All negative, all stereotypes, all void of any kind of background or sociological explanation. And all avoiding the white role in all of this.

Owens has an excuse for everything. Check it out:

> I can hear the blackthinkers screaming, "The white man built the houses and stores! The white man created the system and forced the black man to make a living by taking the bread out of his own brother's mouth!" One look at the HELP WANTED section of any daily newspaper in just about any city in this country knocks that into a cocked hat. So does a look at all the *honest* Negro property owners and Negro entrepreneurs (p. 145 – emphasis added).

How can Owens hear anyone screaming above his bitch-like whining, wailing and lying? He can't hear anything "black" at all because he is too busy directing his ears toward what his white masters are ordering him to say and do! What you just read from Owens is bullshit, and he knew it when he wrote it, when he re-read it and when it was passed off to his editors. He is getting this shit in print because it is saying everything the white man wants to say but won't come right out and say because he knows he'll get his ass kicked. So you can't say it's "racist" if a "black man" says it. That is the new way that these white people have of degrading our people: create a buffer zone made up of negroes who don't give a shit about their own people and make those negroes into "authorities" on the black condition (read: Shelby Steele, Ward Connerly, Raven Simone, Tavis Smiley, Steve Harvey, Whoopi Goldberg, etc.)

Now comes the stroke that kills – the *coup de grace*:

> For the cold fact that almost every Negro, he was moderate or militant, wants to overlook – and that whites just don't know -- is *that today the Negro is the greatest exploiter of the negro.* It starts at the very bottom, with the portable hot-dog vendor who also sells heroin, and goes all the way up to the top, to many of the so-called "Negro leaders" (p. 145 – emphasis original).

In order to exploit someone you have to have power. The definition of exploiter is, "To use selfishly for one's own ends." And what "ends" would the black exploiter have? To make money and then to spend it where? At the white man's stores and establishments. And save it where? At the white man's banks and credit unions. So any black person who exploits another black person is an ally to the white businessman! Where do you think we learned it from?

But the fact is no one exploits black people more than white people. White people even exploit the black people who exploit black people. For instance, take the case of black ministers, the biggest black exploiters of all. And yet Owens doesn't mention them, does he? Nobody takes advantage of the black community more than the black minister because the black church is where most of the black community can be found on any given Sunday! And in every black community where there is a black church there is also poverty, exploitation, hunger, and crime. So the "negro leaders" that Owens gives credit – his fellow Uncle Toms – are far worse than the ones he is talking about in the previous excerpt. It was true then, and it remains true to this very day.

Owens speaks specifically when he defends his white pals. But when it comes to black people there are blanket indictments – like the following one, for instance:

> To show when it comes to the so-called exploitation of the Negro, the black man himself is first in line. The Negro is not the eternal masochist to the sadist white, and he shouldn't think of himself in this way. More than anyone else, he often has a vested interest in his brother's own poverty, ignorance and degradation. And so, in blackthink … (p. 146).

When the trash-talking track star writes that, "More than anyone else, he often has a vested interest in his brother's own poverty, ignorance and degradation," he is describing black ministers and preachers to the "t." The black preacher doesn't even have credibility among his own fellow white preachers. The adage teaches us that "Sunday is the most segregated day of the week." Why is that, Christians? Where is your god when these peckerwoods are wreaking havoc in, around and over black communities across the nation? The only time they pop up is to lead some kind of "prayer vigil" where they can collect some money or get a funeral that they then turn over to a mortuary in exchange for a kickback. It's taking place all over the nation, folks.

> But just the fact that we are human is a key to this whole crisis, too. Human beings can be improved. I write this chapter to say to the black man what I've tried to say to myself for so many years. To paraphrase President Kennedy: Don't ask what the white man

> can do for you – don't even think of it – until you've first done
> every damned thing *you* can do for yourself (p. 146 – emphasis
> original).

The name of the chapter was "Black Man, Heal Thyself." For Jesse Owens to have that title of a chapter and then write what he did is like asking Jack the Ripper to perform a gynecology exam! Look at his own words where he claims that, "I write this chapter to say to the black man what I've tried to say to myself for so many years. To paraphrase President Kennedy: Don't ask what the white man can do for you – don't even think of it – until you've first done every damned thing *you* can do for yourself."

Heal thyself. This sounds like a call for self-reliance, self-determination and what Carmichael and Hamilton referred to as "black power" a year before Owens' book came out. After all, what did they say about black power? To reiterate, "Before a group can enter open society it must first close ranks." Isn't this what "Black Man, Heal Thyself" sounds like? Oh, that's right: when black people with expertise say it, they are "blackthinks." When Jesse Owens says it, he has to attribute the concept to a white man, John F. Kennedy. So in Owens' mind, it is the race of the person making the statement, not the statement itself.

Jesse Owens cannot "heal anyone" or give out advice to do the same. He died in a state of disease – a disease of the mind. He sold out an entire race: *his own.*

Chapter 10: Open Letter to a Young Negro

When I saw the title of this chapter, my first response was, *"why, Jesse, why?"* I continued, "why would you write an open letter to a young black man when you've already castigated and indicted the entire race, already? Why would you write a letter to a young brutha when your book promotes a belief that the black man is his own worst enemy and on some level, white people are misunderstood? Why are you trying to brainwash young black men to become the kind of ass kissing, warm spit carrying, bootlicking muthafucka that you are, Jesse?

And that is what this chapter does: it offers some "young negro" tips on how to be an Uncle Tom. He gives out information that sounds like some house nigger talking to a slave in the back of the big house. And as the Malcolm X quote made clear earlier in regard to the house negro, "He identified himself with his master more than his master identified with himself." And this description fits Jesse Owens like a glove.

This time the opening quote is from the white boy that he defeated in the Olympics, Luz Long. The quote is, "Tell them how the good times between us were" (p. 147). Now here is a fuckin' Nazi, who Owens competed against, one of Hitler's prize "students" and Owens was so starved for white acceptance that he became pals with this "sieg heilin'" sonofabitch! You can't tom much more than that! But quoting a Nazi is not good enough for the bootlicking Owens. His next move is to follow up the quote from Luz Long with a quote from a black man, Bob Teague to begin this chapter:

> "All black men are insane … Almost any living thing would
> quickly go mad under the unrelenting exposure to the climate
> created and reserved for black men in a white racist society .. I am
> secretly pleased about the riots. Nothing would please the tortured
> man inside me more than seeing bigger and better riots every day."
> Those words were spoken by Bob Teague to his young son in
> Letters to a Black Boy. He wrote these letters to "alert" his son to
> "reality" so that the boy wouldn't "be caught off guard –
> unprepared and undone" (p. 147).

Teague was a real black man with a real message. Everything he wrote is something that I agree with almost one hundred percent. The fact is, I think he was rather diplomatic about it. Black people are not insane, but we do suffer from serious brain damage. After four hundred years of an intense campaign of dehumanization, we survived it physically, but were never de-briefed. We went from that physical brutality to the psycho-economic brutality of sharecropping and those who went North faced intense racial segregation in the slums. Who wouldn't be insane after all that bullshit? White people whine and cry when they are exposed to a fraction of what we went through.

For instance, look at the Jews claiming six million of their people were killed and then they insult us by saying it was the worst crime in the history of humanity. Have they forgotten 400 years of enslavement and the fact that over 100 million black people died both during the Middle Passage and during enslavement? Did they forget that their people had a role to play in that slave system, the least of which was not providing many of those ships that African people were loaded onto?

What do you think all this black on black crime is about? If I've got a white mind like Jesse Owens, when I see another black man I see that black man the same way a white man would see him: as my enemy. Back in the day the worst thing you could call another black man was a "black muthafucka." It wasn't the word "muthafucka" that was the major insult – it was the fact that the term was prefaced with the word "black"!

More contemporaneously, you see all these skin lighteners making a comeback under the name of "skin cleanser" (read: Proactiv). You see these women wearing and requesting "flesh-colored" dresses, as if the only flesh was the color of the white man's. It's the same shit: the conk has been replaced with the jheri-curl which has been replaced with hair extensions and weaves. These are all forms of black-on-black "crime" because on various levels we are rejecting our nature, rejecting our very selves! These are the acts of a people who have been tortured and dehumanized!

Owens then poses a series of questions:

> Are his words true? Does a black man have to be just above insane to exist in America? Do all Negroes feel a deep twinge of pleasure every time we see a white man hurt and a part of white society destroyed? Is really something so stinking terrible that it'll grab your heart out of your chest with one hand and your manhood with the other if you don't meet it armed like a Nazi storm trooper? (p. 147).

Jesse would not have to ask these questions if he gave a shit about his own people and his history. If he loved his father the way he claims he did, he would not be selling out to the very people who degraded his father and insulted his family the way they did. He asks these questions in a tongue-in-cheek fashion: they are rhetorical and loaded questions. He has an answer already in his mind. It doesn't matter how the question is answered because this Uncle Tom is going to figure out a way to somehow find the white man "not guilty" of anything. At the same time he paints a picture of black people who stand up and fight as somehow being as maniacal as "Nazi storm troopers."

And do you know why he keeps making these references to Nazis? There are two reasons. The first one is that his claim to fame is the success he had during the Olympics in Berlin, which Hitler and the Nazis hosted. That is why the white man showered him with praise during that time (and, of course, treated him like shit once he returned to America). The second reason is that Jews are the ones behind the publishing of this book! They are probably the ones who asked him to write it, knowing full well that it would be published at the height of the black power movement. They knew that by writing a book so full of "white is right" bullshit, that black ire would be aimed at Owens and not at the real culprits: white folks in general and Jews in particular!

This Uncle Tom then starts babbling incessantly about his relationship with his broad jumping Nazi counterpart Luz Long, and it was so pitiful that I devoted an entire section of this book to it. I address it later. At any rate, this chapter titled "Open Letter to a Young Negro," continues:

> We all get tired. But know yourself, know your humannness, and
> you'll know why you can never finally throw in with bigotry or
> blackthink. You must not be a Negro. You must be a human being
> first and last, if not always … (p. 157).

The words that this bootlicker just shared should have been the title of the book: "You must not be a negro." What??? What else are you going to be when your "negro-ness" is not only your ultimate reality (you were black before you were born) but there are millions of white people who are going to remind you, ever day, that you are black? You can be black and still be a human being. But Jesse isn't convinced of that because he denied his own humanity a long time ago. So starved was he and those of his ilk for integration and the coming of a chariot called "equality," that they forgot all about being black and caring about other black people. They wanted that "one-way integration" now and be damned with black business development, black community growth, black education, black hospitals and clinics and so on.

And look where we are now because of that warped, pro-white thought process: too weak to do anything but wander.

In his letter to black youth, Owens is trying to create a cadre of future Uncle Toms. Check out his "advice":

> Reach back, Harry Edwards. Reach back inside yourself and
> grapple of that extra ounce of guts, that last cell of manhood even
> you didn't know you had, that something that let you stand the
> pain and beat the ghetto and go on to break the records. Use it now
> to be totally honest with yourself. For when the chips are really
> down, you can either put your skin first or you can go with what's
> inside it. (p. 157).

What an asshole! These are the kinds of "Uncle Tom tips" that black kids do not need, not then and not now. Owens is in no position to give Harry Edwards any advice on any subject. Edwards was the intellectual superior to Owens and those like him. Edwards maintained his blackness and consciousness and STILL went on to get his doctorate. And then, once he got it, he continued working to help black people. What does Owens have to offer? What did Jesse Owens do that would qualify him to even consider writing a letter to a "young negro"? The fact is, he is doing the white man's bidding as he always did. And I'm here to expose him, post-mortem, but as they say: better late than never.

Owens' plunge into treachery continues:

> Sure, there'll be times when others try to keep you from being
> human. But remember that prejudice isn't new. It goes way back,
> just as slavery goes way back, to before there ever an America.
> Men have always had to meet insanity without losing their own
> minds. That doesn't mean you should stand still for bigotry. Fight
> it. Fight it for all you're worth. But fight your own prejudice, too.
> Don't expect perfection in your white brother until there's not an
> ounce left in you. And remember that the hardest thing for all of us
> isn't to fight, but to stop and think. *Black, think …* is the opposite
> of *… blackthink* (p. 157 – emphasis original).

Is this how Owens sums up the racial situation? Does he think that we are seeking "perfection" in or from the white man? We are long past and know much better than that. We have centuries of proof that this white man cannot even accord to us some basic respect as human beings! Even his own history shows that when it came to black people we were only counted as "three-fifths" of a man. That was in 1787 and based on the pervasive discrimination and racist acts that you see today in 2016 – some 239 years later – it is clear that this white bastard is not going to change or accord to us anything even *resembling* human rights.

He wants young people to oppose and despite "blackthink," that is, thinking in terms of black people. He wants them to be the same as he is: a man with no soul. Or, as Owens himself put it,

> So be a new kind of "militant," an *immoderate moderate*, one
> hundred percent involved, but as a man, not a six-foot hunk of
> brown wrapping paper, be an extremist when it comes to your
> ideals, a moderate when it comes to the raising of your fist … (pp.
> 157-158).

What is an "immoderate militant"? I'm a wordsmith and I never heard the term. So I looked up the word "immoderate," and guess what it means. To be "immoderate" is "to go beyond reasonable limits: not moderate." But the key word is "limits." And so you have to ask limits set by whom? So you can go beyond limits set by the white man, but do it in a way that is deemed "acceptable." Apply "moderation." In other words, take your time. As a former mentor and instructor of mine used to say, "Put some water in your wine."

And there goes that "brown wrapping" reference again, just like the one he made on page 43. He uses this reference because he thinks black skin color is something that should be removed or ignored. He thinks you can raise your fist and be a "moderate" – the way today's fake-ass white liberals are doing (read: Bernie Sanders). In simple terms he wants young black people to be sellouts and pretend that they don't even see skin color. The final paragraph of this chapter sums up where Owens is coming from:

> Live every day deep and strong. Don't pass up your Olympics and
> *your* Luz Long. Don't let the blackthinkers sell you out for a
> masquerade rumble where the real you can never take off the
> mask. You see, black *isn't* beautiful. *White* isn't beautiful. Skin-
> deep is *never* beautiful (p. 158 – emphasis original).

Look for a white man to love and give credit to, the way Owens did to that Nazi Luz Long. Keep your "mask" on and don't take it off. And remember: black is not beautiful. And remember folks, he said and wrote this shit at a time when black people would run a nigga out of town on a rail if he said that shit to a crowd. So he put his Uncle Tom tips in a book for all to read. And in doing so he hoped to deflate the egos of black youth while giving white kids some semblance of comfort knowing that there were black people out there like Jesse Owens.

And as much as I hate to admit it, I agree with Malcolm X: there's still some house niggers walking around here ….

Chapter 11: Open Letter to All Whites

It only stands to reason that an Uncle Tom could not write a letter to a "young negro" without also including a letter to "all whites." Of course, as I have shown, his letter to the young brutha contained nothing more than tips on how to be a sellout, so what's the difference? At any rate after starting off with a quote, "You mean shit, don't you?" and then attributing the quote to "a white suburbanite," Owens' chapter descends even deeper into the abyss of ignorance.

He devotes a great deal of time to talking about jobs and training. He seems to be begging and expecting the white man to provide the jobs while black people get an education and then look for some white man to adopt them. There is no talk about self-reliance or self-determination; just the Jesse Owens method of integration. Karenga (1967) once wrote that, "The Negro lives on a two-fold economy: he borrows what he wants and begs for what he needs."

It is also in this chapter that Owens admits that he – and his followers (whoever in the hell they are) at "at war" with militant black people. At war? What's wrong with this nigga? I'll tell you what's wrong: he's such an ultimate tom that anyone who isn't willing to kiss white ass is considered an "enemy." That is how deep is treachery runs. And as you read on, you'll read his words and see what I mean.

The chapter begins with a story that sounds like something out of Oliver Twist (for reasons too numerous to mention here). At any rate, check it out:

> During the last Olympics, a number of Negro athletes became
> close with white fellows on the team. This was the rule, by the
> way, not the exception … They cheered each other on during the
> competition, ate together off the field and just did a lot of walking
> and talking – finding out how much they had in common. When it
> came time to go home, the white fellow asked his negro pal to
> come to his house and stay for a week. "I know Dad would love to
> have you," he added. The Negro nodded quietly, "But would he
> give me a job?" he said sarcastically (p. 159).

How would Owens know how "close" black men got with their fellow white athletes? Appearance is not essence, and the black people that Owens didn't like are the ones he ignored. How are you going to have an integrated and happy Olympic team and then come back to the U.S. and face housing segregation and unemployment? You would have to be an Uncle Tom of Jesse Owens' ilk to be able to show progress in such a context.

Now check out this bullshit story, which consists of two unnamed athletes. He claims two athletes were on the team and the white boy asked his "negro pal" (how does he know they were "pals"?) to come to his house and stay a week. The brutha agrees but asks the white boy if his father would love to have him over so much "would he give me a job"? That is bullshit. No black kid would have the guts to make such an exponential jump in logic: "yeah I'll visit – by the way, can Pops get me a job"? Only an asshole like Jesse Owens would even make the attempt to pin such a lie on a black kid.

But in order to complete the moral of his story – that being that "the white man will give a nigga a chance," he has to lie. Then, he completes his fairy tale:

> The white athlete was shocked. But then he thought it over and
> saw the point. He still asked his buddy to come to the house, but
> only after he'd phoned his father from Mexico City and secured a
> job interview for the friend. As it turned out, the man did give his
> son'[s pal a job. But not because the Negro was a friend. Because
> he was competent and eager to work. In less than two years, the
> young man has been promoted twice and is making $16,000
> annually … (p. 159).

How does Jesse know all this? I'll tell you how: because it exists only in Jesse's fantasies. And when you're making shit up as you go, anything is possible! So somehow this kid calls his father and gets a black kid an interview. So the black kid got a job. And in Jesse's fantasy, two years later the kid was earning $16,000 a year. How does Jesse know how much this kid made? How does he know what took place two years AFTER he (Jesse) had left the Olympic games? This is another bold-faced lie that should never have been printed. And that's why the key characters remained anonymous: Jesse could not name them because they never existed in the first place!

And then Jesse gets to the point he is trying to get across to a gullible American public:

> Yet it never would've happened if the Negro hadn't come out and asked for that job. His white brother would've had him out to the house for a week, would have had him waited on hand and foot and the father would have loved having him there. But they never would have dreamed of offering work to him. And work is the most important thing, more important even than friendship (p. 160).

His "white brother"? If the muthafucka was his brother, why did the black kid have to even ask? But this is a slave doing the talking and it's proven when he concludes that, "work is the most important thing, more important even than friendship." Work. Ain't that a bitch? This is what Owens has in a chapter that is supposed to be an "open letter to all whites." He wants black people to beg white people for jobs. And he wants white people to believe that if they give black people jobs, black people will kiss their ass in return. This seems to be the Jesse Owens message (not to mention his philosophy on life). And he admits it – check out the following:

> It was for me in 1936, too. I told you how I came home from the Olympics to the irony of parades and poverty. But why I came home when I did is part of that story too. (p. 160).

Such an ass kisser, an allegation proven in the following excerpt:

> I was walking off the track with Ralph when Larry Snyder crossed over to us. There was a strange look on his face. "Keep washing your sweat clothes, guys," he said. "I just got a telegram. The AAU wants you to run in Sweden tomorrow." I didn't say anything for a full minute. If there'd been an AAU official there, I might have hit him. The AAU simply didn't understand. Just as they often don't understand today … (p. 162).

Owens says that if there had been an AAU official there he "might have hit him." Oh really? Nowhere in this bullshit book does he ever strike anyone, let alone a white man. But now he grows balls, and do you know why? Because he knows he wouldn't do it, that's why! He's certainly had more than a few chances to kick some white ass, hasn't he? Did he take advantage of the chance? Hell no.

he's too busy dogging out black men who are trying to make a difference. And his cowardice is only surpassed by his on-going mis-perceptions of reality.

For instance he writes that, "The AAU simply didn't understand. Just as they often don't understand today …" Muthafucka, the AAU *does* understand! That's why it's called an "amateur" association so that they don't have to pay niggas like you and STILL get you to run, jump, dunk, and throw for them! It's a modern-day slave system for desperate young people with talent – and the only people getting paid are white coaches, trainers and the like. The AAU understands a "good nigga" when they see one. And that's why they felt totally within their rights to infringe upon Owens' free time and his life. They had done it before – why not believe that they had the right to do it any time they chose to?

And Owens *continues* to keep giving white folks the (undeserved) benefit of the doubt:

> They'd never thought of finding me a job somewhere for when I
> got home and *then* asking me to run "one more time" and one more
> time after that. They'd never dreamed of trying to break a Negro
> into professional baseball or football. I would have been the
> perfect guinea pig with my "world's fastest human" reputation.
> No, they thought of me as their performing money, a running
> machine that never broke down and that would do some p-r work
> for America while mainly doing a lot more good for the old AAU.
> (p. 162).

Why would they respect him enough of him to give a shit about his feelings or schedule? He's shown them by his own actions that he's their willing thrall. He has no idea about what white people "never dreamed of," but one thing is for sure: they didn't dream of making his black ass rich, did they? They knew he was married and had children, didn't they? Did they give a shit? Hell no. So not only were they disrespecting him, but they were also shitting on his family – the same way that white man John Cannon did back in the day when he told Henry Owens, "Your sons will never amount to anything – just be grateful if they *survive!*"

And even in this repetition of racist history, Jesse remained a bootlicker – by choice. Even when Jesse decided to take a stand, he still finds a way to give the credit to some white man:

> Well, the money wasn't going to perform anymore. He'd lost at
> Cologne, and he wasn't going to make a habit of it at Stockholm
> and at the next place after that and the next and the next. Not that it
> was the losing that hurt most. It was what Pierre de Coubertin, the
> founder of the modern Olympics had said: "The purpose is not

winning, but fighting well." I didn't have any more of that kind of fight left in me (p. 162).

Angry because he lost a race and now he's going to pretend as if he has a shred of dignity. Then, when he decided to exercise some kind of temerity, look what his good buddy the white man did to him:

> Then I went and did it – sent a telegram to the AAU. It said: *"Sick and underweight. Cannot compete in Stockholm. Family waiting for me. Going home. Jesse Owens."* Two hours later I got a telegram back from them. It notified me that I was suspended from the Amateur Athletic Union and I was never again to compete as an amateur athlete for the United States (pp. 162-163 – emphasis original).

Did he learn anything from this kind of treatment? Evidently not. He kept right on tomming and didn't miss a step. The fact that he sent a telegram and had to tell a lie in order to attempt to get out of going to Stockholm, shows how gutless he is. And did the white man give a shit about his alleged sickness? Hell no. So on the one hand you have a lifelong Uncle Tom and sellout and on the other hand, white racist bastards who really don't give a shit. And both are facing each other in an arena that is dominated and controlled by the latter entity. Guess who wins?

Jesse is no economist or job specialist, but he's always talking about "work" and the "workplace." In doing so, he makes just that much more of an ass out of himself. For instance, where he makes the following claim:

> First, a Negro doesn't want just any job. Like a white man, he wants the right job. Second, the right job more and more in our society is the one that requires training. There are fewer and fewer ads for laborers and more and more for computer specialists … Or take a look at Dave Albritton. Last year he finally opened a bank in Ohio. It took him three years from the time he'd gotten the money. Because he didn't have the Negroes to work in it (p. 163).

Again, when he attempts to speak for black people (which he is not even remotely qualified to do), he has to use the white man as the standard. Just because the white man wants the right job doesn't mean that the black man who wants the right job is going to get the same access or opportunity. This is true because the people in charge of providing the jobs are the same race as that white man is! To them the "right job" for a black man is no job; if they can't get that across then they'll find one that is menial, hazardous and low-paying. The right job for the white man is any job that white man applies for because in addition to being white in a society that rewards whiteness, he also has the benefit of society-wide "white privilege."

And then there's that "I can't find any qualified niggas" bullshit rap that white people use. Look: do you think that even half of the white people who have jobs are qualified for them? You've seen them: idiots for the most part. They got hired because of somebody they knew, not WHAT they knew! They come in cold and get training and get to learn on the job if they come across something they can't handle. The concept of "no qualified blacks" is buying them even more time to *disqualify us!*

Even with racism staring him right in his face, Owens seems to think that the problem is with black people:

> Training, training, training – that's what it's all about in our economic society today. The white conservatives with their grandiose ideas of "black capitalism" don't realize that a man without the means to gain capital is never going to be a capitalist. The white liberals with their bleeding hearts and paternalistic handouts don't see that socialism and self-reliance can never make it together (p. 164).

It's not an either or situation and the options that Owens just gave show how off-kilter his thinking is.

For one thing he opines that, "that a man without the means to gain capital is never going to be a capitalist." Even if a black person has some capital and even if he thinks like a capitalist, race trumps capital accumulation. Look at all the rich black people that get their asses kicked, get discriminated against, and get imprisoned. Anybody can be a capitalist; as Karenga (1967) wrote, "When we speak of blacks being capitalist, we are speaking philosophically, not economically." In other words if you can exploit your fellow man, you have met the basic pre-requisite for being a capitalist. Black people can get jobs and can even be considered middle class, but it is the white man who continues to sit in judgment. And as far as he's concerned, a nigga with a million dollars is still, first and foremost, a nigga.

Secondly, he talks about liberals , socialism and self reliance. White liberals don't have anything to do with black self-reliance. They just run their mouths. Black self-reliance requires, in my view, eliminating white folks from the equation. Their ultimate goal is to foster black dependency so their emphasis and direction are antithetical to what black self-reliance is all about. That's why the key to black power, as I quoted earlier, is to first of all "close ranks." Owens doesn't understand this because he believes in opening up his heart, his home and probably his ass crack to his white buddies.

He relies on the white man's "charity" more than he says the black militants do. He writes,

> Give jobs before friendship. Give speeches only if you're provided training to make the message of those speeches work. But at the same time don't throw in with the blackthinking "we don't need whites for our friends" party line. Whites *can* help the race crisis on a level ultimately as important as the economic one. But not the way they've been doing it (p. 164).

In his open letter to white people, Jesse gives them far more power than they deserve. But he can't avoid knocking black people who think in a less than passive way, can he? When he says that whites CAN help the race crisis that is as important as the economic one, he is in error on a number of levels.

First of all, the "race crisis" is one that generates comfort and revenue for white people. The more they "steer" black families to certain areas, the more they discriminate against us, the more money they can make from poverty pimp programs. The more they devalue the land that black people live on, the more they mis-educate minority kids, the more they continue to stir the pot that is boiling. And when that happens everything that will get torn down or burned is insured to the hilt. So they benefit from every crisis because they created it, they maintain it and on various levels, they benefit from it.

Secondly, the concept of giving jobs before friendship. The fact is, we don't really need the friendship. The jobs are going to help the white economy so when they discriminate, they are jeopardizing the size and quality of their own work force. When they reject black dollars, they are harming their own revenue streams. Today in 2016, they have come to know that. But the friendship thing is something you don't see on any black list of "what we want" or "what we demand." Just check them out. The only nigga talking about friendship is that Uncle Tom Jesse Owens.

And yet Owens knows that the odds of racial reconciliation are slim and none. He *almost* admits it in the following passage:

> Frankly, I don't know that any Negro old enough to read this will ever live in a world without the gut reactions of prejudice staring him in the face. I don't know that any white reading this, even if he starts now to try and free himself of his bigotry, will ever be able to succeed more than a small percentage of the time. But I do know that those few successes will count for a lot. And the failures will be a *different kind* of failure (p. 166).

"The gut reactions of prejudice" don't just stare the black man in the face. Prejudice as he calls it, is not just a reaction – it is a way of life for all human beings. If I know that a particular woman can't cook and I avoid it and then tell her she can't cook worth a shit, that's not "pre judging" her. That's a reaction and a statement based on facts as I see them. So "prejudice" in and of itself is not an issue. What Owens means is *racial* prejudice" or more specifically, racism. And when it comes it's not just a reaction: it is based on a long-time anti-black philosophy and is backed by institutions.

Furthermore, Owens is also confused when he writes, "I don't know that any white reading this, even if he starts now to try and free himself of his bigotry, will ever be able to succeed more than a small percentage of the time." Why would a white person spend time trying to free himself from something (bigotry) when it is a part of his being? What does he stand to gain? Even these white grandparents whose daughters have brought a black man home or who have given them mixed grandchildren cannot free themselves of their bigotry – they just target it differently. Owens, as he has done throughout the book, continues to give white people far more credit than they deserve because he continues to short-change and misunderstand the underpinnings and depth of white racism.

Because of what I just accused Owens of, it only stands to reason that he would make statements like the following one:

> Only when you're totally committed to fighting whitethink can you battle blackthink. But don't make the mistake of feeling then that blackthink is any less insidious than the white brand of bigotry. If Rap Brown and Harry Edwards were the only kind of blackthinkers, the war against them would already be won ... (p. 168).

Why would a white person want to "fight white think"? What else do they know. In their universe, the "white way is the right way." They lose nothing by going through life hating black people but pretending like they don't. I can understand why they would want to battle "blackthink" because it is the key to stripping through the maze of lies and bullshit that white people have heaped upon black people for four centuries. But then Owens makes a major mistake.

He informs white people in his "letter" to them that they should not "make the mistake of feeling then that blackthink is any less insidious than the white brand of bigotry." What? Even if "blackthink" were insidious, it is not backed up by the cops, the military, the courts, prisons and an ideology of hate the way "whitethink" is! Owens has it twisted and he is telling the white people things that will only lead to them getting their asses kicked if they attempt to apply it! Instead he tells them, "If Rap Brown and Harry Edwards were the only kind of blackthinkers, the war against them would already be won."

And that was the beauty of the movement. We had our Rap Browns, Stokelys and Huey Newtons, but we also had the more accommodationist Martin Luther Kings and Ralph Abernathys. The white man had to choose between the lesser of two evils. But with Owens telling him that "there are more types of blackthink so be careful," *he is warning the enemy of our race of our strategies and tactics!* He has, once again, betrayed the race! And he continues with his "warning" to his white brothers (read: "masters"):

> The blackthinkers who really count are much more difficult to
> spot and to fight. They're not just black militants who actually feel
> that their kinky hair makes them superior to whites just as Hitler's
> Aryans used to feel superior because of their wavy blond hair. Nor
> are they only white women hung up on the Negro's supposed sex
> prowess. They're people like me – or *you* (p. 168-emphasis
> original).

He's telling the white man what he (Owens) believes black people are doing and the "threat" that black people pose. He is exposing our people to the enemy of our race at a time when black awareness was at an all time high. But as Shakespeare once wrote in his play about the life of the legendary Roman leader Caius Marcius Coriolanus, "Though those that are betray'd do feel the treason sharply, yet the traitor Stands in worse case of woe." Surely, Jesse Owens feels the woe that Shakespeare is referring to because not only did he practice and live a life of treachery, but he committed it to paper and pen for the world to see.

Let me also point out here that on several occasions, Owens has mentioned white women and their relationship to or belief in the black man's "sexual prowess." What about the white man? How about his belief that all black women are whores and how about his historical rapes of them? No mention. So he would rather stereotype and degrade his own race than to tell the truth about the white man who is hated the world over for the rapes of women of color.

Moving on:

> It was out of fear that the whites bought subscriptions to magazines
> they didn't want. They were paying off. Here was a tall Negro boy
> walking up to their manicured lawn. Fear. But wait – he only wants
> me to spend eight dollars on *Harper's*. What a small price to pay,
> eh? Give in, pay it. Be thankful he's here to sell subscriptions and
> not to set fire to the house. Pay the blackmail (p. 169 – emphasis
> original).

Although speaking metaphorically, he nevertheless accuses black boys of the crime of "blackmail," does he not? It is not fear that makes the white man buy those magazines: it is guilt. Not only that, but it's not as if the black kids were selling Ebony, Jet or Sepia! They were selling white magazines to white people who were safe in white neighborhoods. And yet because a black youth is present, the Uncle Tom Jesse Owens finds something wrong with it. But more blame is a'comin':

> And the Negroes? They knew it. That's' why they picked the neighborhoods they did. They knew that they had blackthink going for them, that the threat of riot was right underneath the polite smile and list of publications. But they don't want to riot. They could get hurt. They don't want to waste time demonstrating. They want to make money, or go to college, maybe just buy a shiny car. And they want to do it by climbing on someone's back. They want to stay right smack in the middle of the Establishment by using the threat of militancy (p. 169).

Owens is reinforcing the very stereotypes that white people use to justify their hatred and fear of black people. From the "threat of riot" and "buying a shiny car" to "climbing on someone's back," he is writing from a position of hatred. This letter to white people and the book are nothing short of a temper tantrum.

Owens is sick. He then transitions his letter and writes about this white bitch named Karen who was married to a white man but had an affair with a black man. The brutha fucked her but then moved on. Here is what Owens claims took place:

> … after he's broken up with her , he came to me for advice on a business mater. He go to talking, and before I knew it he was telling me about it. "She's so bright and such a beauty," he said. "But she's sick inside, Jesse. I hated to, but I finally had to end it." "How is she sick?" I asked. He hesitated for a moment. "She's one of *those* women," he said. "She .. needs pain. She always wanted me to hit her before I … made love to her." (p. 170 – emphasis original).

Why include this in the book? He protects the names of the people because I doubt if either of them ever really existed. But this does show Owens' preoccupation with interracial sex – just like his white male master. In the old days the segregationist slogan was, "The key to the classroom is the key to the bedroom." Owens has taken it one step farther: "The key to according black people human dignity is the key to riots and destruction."

He closes out his "letter" to white folks in the following paragraph:

So what I'm really saying is to give yourself a chance. And give us
a chance with it. Maybe we *do* have rhythm. Maybe our sweat *does*
have a different odor. Well, it's too bad you don't have rhythm.
And your sweat smells different to us. Who in the hell cares? I
don't. Because I know all the other things we have that matter so
much more. They're the same things you have. They're what being
a human being is all about (pp. 170-171 – emphasis original).

He wants white people to give themselves a chance. That's like asking
Warren Buffett to give himself a loan! These peckerwoods don't need any more
"slack" than they've already assumed. They've been getting by for far too long as
it is. Owens talking about the different smells of sweat and that other foolishness
that he mentions as he closes out this chapter are the remarks of a man gone mad.
He is so frustrated and angry that he cannot be white that he writes a book claiming
that he actually had a life as a white man! Then he betrays black people,
stereotypically degrades black youth, and basically works to promote race
treachery and one-way integration.

With all this having been done, we come to the final chapter, and the title is
as nebulous and disingenuous as most of Owens' statements.

Channel 12: We Shall Overcome – If

This mind numbingly confused asshole and his tommishness have to end.
This last chapter of the book also begins with a quote, and this one comes from
another racist muthafucka. Alan Paton, the author of *Cry, the Beloved Country*, is a
South African. He is known for opposing apartheid but in my view he was still a
racist muthafucka. Just because his people take eight steps backwards and he
comes along and tapes one step forward, that ain't no "progress" in my book!

Of all the people who could be quoted, Owens goes from a quote from a TV
show ("The Big Valley") to a white boy named Thorpe and now Alan Paton. Jesse
said that his co-writer was white: I think the white boy wrote the majority of the
book with the intention of castigating black people using Jesse Owens as a
smokescreen. Sure, Jesse was a tom, but he wasn't the sharpest knife in the drawer;
a lot of this shit could only have been known by someone who was a scholar while
in college, someone who was well-read. That counts Jesse out without a doubt.

Now check out how this final chapter, "We Shall Overcome – if" begins and
the quote selected by Owens (and his white master):

> *"The great valley of the Umizimkulu is still in darkness, but the*
> *light will come there. Ndotsheni is still in darkness, but the light*
> *will come there also. For it is the dawn that has come, as it has*

> *come for a thousand centuries, never failing. But when that dawn*
> *will come, of our emancipation, from the fear of bondage and the*
> *bondage of fear, why, that is a secret."*
> ■ *Alan Paton in Cry, The Beloved Country*

A quote from a racist who uses color-coded imagery (all that reference to "darkness" and the coming of the "light" and this black sonofabitch puts it in print while claiming to give a shit about improving race relations and changing the attitudes of people. He's playing right into their racism with his own choices.

The chapter begins:

> What color is Utopia? I know – how can a negro ever use the word
> Utopia? But even with the violence that is exploding around us,
> even though it's taken hundreds of years to produce the mess we
> got ourselves into and is going to take a bell of a long time to get
> completely out. I think there are signs that someday a realistic kind
> of" Utopia" actually will come about (p. 172).

Nobody even thought about the word "utopia" except for Owens: since he is so in love with white people and since he views them as his "god," it would only stand to reason that he would consider America as a place that has the potential to be a utopia. As you know, a "utopia" is, "an imagined place or state of things in which everything is perfect." Black people know that this place will never even come close to being perfect, at least not for us. As the old reggae song goes, "White man's heaven is the Black man's hell." Therefore, when Owens claims that "someday a realistic kind of utopia actually will come about," he is out of his ever-lovin' mind.

We shall over come – if WHAT, muthafucka? How can anybody overcome with a coon like Owens offering up the following sentiments:

> That the young are so serious about things – unfortunately
> sometimes even to the point of violence - is one hopeful sign. I
> hate, really hate, their ravaging universities and clubbing
> professors, but I also think the deeper meaning of everything from
> hippie to yippie is that some things much more basic than college
> curriculums have to be changed in this country. The days of
> Establishment for Establishment's sake are over. Today's youth
> aren't going to live their lives by any races that were run in 1936.
> (p. 172).

You twisted sonofabitch. He's restricting the situation to the college campus and even in that limited context he is exaggerating what was taking place. We never "ravaged" any universities or clubbed any professors. If professors got in the way or were caught calling us "nigger," maybe we would have. But Owens is painting a picture of a revolt that exists in his head: black students were organized on those campuses and even when violence was used, it was directed at particular buildings, the ones that were the sites where the racist activity may have directly impacted black students (e.g., the athletic department, the student union, etc.).

There is a form of argument called "the straw man." This is where you think you are refuting an opponent's argument while actually refuting an argument that was not made in the first place. So when the spaced-out sprinter writes that, "Today's youth aren't going to live their lives by any races that were run in 1936," the fact of the matter is: nobody even assumed they would. Nobody even used the analogy of a "race" to describe what is taking place in America. Only a trained gladiator, an Uncle Tom would continue to see reality within the context of the sport that he loves so dearly.

He concludes the book with a story as senseless as the rest of his concepts:

> The collection box went from person to person, row to row to row
> and finally back to the front. The preacher shook hands with the
> people as they field out. When he was alone, he opened it up.
> Inside was one coin – his own gold piece. He stood there silently
> for a long moment, fighting to hold back the tears. Then, slowly,
> his expression changed. Something like a smile touched his mouth.
> "You know, baby," he whispered to himself, "it's too bad you
> didn't put a lot more into that thing. 'Cause if you did, you
> would've have a lot more to take out" (p. 175).

What??? First of all the collection plate is based on some bullshit that the preacher fed a group of people who were clueless to begin with. Then, if you put money into it you are endorsing the bullshit you just got fed. Putting more money into the collection plate only feeds the minister and pays his bills – not yours. You remain poor and when you walk outside, the community has not changed one bit. But that's what religion does: it makes people more conservative and has them believing that, "God will handle it."

Blackthink is a book that should be read in any political science class or better yet, a Black Studies class that deals with various perspectives on race. The book is a case study in black low self-esteem and self-hatred. I've provided you with what Owens wrote and my response to his words. Now, you can judge for yourself.

Sidebar I:
About Jesse Owens and Dr. Martin Luther King, Jr.

The late W.E.B. DuBois once wrote, "A little less complaint and whining and a little more dogged work and many striving would do us more credit than a thousand civil rights bills. WEB DuBois." I am sure Dr. King read this statement but it is clear that he didn't agree. He did a lot of talking and a lot of writing, but had no coherent program (other than helping ministers leech for the collection plate in churches around the country) that black people could rely and depend on for personal, financial or cultural development.

In the chapter "I Know Because I've Been There," I intentionally passed over the huge amount of space given to Dr. Martin Luther King, Jr. for a reason. And that reason is that I believed that Owens' views on King, and his alleged connection to him go a long way toward Owens transforming into and remaining the bootlicker that he was. And not only that, but King's influence also got a lot of people into that state of mind, what I call "one-way integration" mindset. And as a result, a teaching moment makes itself available and following are both Owens' and my own views on King, nonviolence, and racial politics. Therefore, a section of this book devoted to my perspectives is most worthy here.

For instance, on page 103 Owens writes,

> Martin Luther King, Jr., of course, was another person who made a huge difference in my life. I met him before he ever rose to worldwide prominence, and one of the things he showed me better than anyone else is that fame can't change a man who's really a man. Someone once said Martin combined the best of Joe Louis and Ralph Bunche. That would make him a human saint. He was. As one writer said, he had the "ability to achieve instant slum clearance by his very presence." (p. 103).

If they were so close, did Owens know that King was in love with and engaged to marry a white woman before he was "forcibly" introduced to Coretta Scott? King's love for that white woman is evidence that he had something in common with Owens because even though Owens married a black woman, his mind was obviously white. And King, in promoting that integration bullshit, surely thought or believed that the white man's ice was colder than our ice.

Therefore when Owens makes the claim that, "Martin combined the best of Joe Louis and Ralph Bunche. That would make him a human saint," he is wrong: that makes him an even bigger Uncle Tom that I thought he was and that most black people knew him to be. Joe Louis was definitely a white man's "nigger:' and as for Ralph Bunche, We must fight as a race for everything that makes for a better country and a better world. We are dreaming idiots and trusting fools to do anything less.

He was not an overt Tom like Owens, but he chose to flee rather than address racism, and he surely had the power to do so. According to Niven (2016):

> Bunche was clearly the unequaled choice for the State Department post, but he turned Truman down, initially stating that he wanted to continue his work at the U.N. But it was soon revealed that his decision was driven by an intense opposition to living and working in Washington, D.C., and its Virginia suburbs, where he would have had to face the daily indignities of Jim Crow.

So he did something more than what Owens would or could have done. Bunche made history and although he was a system oriented "coon" in many respects, he wasn't as bad as Owens was. Not by a long shot. Even his reasons for doing what he did had the sound of "coon-ism." Check it out:

> He had endured racial slights during his years at Howard and in the State Department. But as he told his friend and former colleague at State, Dean Rusk—sent by Truman to lobby him—one particular incident explained why he could not return to segregation and second-class citizenship in Washington. The case involved the family dog, which had died. The Bunche children wanted to have the pet buried in a pet cemetery, but when their father went to make the arrangements, he discovered that the cemetery was segregated, with one section for the pets of white owners and a separate space for the pets of African Americans. In a Fourth of July radio broadcast, Bunche declared in public what he had told Rusk and Truman in private: that "living in the nation's capital is like serving out a [prison] sentence for any Negro who detests segregation and discrimination." (Niven, 2016).

At least Bunche had the balls to say how he felt on radio. Again, he was far more of a black man than Owens ever was. It was therefore noteworthy that I make this point because when an Uncle Tom chooses a friend, the tendency is for us to assume that the friend is also a sellout. This was not quite the case when it came to Ralph Bunche.

In my view, Dr. Martin Luther King, Jr., was another story. As Owens put it,

> Martin came along at a time when I needed him personally. Life hadn't been any nonstop parade for me after getting on my feet from bankruptcy. I'd worked hard in the late forties and early fifties, was making ends meet and helping Ruth to raise three daughters, but I still felt I hadn't really found myself. That wasn't easy for a man of forty to admit to himself, but in a way I didn't feel forty. It was as though I'd had two lives, the first ending with the Olympics and riches and then bankruptcy. I'd begun a new life

after that, but hadn't really had time to stop and figure out how
best to live it … (p. 103).

Forty years old and barely holding on – after winning four Olympic gold
medals. I hope this is a lesson to the young people who Owens is trying to get to
kiss his ass and the ass of the people who made his life a living hell. How can he
write the shit he has written, experience what these white people put him and his
father through, and still be in such a situation? In most cases doesn't Uncle
Tomming pay? That's what your leadership, then and today, seems to want you to
believe. That's why they promote "education" – so that you can go to school to
learn how to be a good nigger, how to get to work on time and how to submit to
(white) authority. Owens did all of these and look at what he just shared: he sounds
like a homeless bum who just got back from the war.

At any rate he further claims that,

> Martin helped me through that most difficult time. I'm not saying
> we were the closest of friends. You didn't have to be close to
> Martin to have him hit you where you lived. Just being a human
> being was enough for that. I opened up to him one night after he
> spoke in New York. I didn't mean to. I just meant to discus civil
> rights with him for half a minute and let him catch his plane … (p.
> 104).

In other words, Owens was spilling his guts and begging for advice. He
looked up to King the same way most Black people did – and still do. And for
what? Because he pushed that Christianity line and told black people never to hit
back when attacked? Because he convinced black people that sitting next to a
peckerwood on an integrated toilet stool was a sign of progress? And to this day in
2016, we still pay for *that* little mistake! King had no business giving anyone
advice other than that Bible-based bullshit that most ministers pawn off as "life
lessons." And black people, so starved for acceptance, eat it up by the barrel fulls.

Owens is treating King as if he is some kind of prophet. Check it out:

> But all at once it came out. And it wasn't embarrassing, because
> you couldn't feel any demeaning emotions when you were with
> Martin. The hurry to catch his plane vanished. He motioned me
> aside as if there were all the time in the world, even though the
> whole thing probably took only a few minutes … (pp. 104-105).

King knew Owens won those gold medals, so don't think he was showing
this kindness just for the sake of "Christian brotherhood." King probably knew that
somewhere down the line he could bring Owens in as a speaker at a fundraiser.

King was just as money hungry as any other minister, make no bones about that. And Owens claims that the following conversation took place:

> "I think I understand, Jesse," he answered when I was through talking. Thank god! Someone who didn't say it's all right, not to knock my life because I'd had it so much better than most Negroes, someone who didn't ask me to stop rocking the boat of my own spirit. "I never knew you that well," he went on. "But I always thought you might have to meet this problem someday. You were like a child prodigy who couldn't go on with what he'd done. And a man must have his work before anything else." (p. 105).

Again, we know that Owens is lying because there is no way he could have remembered this conversation in such detail. He remembers every word of Luz Long, every word of his high school track coach and the like. He's just embellishing reality because he knows that his life was pretty much the story of a sellout. He claims that King said, ""I never knew you that well … But I always thought you might have to meet this problem someday. You were like a child prodigy who couldn't go on with what he'd done. And a man must have his work before anything else."

Bullshit. If King said that than it is clear that he, like Jesse, did not know his ass from a hole in the ground, either. Two opportunists talking to one another – what can you expect to be produced other than some free ass-kissing tips? Moving on:

> "What *do* I do, Martin?" I asked. "It's too late for me to go back to school." He thought a moment. "All I can tell you is to build on what you know, what you love. You can't run anymore, but isn't there something larger, something related to that part of your life, which you can use as an anchor for the new?" (p. 105).

Of course there was: he could devote his entire life to being an Uncle Tom! After all, that's mostly what he had done for much of his life, was it not? As Owens explains,

> Then he was gone, on his way to the airport, and I was left alone to catch my own plane in two hours. But what he had said opened up a new way of thought for me. It didn't happen with any flash of light. It took months, years. Yet slowly I began to see that I wouldn't have to cut myself off from my past completely in order to have a future. I did have something to build on (p. 105).

Owens sounds like a mis-guided kindergarten bitch! He's a grown man. What does he mean he was "left alone"? Where is his wife in all of this? Where are his other Uncle Tom buddies at? Where are his white pals who he seems to love so much? He claims to have a plan but instead of going into detail, he goes back to talking about King and this time he just has to interject the name of Malcolm X:

> People knew Martin wasn't putting on. I remember how we were together once watching a TV clip of Malcolm X in his early days. I was studying Martin's face, not the film. Suddenly he noticed. "What is it, Jess?" he said. "I – I thought I saw hate in your face, Martin." He was silent for a time, as though this was something he really didn't want to admit but had to because he wouldn't be dishonest no matter what the circumstances. "You did," he said. "Whenever I hear Malcolm and a couple of others, I begin to hate the white man, too. But just for a little while, Jesse, It doesn't change anything when I get up and go out among them." (p. 106).

What people? Who is Owens speaking for? What gives him the right to act as if he knows King so well when he admitted that he didn't know him that well at all? He claims to have told King that he saw hate in his face. How would be know? He's acting like a bitch hung up on King. Then he uses his photographic memory – in other words, lies – to make it sound like King confided in him and said, ""Whenever I hear Malcolm and a couple of others, I begin to hate the white man, too. But just for a little while, Jesse, It doesn't change anything when I get up and go out among them."

Now, I don't believe a damn word that Jesse said. But what if it did happen? What does he hope to gain by sharing this information with the reading public? King allegedly saying that he "begins to hate the white man" runs totally counter to what Owens and King stood for – which was love of the white man. Why is Owens "snitching" on King? Why is he sharing something that may have never have been known? I believe Owens is lying and if he's not, then he is trying to prove an "integrationist" point: that King may have been capable of hating the white man, but when he comes to his senses, all he can do is love him. In the final analysis he has to "go out among them." He sure did – because that is where the money was at.

Owens continues:

> So Martin wasn't infallible. I think a few of his statements on the Vietnam War were confusing, for instance. They tended to make some people think that most negroes wouldn't want to fight for their country … I feel he was frustrated at the time – his ideals were always so much larger than immediate reality could satisfy – and for one of the few times he was lashing out in his own way … (p. 106).

Owens doesn't know what the hell he's talking about. The situation surrounding King was much simpler than the bullshit complexity that Owens is trying to feed into it. Simply put, King got too big for his britches. When he was telling black people not to fight back, to let white people put knots on their heads, to sing "We Shall Overcome" and let police dogs bite us all up in the ass, this was great for the system. But when he started thinking that he could move beyond the borders of America and start getting involved in American imperialism and world politics, that is when they decided he had to go. It's no more than that.

As a person who has read Jesse Owens' words would give a shit about his views on nonviolence, he offers them anyway. Check out the following passage:

> Most of all, I disagreed with Martin on nonviolence. It might sound ridiculous to say you idolized Martin Luther King, Jr. and then say you're against nonviolence, because that is supposed to be what his movement and ideas were all about. In one way they were. For Martin was just about the gentlest, kindest man I've ever known. Yet Joe Louis made his living as a fighter, and it never changed him. I think Martin should have fought back more, too. If he had been prepared to defend himself, others might not have found him so vulnerable … (p. 106).

This muthafucka has the gall to talk about someone "fighting back more"? And then he adds that if King had fought back more and had been prepared to defend himself, "others might not have found him so vulnerable." Talk about the pot calling the skillet black! Owens is the most cowardly "negro" I've read about in some time. He wants to be white so badly that he denies his own blackness. He falls in love with Nazi white boys and any white man who will give him the time of day. Any reference or inference that he made in this entire book about defending himself or his family is limited to what he "should have" or "could have" done. In fact, King may have promoted nonviolence, but he was no coward; Owens was nonviolent AND cowardly!

Closing out this one-way love affair that the tricked-out track star has with King, he writes:

> I loved Martin Luther King, Jr. He was almost young enough to be my son, but he left me with a legacy I can never repay. Yet I wish Martin had had a dozen bodyguards when he stood out on that balcony in Memphis. I think it would have been wiser, kinder to all of us, if that incomparably wise, kind man were here today to help this country as he helped me (p. 107).

And this is what makes it worse. King was young enough to be Owens' son, which means Owens should have been more of a mentor. Instead, all he did was leech, beg for answers and whine about his situation. What does this say about Owens' character?

Now, we go from Owens as the leech and milquetoast to Owens as the straight up Uncle Tom. The second "sidebar" deals with his views on the German Olympian, the "Nazi," Luz Long.

Sidebar 2:
Jesse Owens, Adolf Hitler and Luz Long

We all know who Adolf Hitler is. Fewer remember the name Luz Long (Hitler's champion) – is the Nazi that was competing in the broad jump during the 1936 Olympics, and his main competition was none other than the "American negro," Jesse Owens. The difference is that Long was white and committed to something; Owens was black and was committed to Luz Long. Or at least that is the way it sounds to me in the chapter titled, "Letter to a Young Negro" (reviewed earlier) where Owens seems to be giving out Uncle Tom tips to young black people. And his "love" for Luz Long is at the basis of his uncle tomfoolery.

Following are my analyses of his comments about both Hitler and Long, extracted from the aforementioned chapter. Remembering that both men were in the Nazi Party (Hitler and Long), read along and check out my analyses as I prove that when it comes to super-toms and confused sellouts, Jesse Owens reigns without rival.

On page 149 he offers the following:

> I was up against it, but long before I came to the broad jump.
> Negroes had gone to the Olympics before, and Negroes had won
> before. But so much more was expected of me. Because this was
> the time of the most intense conflict between dictatorship and
> freedom the world had ever known.

Owens is trying to live up to his "super hero" billing, but that was all a façade. He was being given play because he represented America, not because he was a black man. Hitler and his people were not the only racist white bastards who had a belief that black people were somehow more "ape" than human. Hitler and his crew were not the only ones who believed that black people were inferior. So when Owens talks about an "intense conflict," he is somewhat confused: it matters not if the white government is a dictatorship or a self-professed "democracy," what you have to look at is the way they treat US. And in both cases, black people were treated like shit.

Owens continues:

> Adolf Hitler was arming his country against the entire world, and almost everyone sensed it. It was ironic that these last Olympic Games before World War II was took split the earth were scheduled for Berlin, where he would be the host. From the beginning, Hitler had perverted the games into a test between two forms of government, just as he perverted almost everything else he touched. *Almost* everything else (p. 149).

How can Owens make these statements about Hitler when the government that he was representing – America – had contaminated, perverted, distorted, corrupted and defiled almost every culture and society it had come into contact with? Owens is living in the heart of a racist American Octopus, but wants to leave the heart and throw stones at its tentacle-gripped colleagues! What an asshole!

He writes,

> The broad jump preliminaries came before the finals of the other three events. I was in – the hundred-meter and two-hundred-meter dashes and the relay. How I did in the broad jump would determine how I did in the entire Olympics. For here was where I held a world record that no one had ever approached before except one man: Luz Long, Hitler's best athlete (p. 149).

He's building up the suspense and like the true pussy he was, it seems to me that he was thoroughly intimidated – or maybe it was love. Why do I say that? Just read the following description by Owens of Long:

> Long, a tall, sandy-haired, perfectly built fellow (the ideal specimen of Hitler's "Aryan supremacy" ideal, had been know to jump over twenty-six feet in preparing for the Games (p. 149).

Owens sounds like a faggot! Perfectly built? And what does the fuckin' color his hair have to do with it? And if Owens believes that Hitler's Aryan supremacy concept was fucked up, then wouldn't it stand to reason that anyone who was a "perfect specimen" of that concept would be equally fucked up? As Owens talks and writes in retrospect, it is clear that he has a thing for this German. He doesn't go into that much detail about a single black man in this entire book, not even his father (who he devoted an entire chapter to). When it's black men it's the negative, it's poor judgment, its squalor and even rape. But here is a fuckin' Nazi, who hates his damn guts, and all he can do is build him up.

Owens displays fear in every word:

> No one knew for sure what he could really do because Hitler kept
> him under wraps. But stories had filtered out that he had gone as
> far as I had, farther than anyone else in the world. I was used to
> hearing rumors like that and tried not to think too much about it.
> Yet the first time I laid eyes on Long, I sensed that the stories
> hadn't been exaggerated. After he took his first jump, I knew they
> hadn't. This man was something. I'd have to set an Olympic record
> and by no small margin, to beat him (p. 149).

More signs of "love" if you ask me. What would prompt a man to make the following statement about another male: "Yet the first time I laid eyes on Long, I sensed that the stories hadn't been exaggerated." He sounds like a bitch describing her first date! In my view, as a former high school athlete of some caliber, I never felt anybody, white or black, was "better" than me on the court. I threw out statistics because those were garnered based on some other muthafucka guarding this guy. If he was so great, he would have to show ME, and I wasn't going to glance over at him during warm-ups and fantasize about him the way Jesse Owens admits he did with Luz Long.

Owens' problem is that he craves, seeks and desires the "white stamp of approval" – even if the white person is the leader of the Third Reich:

> I looked over at where the German ruler had been sitting. No one
> was in his box. A minute ago he had been there. I could add two
> and two. Besides, he'd already snubbed me once by refusing the
> Olympic Committee's request to have me sit in that box. This was
> too much. I was mad, hate-mad and it made me feel wild. I was
> going to show hm. He'd hear about this jump, even if he wouldn't
> see it! (p. 150).

Hitler never "snubbed" that black muthafucka! A "snub" is when you, "rebuff, ignore, or spurn disdainfully." In other words, the person you snub has to be of some significance to you before you "ignore" them. Are you snubbing a dog when you walk past it on your way to take a shit? No. It's a fuckin' dog! And that's the same way these Nazis felt about black men in general. Owens is giving himself far more credit than he deserves. If he wants to see someone "snubbing" something, he should look at the way he treats his own black brothers and sisters!

Like a bitch that has been rejected, he writes in regard to Hitler, "I was mad, hate-mad and it made me feel wild. I was going to show hm. He'd hear about this jump, even if he wouldn't see it!" Isn't this what women do to men? When we cut them loose or things don't work out, do many of them not go out of their way to make sure we "hear" about something they've done (like sucking the dick of your best friend or maybe come into some big money)?

It's all about the power that the white man has over Owens that lies at the crux of his very being. Born poor in the South and having seen what he's seen, you would think a peckerwood would be the LAST thing on this black muthafucka's mind. But nope. Just the opposite. And look at the way he describes his Olympic broad jump:

> I felt the energy surging into my legs and tingling in the muscles of my stomach as it never had before. I began my run, first almost I slow motion, then picking up speed, and finally faster and faster until I was moving almost as fast as I did during the hundred-yard dash. Suddenly the takeoff board was in front of me. I hit it, went up, up high – so high I knew I was outdoing Long and every man who ever jumped … (p. 150).

This muthafucka got a boner! Look at how he describes the *physical reaction* he has to the mere *thought* of the white man! When another person affects your thoughts and physiology to such an extent and degree, something is happening to you on an emotional level. Jesse Owens is obsessed with whiteness to the same degree that he despises his own blackness. And he despises blackness because as far as society is concerned, that is what keeps him from being white!

He admits that he was losing his mind over this white man:

> But they didn't measure it. I heard the referee shout "Foul!" in my ears before I even came down. I had run too fast, been concentrating too much on a record and not enough on form. I'd gone half a foot over the takeoff board. All the newspaper stories and books I've ever seen about that Olympic broad jump had me fouling on the next of my three tries, because the writers felt that made the story more dramatic. The truth is I didn't foul at all on my second jump (p. 150).

If the media lied about him, why didn't he sue? Why didn't he file libel charges? Why didn't he say something about "defamation of character"? You know why? Because it was peckerwoods doing it, that's why. Even when it comes to his own reputation, this ass backwards alley cat just can't seem to see the system and these white people for what they are. He is too busy attacking black people who are trying to stand up to the very system that he (Owens) obviously loves!

Continuing:

> I had one jump left. I looked around nervously, panic creeping into every cell f my body. On my right was Hitler's box. Empty. His

> way of saying I was a member of an inferior race who would give
> an inferior performance. In back of that box was a stadium
> containing more than a hundred thousand people, almost all
> Germans, all wanting to see me fail. On my right was the broad
> jump official. Was he fair? Yeah. But a Nazi. It came to a close
> call, a hairline win-or-lose decision, deep down didn't he, too,
> want to see me lose? Worst of all, a few feet away was Luz Long,
> laughing with a German friend of his, unconcerned, confident,
> *Aryan* (pp. 151-152 – emphasis original).

Of course Long was unconcerned. Just like Hitler was. And why? Because Jesse Owens was a sub-human as far as they were concerned. The same love and lust that he had in his mind and heart for them they held an equal amount of disdain-and-how-dare-you for him. And he was so obsessed with the "record" that he couldn't see it. And even in that record was whiteness: he knew that if he won, the white people in America would see him as "one of them." As we now know, nothing could have been further from the truth.

When his ass is in a sling, even his bootlicking contains a scintilla of racial consciousness. Check it out:

> They were against me. Every one of them. I was back in Oakvill
> again. I was a nigger … Then the panic was total. I had to wait in a
> little circle to keep my legs from shaking, hold my jaw closed tight
> to stop my teeth from chattering … And this is what it all comes
> down to, I thought to myself. *Ten years and 4,500 miles to make a*
> *nigger of myself and not even reach the finals!* (p. 152 – emphasis
> original).

So if he cannot curry favor with white people, he is more than willing to admit that he is a "nigger." The fact is, he was a nigger all along, but refused to admit it. He was so busy pointing fingers that he couldn't see the forest for the trees. And during this major point in his life, he does what Black Christians do when they claim that they are turning their lives over to God or some other invisible deity: Owens turned his over to the Nazi, Luz Long:

> Suddenly I felt a firm hand on my arm. I turned and looked into the
> sky-blue eyes of my worst enemy. "Hello, Jesse Owens," he said.
> "I am Luz Long." I nodded. I couldn't speak. "Look," he said.
> "There is no time to waste with manners. What has taken your
> goat?" I had to smile a little in spite of myself – hearing his mixed
> up American idiom. "Aww, nothing," I said. "You know how it
> is." He was silent for a few seconds. "Yes," he said finally, "I
> know how it is. Now, *what has taken your goat?"* (pp. 152-153 –
> emphasis original).

This white boy is grilling this nigga! And Jesse is considering a favor or some kind of act of love. That's not what is taking place: Long wants Owens' best effort because he wants to beat it. No excuses. He knows an Uncle Tom when he sees one. The Nazis studied black behavior and knew all about racial intimidation. Despite all the pressure, when the white man acknowledges his existence, look at the reaction and mood change:

> I laughed out loud this time. But I couldn't tell him, him above all. I glanced over at the broad jump pit. I was about to be called. Luz didn't waste words, even if he wasn't sure of which ones to use. "Is it what Reichskenzler Hitler did?" he asked. I was thunderstruck that he'd say it. "I –" I started to answer. But I didn't know what to say. "I see," he said. "Look, we talk about that later. Now you must jump. And you must qualify." "But how?" I shot back. "I have thought," he said. "You re like I am. You must do it one hundred percent. Correct?" I nodded. "Yet you must be sure not to foul." I nodded again, this time in frustration. And as I did, I heard the loudspeaker call my name (p. 153).

Again, there is no way that he would have remembered these conversations and statements on a word for word basis. He's embellishing what took place just like he exaggerates throughout the book. Even when he attacks his enemies, the "blackthinkers," he lies about their motives, values and goals. Why? Because Jesse Owens is a dyed-in-the-wool idiot. He didn't even graduate from college. He just went there, went to practice and like a true "coon" ran and jumped for the white man. And look what it got for him.

Now you might counter, "Yeah, but look at what he did – he went down in history." And I would tell you, "So fuckin' what? Lassie, Shrek and Godzilla are historical figures too, but when all is said and done, didn't the white man ultimately control them? According to Owens,

> Luz talked quickly. "Then you do both things, Jesse. You re-measure your steps. You take off six inches behind the foul board. You jump as hard as you can. But you need not fear to foul. All at once the panic emptied out of me like a cloudburst. *Of course!* (p. 153 – emphasis original).

So in reality, Luz Long is the reason why Jesse won the broad jump. Here it is in his own words, in his own book. This muthafucka is such a tom, such a sellout, that the greatest "accomplishment" in his life is attributed to a Nazi. And now you can see one more reason why the sub-title of the book is "My Life as a Black Man and White Man." And judging by the weight of compliments that he gives to the latter group and the insults hurled at the former group, it is clear which group this spook in spikes wants to belong to, is it not?

His "story" continues:

> … The next day I went into the finals of the broad jump and
> waged the most intense competition of my life with Luz Long. He
> broke his own personal record and the Olympic record, too, and
> then I – thanks to him – literally flew to top that. Hours before I
> had won the hundred meters in 10.3, and then afterward the 200
> meters in 20.7 and helped our team to another gold medal and
> record in the relay (pp. 153-154).

"Thanks to him." History will remember these statements. Owens just further disqualified himself. He already was a shitty human being, but now this? Taking credit for that victory when, in his own words, Long was his inspiration, motivation and mentor? Now comes what I view as nothing short of a damn love story:

> During the evenings that framed those days, I would sit with Luz
> in his space or mine in the Olympic village and we would form an
> even more intense friendship. We were sometimes as different
> inside as we looked on the outside. Bu the things that were the
> *same* were much more important to us (p. 154 – emphasis
> original).

Does this or does this not sound like a homoerotic relationships? The problem is not that he "sat" with a Nazi in "his space or mine", but he calls it an "intense friendship." Now this book was edited by a white man and looked over by publishers who were either Jews or Jewish-influenced. They saw this black man paying all this attention and giving all this love to a Nazi. Then this same black man writes of he and this Nazi that "the things that were the same were much more important to us."

What were those things? Nazis hate niggas and Americans. Owens hates himself. Is that where the agreements were strongest? Of course not because it seems that Luz Long cared more about Owens that Owens cared about himself. And yet here he is using his book to continue to kiss this white man's ass. Next, he goes into even greater detail:

> We talked, of course, about Hitler and what he was doing. Luz was
> torn between two feelings. He didn't believe in Aryan supremacy
> any more than he believed the moon was made of German cheese,
> and he was disturbed at the direction in which Hitler was going.
> Yet he loved his country and felt a loyalty to fight for it if it came

to that, if only for the sake of his wife and son. I couldn't
understand how he could go along with Hitler under any
circumstances, though, and I told him so (p. 154).

What a hypocrite. Here is Owens talking about Luz Long and swearing that Long didn't believe in Naziism. And yet here he was. Long looked at black ass Owens and knew of the problems that black people in America were facing and I'm sure he was thinking "why is this nigger running to represent a country that hates his guts"? Owens acts like he speaks for long when he says that Long loved his country and felt a loyalty to fight for it if it came to that, but that is more than Owens had: Owens showed loyalty for a country and was committed to defending and representing a country that could have cared less about him. One man had character of his convictions (Long) and the other one didn't have a shred of dignity (Owens).

Owens acts like some kind of "cross-cultural psychic" as he reads motivates and sub-text into Long's actions, attitudes and statements. For instance, the following:

> He wasn't angry when I said it. He just held out his hands and
> nodded. He didn't' explain because he didn't understand
> completely himself, just as I couldn't explain to him how the
> United States tolerated the race situation. (p. 154).

The reason why Owens couldn't explain how the United States tolerated the race situation is because he is looking at the situation ass-backwards. The U.S. wasn't "tolerating" the racial situation: this country created it, shaped it and maintained it. These are facts that the Uncle Tom Jesse Owens doesn't (or can't) accept. So he makes it look like the racial situation is something that has a life of its own and white people in American are trying their "garsh-darndest" to work things out "for the negro people."

Moving on with Owens' reflections, which are beginning to sound an awful lot like lyrics from the song, "The Way We Were":

> So we sat and talked about these things, some nights later than two
> Olympic performers should have. We didn't come up with any
> final answers then, only with a unique friendship. For we were
> simply two uncertain young men in an uncertain world. One day
> we would learn the truth, but in the meantime, we would make
> some mistakes. Luz's mistake would cost him too much (pp. 154-
> 155).

Here we go again with the homoeroticism, words that got through editing and scrutiny by Owens' white friends. They know what he was sounding like. These are things that even Long's fellow white colleagues would not dare share with the public. And here we have some "coon" sharing that, "We sat and talked about these things, some nights later than two Olympic performers should have." Really? How does he know what should have been done? And if he felt that way why did he do it and why did he share it in this book? And when he adds that he and Long were "simply two uncertain young men in an uncertain world," he sho' nuff sounds gay now! How far did this "bonding" go? What took place as these two lonely, confused men looked to each other for security and solace? Hmmmm. Sounds like "Brokeback Mountain" to me!

Now comes the on-way integrationist bullshit which is, as we now know, the foundation for Owens life and his book:

> Yet we didn't make the mistake of not seeing past each other's
> skin color to what was within. If we couldn't apply that principle
> to things on a world scale, we still could live it fully in our own
> way in the few days we had together, the only days together we
> would ever have. (p. 155).

In my book it sounds like these two guys were fuckin'! Look at the wording and see for yourself; it sounds like a love scene from some date movie: " … If we couldn't apply that principle to things on a world scale, we still could live it fully in our own way in the few days we had together, the only days together we would ever have." What?! "Misty, water-colored memories" like a muthafucka! I don't know how Long felt, but can there be any doubt that Owens was in love with this white man? Read his words again and then think back into your own younger days when we would exchange "love letters" with people we were dating or wanted to date. Could they have possibly had any more depth than you just read?

And it gets even deeper! Check out the following:

> We made them count. We crammed as much understanding and
> fun as we could into every hour. We didn't even stop when we got
> out on the track. Luz was at my side cheering me on for every
> event, except the broad jump, of course. There he tied to beat me
> for all he was worth, but nature had put just a little more spring
> into my body and I went a handful of inches farther (p. 155).

"Crammed"? "Understanding and fun"? "He had put just a little more spring into my body"? "I went a handful of inches farther"? Man, this are homosexual references, man! Did his wife read this shit? Have his children seen this crap? Doesn't he (Owens) have a shred of manly respect left? This shit is in public libraries, on university campuses and is being read by young black men! And with today's crop of black men already teetering on the "down low" fence, this is the kind of shit that just might put them over!

Sounding like a scene from the movie, "The Proposal," pay close attention to the excerpt that follows:

> Luz and I vowed to write each other after the Games, and we did.
> For three years we corresponded regularly, though the letters
> weren't always as happy as our talks at the Olympics had been.
> Times were hard for me and harder for Luz. He had had to go into
> the German army, away from his wife and son. His letters began to
> bear strange postmarks. Each letter expressed more and more about
> what he was doing … It was Luz's world, just as the South had
> been the only world for so many Negroes (pp. 155-156).

Letters? How many niggas do you know who write letters to people other than relatives, girlfriends or wives? And even then it's because they're either locked up or in the military! This black muthafucka is writing letters to this white boy just for the sake of "kicks"! What the fuck is wrong with THIS picture? This is some truly sick shit – he seems more concerned about Long's relationship with his white family than he (Owens) is about his own black wife and kids. A truer ass kisser had never been born.

Moving on:

> The last letter I got from him was in 1939. "Things become more
> difficult," he said, "and I am afraid, Jesse. Not just the thought of
> dying. It is that I may die for the wrong thing. But whatever might
> become of me, I hope only that my wife and son will stay alive. I
> am asking you who are my only friend outside of Germany, to
> someday visit them if you are able, to tell them about why I had to
> do this, and how the good times between us were. Luz" (p. 156).

Did Owens keep the letters that Long wrote to him? And look at how much gall it had to take for this Nazi to ask a black man thousands of miles away to "someday visit" his family and tell them why he (Long) had to do what he did. But more importantly, he wants Owens to tell his family "how the good times between us were." What??? You see what I'm saying? This white man wants a black man who he says is his "only friend outside of Germany," to do this for him. This is a love affair, plain and simple. No white man would trust a black man with his wife or kids while he (the white man) was off doing who knows what!

Like a jilted lover seeing an opening for another "chance," Owens offers up the following:

> I answered right away but my letter came back. So did the next,
> and the one after. I inquired about Luz through a dozen channels.
> Nothing. A war was on. Finally, when it was over, I was able to get
> in touch with Luz's wife and find out what had happened to him.
> He was buried somewhere in the African desert (p. 156).

Luz got killed, but that didn't mean that Jesse didn't spend an inordinate amount of time calling around (long distance calls) and running up bills trying to find him. He finally got in touch with Long's wife and found out that his white pal was dead. This is some of that "Brian's Song" bullshit where tomming ass Gale Sayers tells the audience, "I loved Brian Piccolo, and I want you to love him, too." The white man who was vying for his job at running back, and yet he falls for him. The white man who thought it was a sign of "closeness" to use the word "nigger" and to joke that when he had a son he was going to name it after Sayers – "You know, SPADE Piccolo." Is there any wonder why the black women of today see black men as "mitches" and as the types of males that cannot be depended upon?

In what is the last paragraph (thank God!) that deals with Long, I was able to locate something on page 156 of Owens' book. Sounding like some kind of philosopher or moralist, Owens shares,

> Luz Long had been my competition in the Olympics. He was a
> white man - a Nazi white man who fought to destroy my country. I
> loved Luz Long, as much as my own brothers. I still love Luz
> Long . I went back to Berlin a few years ago and met his son,
> another fine young man. And I told Karl about his father. I told
> him that, though fate may have thrown us against one another, Luz
> rose above it, rose so high that I was left with not only four gold
> medals I would never have had, but with the priceless knowledge
> that the only bond worth anything between human beings is their
> humanness (p. 156).

This coon gives a white Nazi credit for what few accomplishments he (Owens) had by claiming that he was left with "four gold medals I would never have had." How does he arrive at this conclusion? Long wasn't running against him in the relays or the sprints. Wait a minute, I get it! Having Luz Long in his life was Owens' version of having met Jesus Christ! Just meeting Long gave him the strength and power to win those medals! That's it. As had been Owens' lifelong tendency, any white man who pays him attention becomes his god!

His first name may have been "Luz," but in the end he didn't lose. He kept his dignity and did what he had to do. *The real loser then, and up until the end of his life, was Jesse Owens.*

Conclusion

It is akin to what the late journalist Bill Moyers once said: "In one way or another, this is the oldest story in America: the struggle to determine whether 'we, the people' is a spiritual idea embedded in a political reality – one nation, indivisible – or merely a charade masquerading as piety and manipulated by the powerful and privileged to sustain their own way of life at the expense of others."

Following the assassination of Dr. Martin Luther King, Jr., Owens' self-hatred, ignorance and true tommishness came to the fore and is reflected in the following fantasy-laden comment:

> So I tried those few days in April to come over, Harry Edwards. I needed something, somebody to hate. I wanted to feel there as an easy way out. It was tempting, awfully tempting, to turn my back on my white brothers who so often hadn't been brothers, who had let this happen, maybe made it inevitable. But not tempting enough. The Negro can never catch his precious quicksilver by making his hand into a fist (p. 22).

He is truly confused and cowardly. When he writes that, "It was tempting, awfully tempting, to turn my back on my white brothers who so often hadn't been brothers, who had let this happen, maybe made it inevitable." The fact is, they had NEVER been his brothers. It is as Malcolm X taught, "believe in the brotherhood of all men, but I don't believe in wasting brotherhood on anyone who doesn't want to practice it with me. Brotherhood is a two-way street."

And Jesse Owens, if you look at his own words, is no "brother." In fact, even the white man is ashamed of him. In 1984 there was a TV-movie called, "The Jesse Owens Story." And who played Owens? The real-life Uncle Tom Dorian Harewood. It was the perfect choice because Harewood's natural tommish tendencies shown through the role and presented Jesse Owens, at a time when Ronald Reagan was already wrecking black lives, as he really was: an uninvolved sellout. There is an attempt at revisionism with the release of the 2016 movie, "Race," but it bombed.

In the final analysis, having read this book and analyzed the life of Jesse Owens, I have to come to the conclusion that Jesse Owens was WHITE. His values and pursuits were white and so were his goals. And remember what Karenga (1967) once wrote: "White doesn't represent a color; it represents a mentality that is anti-black." And so it is with Owens: his mind is white and I've given you scores of examples that this was the case all the way up until his death.

References

Ashe, Arthur (1998). *A Hard Road To Glory: Track and Field*. New York, New York: Amistad Press.

Baker, C. Daniel (2013, November 28). African-American's Buying Power Projected to be $1.1 Trillion By 2015. *Black Enterprise*

Kirkus Reviews (1969, March 1). Dionysus. Retrieved from https://www.kirkusreviews.com/book-reviews/roderick-thorp-2/dionysus/

Muhammad, Abdul Mu'Min (2010, December 8). Sharecropping cotton for the modern 'pharaoh'. *The Final Call.*

Muhammad, Derrick. (2012, January 3). The secret relationship between rappers and Jews. *The Final Call.*

Niven, Steven J. (2016, February 8). Ralph Bunche: A Diplomat Who Would Not Negotiate on Race. The Root. Retrieved from http://www.theroot.com/articles/history/2016/02/ralph_bunche_a_diplomat_who_would_not_negotiate_on_race/

Owens, Jesse. (1970). *Blackthink: My life as a black man and white man*. New York, New York: William Morrow and Company, Inc.

Wikipedia (2016). Joe Louis vs. Max Schmeling. Retrieved from https://en.wikipedia.org/wiki/Joe_Louis_vs._Max_Schmeling

Wikipedia (2016). Rheingold Beer. Retrieved from https://en.wikipedia.org/wiki/Rheingold_Beer

Wikipedia (2016). Nat King Cole. Retrieved from https://en.wikipedia.org/wiki/Nat_King_Cole#Experiences_with_racism

CANDACE OWENS

You're never too young to sell out it seems. You may not have heard of this sistah but like Star Parker, she's a staunch conservative and uses every means at her disposal to promote it. According to Wikipedia (2018), "Candace Owens ... is an American conservative commentator and activist. She is known for her pro-Trump commentary and her criticism of Black Lives Matter and of the Democratic Party.[2][3][4] She is the Director of Urban Engagement at the conservative advocacy group Turning Point USA."

Another Jemima who wants to get involved in urban life (remember Candace Parker?). These bitches don't seem to understand what it takes to run an organization or start a movement. The only component they have is the "communications" element. They are still missing the ideology – which is the white man's way of thinking and that's not going to be of benefit to them in the long run; they're missing resources because they scrounge to sell articles and speaking gigs to get chump change to pay for their draws and keep the lights on. Living on a bologna and cheese economy when they're in a caviar and prime rib environment.

Who is she? Check out her resume and get ready for yet another "po' li'l black girl who made it big" story:

> Born to an African American family and raised in Stamford, Connecticut,[5] Owens is a graduate of Stamford High School ... She was raised by her grandparents **after her parents divorced** ... In 2007, while a senior in high school, **Owens received hurtful and threatening racist phone calls that were traced to a car in which the 14-year-old son of then mayor Dannel Malloy was present** ... Owens' family sued the Stamford Board of Education in federal court alleging that the city did not protect her rights, resulting in a **$37,500 settlement** ... Owens was pursuing an undergraduate degree in journalism at the University of Rhode Island **but left school after her junior year** ... Afterwards, she **worked for** *Vogue* magazine ... In 2012, she took a job as an **administrative assistant** for a private equity firm ... (Wikipedia, 2018)

Ain't this a bitch? Her scratch-and-claw journey up the ladder to public renown is almost as pitiful as her educational background. But let me not get ahead of myself. Let's break down six (6) concerns I have with the previous excerpt.

First, the fact that her parents divorced. What is the purpose of mentioning that when indeed, her grandparents did an adequate job of raising her? What this tells me is that she had chance to give up booty and take over her own growth and development because the elders couldn't keep up with her. That's how it usually goes.

Secondly, that lawsuit about a threatening racist phone call being "traced" to a 14 year old. So fuckin' what? Traced to whom? Is a call like that the basis for an actual lawsuit? Making terrorist threats is nothing unique or sui generis! But when you're a Jemima and you're trying to establish enough street cred to convince the white man that you are worthy of hiring and trusting, then this is the kind of shit that you capitalize on.

Third, the size of the settlement – chump change! Just like that nickel and dime payments doled out to Diamond and Silk. These white people know that if they can't buy a nigga, they can sure enough rent one! But that was probably the money that she used to get into Rhode Island, and she couldn't even hack it there. Another "well I went to college" story without stating that you never finished college, which was the whole purpose. The degree – remember, heifer?

Fourth –and a continuation of point number three - she never finished school. You know I find that interesting about Facebook as well. When these so-called successful people are asked about their education, they merely put that they "attended" this college or that university. Just like these negroes who are leaders – "I went to college." So what? The question is, did you finish and what did you do while you were in college to positively impact on black life?

Fifth, it says she "worked for Vogue." Name the position. Name the job responsibilities. Who did you report to? Were you a janitor? Did you work in the mailroom like Damon Wayans (another sellout) did in the 1992 movie that he did with a fellow Jemima Stacey Dash ("Mo' Money"). Was she just a token hire or a fake ass "intern"? Was it college work study? What? What? What?

Sixth, the was an administrative assistant at "a private equity firm." Which one was it – Dewey, Cheatem and Howe? How big was the firm? As an administrative assistant, was all she did was type and take messages? To far too many black people this is an impressive list of credentials. To me – this woman couldn't be a leader or advocate of any kind of movement I was involved in unless it was a bowel movement!

And like the other script-flipping Jemima types, she starts off one way, smells money to be made, dumps what little values she had, and becomes a lackey for the system:

> Prior to 2017, Owens ran a website that frequently criticized conservatism and mocked then-candidate Donald Trump … By 2017, she had become prominent in conservative circles for her pro-Trump commentary and for criticizing liberal narratives around structural racism, systemic inequality, and identity politics (the kind of content that her website previously trafficked in).(Wikipedia, 2018)

She starts off as a critic of the right wing and Donald Trump. But that was BEFORE 2017. Once he got in office, she saw there was money to be made, and like most Jemimas – Diamond and Silk, Omarosa Manigault and Candace Parker to name but a few – they flipped and ran behind the white man. These Jemimas have a common trait: they are willing to make themselves look like hypocrites and coons in exchange for some radio, television or newspaper time. That's what it's all about, because even notoriety translates into cash when all is said and done.

Continuing:

> In 2015, Owens founded the website Degree180 … The website frequently posted anti-conservative and anti-Trump content, **including mockery of his penis size …** Owens said in one of her postings that it was "good news" that the "Republican Tea Party ... will eventually die off (peacefully in their sleep, we hope" … In one article she wrote that the antics of the Tea Party Movement were "bat-shit-crazy" … When *Buzzfeed News* in May 2018 reported on the anti-Trump content on Degree180, Owens described the Buzzfeed reporter as a "despicable creature" and **alleged that Buzzfeed had threatened the former writers of Degree180 (something which Buzzfeed rejects)** …. (Wikipedia, 2018 – emphasis added)

Making fun of a white man's dick usually doesn't bother him because he knows its true. But in the case of the ultra-sensitive Trump, she's lucky she wasn't locked up. Then she lied on Buzzfeed the same way that Diamond and Silk had lied on Facebook. No evidence, no proof – just allegations. But she was a long way from being "done" with her Jemima mission:

> In 2017, Owens began posting politically themed videos to YouTube … **She launched Red Pill Black, a website and YouTube channel that promotes black conservatism in the United States …** On November 21, 2017, at the MAGA Rally and Expo in Rockford, Illinois, Turning Point USA founder Charlie Kirk announced her appointment as their **director of urban engagement …** Turning Point's hiring of Owens occurred **in the wake of allegations of racism at Turning Point.** (Wikipedia, 2018 – emphasis added)

These Jemimas wait in the wings until the white man inevitably gets his nuts in the wringer. Then he needs a token, a "coon" who can be marched out to claim that he's not a racist or guilty of racism. That's what Omarosa did in her early days with Trump, and that's what Star and Diamond do. Ms. Owens is no exception as you can see. She promotes "Black conservatism" which is not in itself bad. Black people ARE conservative on a lot of social issues because of that Christian tradition, a dogma that teaches black people not to upset the apple cart.

And she got her appointment as "director of urban engagement." Another long title along with a set of keys that probably didn't fit anything. Just like Omarosa was appointed to a "created position" called "Assistant to the President and Communications Director for the Office of Public Liaison," and at the same time Her title was assistant to the president and communications director for the Office of Public Liaison and was placed in charge of the White House Office of

HBCU Initiatives out of the Department of Education. It was placed into the Executive Office of the President.

The "urban engagement" is just a fancy of saying "nigga issues." That's what these white boys do: they appoint people to handle issues that are majority black and then deny the same people the resources to do the job properly. That is what is going to happen to Dr. Ben Carson, another lackey who doesn't know his ass from a hole in the ground, who is in charge of Housing and Urban Development.

Only when Turning Point was charged with being racist did Ms. Owens get marched out. But toms stick together, even across industries:

> In April 2018, Kanye West tweeted "I love the way Candace Owens thinks."[17] The tweet was met with derision among some of West's fans … In May 2018, President Donald Trump stated **that Owens "is having a big impact on politics in our Country...**She represents an ever expanding group of very smart 'thinkers,' and it is wonderful to watch and hear the dialogue going on...so good for our Country!" (Wikipedia, 2018 – emphasis added)

Trump was then and continues to be a lying sack of shit. That woman didn't have any "big impact on politics" by any stretch of the imagination. Influence peddlers don't get things done – only power brokers do. Owens was and remains a Jemima and gets paid for doing just what she does: intellectually masturbate and talk to the gullible masses.

It's only a matter of time before these Jemimas overstep their rhetorical boundaries and begin delving onto areas that they have no business discussing. Just like Whoopi did when it came to defining "rape" and just like Stacey Dash did when (along with Raven-Symone) somehow became experts on black culture and black history month, Owens committed a similar act. Check out the following:

> In May 2018, Owens suggested that **"something bio-chemically happens" to women who do not marry or have children**, and she linked to the Twitter handles of Sarah Silverman, Chelsea Handler and Kathy Griffin, saying that they were "evidentiary support" of this theory … Silverman responded, saying "It seems to me that by tweeting this, you would like to maybe make us feel badly. I'd say this is evidenced by ur effort to use our twitter handles so we would see. My heart breaks for you, Candy. I hope you find happiness in whatever form that takes." … Owens responded, accusing Silverman of supporting terrorists and crime gangs. (Wikipedia, 2018 – emphasis added)

What Owens was basically saying was that a woman is no thing without a man to marry or children, provided by the man. This is akin to Barbara Acklin's 1968 jam, "Love Makes a Woman" or Aretha's "You Make Me Feel Like a Natural Woman." This is all derived from that bullshit theory of Adam and Eve and Eve supposedly being formed out of Adam's rib. Ain't that a bitch?

But her views are what keeps her going. For instance one source documents the following:

> By 2017, Owens had become a pro-Donald Trump conservative commentator … *The Guardian* has described her as "ultra-conservative", the *Daily Beast* has described her as "far-right", the *New York Magazine* and *Columbia Journalism Review* described her as "right-wing", and the *Pacific Standard* described her as "alt-right" … Prior to 2017, she ran a website that frequently criticized conservatism and mocked then-candidate Donald Trump … She has characterized Trump as the "savior" of Western civilization … She has argued that Trump has neither engaged in rhetoric that is harmful to African Americans nor proposed policies that would harm African Americans (Wikipedia, 2018)

When you find a black woman who is deemed "ultra conservative," you have a true, full-fledged Aunt Jemima on your hands. When you consider a psychotic like Trump to be the savior of Western civilization, that is a trap. People know that Trump is so bitch-like that if you give him a compliment, it will go straight to his head and he will let you into his fold. She is sending a message to that racist that she loves him more than he loves himself.

And, like most Jemimas, she is a pathological liar. In my book Donald Trump as White Male Prototype, I list a plethora of lies that Trump has told, and that was a year back, before the New York Times revealed that he had told more than 3,000 lies since his inauguration! So we know that Owens is an opportunist and, like Omarosa Manigault, will say and do anything to curry favor with the white power structure.

And these Jemimas also turn against their own race in a direct way. For instance,

> Owens did not vote in the 2012 and 2016 elections, saying in June 2018, "his is the first time I've been politically inclined and active." … She has called for the imprisonment of Hillary and Bill Clinton, former FBI director James Comey, and special counsel Robert Mueller, as well as TV anchors such as Jake Tapper, Rachel Maddow and Anderson Cooper. (Wikipedia, 2018)

Now we know who ran for President during this period: none other than Barack Obama. But some reason this Jemima didn't vote, which is her right. But then to turn around and shower someone like Donald Trump with hosannas of praise is going too far. Like the white conservatives she calls for the imprisonment of Bill and Hillary Clinton (both of whom are two-faced peckerwoods who did black people a grave disservice), and like Trump, calls for locking up James

Comey along with members of the media. Whatever Trump says, she does. He says "jump, nigger," and she asks, "how high?"

And her views on race are equally jejune, although some of them I tend to agree with even though it is for different reasons. Let's go through a few of them. To begin with,

> Owens is known for her criticism of Black Lives Matter … She has described Black Lives Matter protesters as "a bunch of whiny toddlers, pretending to be oppressed for attention" … Owens has argued that African Americans have a "victim mentality" and often refers to the Democratic Party as a "plantation … She has argued that the American left "like black people to be government-dependent" …. Owens has argued that black people have been brainwashed to vote for Democrats (Wikipedia, 2018).

Some of the things that this woman is opposed to are areas where I have similar concerns – just for different reasons. I am skeptical of black groups that make generic appeals to white people's non-existent morality. Black lives have always mattered, but when you make the fact a slogan to generate social interest, you are basically saying that black lives don't matter and we need white approval to affirm black humanity. Besides that, they appear to be linked to the homosexual lobby and that is a group with a whole different set of issues and I think black people need to iron out our own problems and leave the rump roasters to fend for themselves.

But it just seems in the case of Owens that whatever Trump opposes is what she opposes. Black people do have a "victim" mentality and that is because we are victims. But pointing it out to the culprit – the victimizer – is like running from the wolf to the fox! In fact, the Jemimas I 've mentioned have exponentially increased the victims mentality to the point where they act and sound like handicapped lab rats. They are the ones constantly looking for a conservative/white cause to "adopt" them.

And she is right when she says that black people have been brainwashed. But not just by the Democratic wing – by white people in general. Look back to enslavement and study the 350 years of dehumanization that black people were exposed to. If that wasn't a cultural brainwashing of sorts, then I don't know what is. But it gets worse:

> She has argued that police violence against black people is not about racism … According to *The Guardian* and the Daily Beast, Owens has referred to police killings of black people as a trivial matter to African Americans … (Wikipedia, 2018)

What?! If shooting unarmed black men in the back is not about racism, then what is it: some kind of new police bullet disposal project? And if she says what she is cited as saying about black people thinking that those shootings are a trivial matter, then she is as out of touch with the black community as most Jemimas are. The white man knows all this – he just needs to re-direct black ire from his racist ways and words to someone else stupid enough to promote his policies – and Jemima will bail him out every time!

Moreover,

> After the 2017 Unite the Right rally in Charlottesville, Virginia, Owens said that **concern over rising white nationalism was "stupid"** … Owens rejects the scientific consensus on climate change … **She has called climate change a lie used to "extract dollars from Americans."** … Owens described the #MeToo Movement - which was an international movement against sexual harassment and assault - as **"stupid" and said that she "hated" the movement** … Owens wrote that the #MeToo Movement was premised on the idea that "women are stupid, weak & inconsequential." … **She is critical of feminism.** (Wikipedia, 2018 – emphasis added)

She is towing the conservative line and backing up everything that the racist President Donald Trump believes in. At a time when the nation is seeing its own racist past in full view (sans denial), here comes some Jemima marching out and claiming that concerns over rising white nationalism was "stupid." I'm sure the Jews thought the same thing before Hitler marched them into the concentration camps and gas chambers.

Climate change is real to anyone who is alive and breathing. And in my view it appears to be getting worse. The worst expenditure that can be made by a television station is to hire a full-time weather reporter. Part-time maybe, but full time is a waste of funds. And some of these stations carry three and four meteorologists. Weather is too unpredictable and can even avoid detection by Doppler Radar and those other gadgets. To doubt that global warming is a lie flies in the face of reality.

According to the December 6, 2017 issue of the **Huffington Post**, 14 cities "could disappear over the next century because of global warming." Which ones are they? Miami (FL.), Fort Lauderdale (FL), Boston (MA), NY, Atlantic City (NJ), Honolulu (HI), New Orleans (LA), Sacramento (CA), San Diego (CA), Los Angeles, (CA), Charleston (SC), Virginia Beach (VA), Seattle (WA) and Savannah GA). That's right. So if they "could disappear" in a century that means that the actual process of disappearing is taking place even as we speak. And yet people like Candace Owens are out there calling this reality "a lie."

I agree with her about the MeToo movement because white women have co-opted it from the black woman who began it all. Feminism is also the white woman's domain for the most part. But Owens is a woman who backs the Trump agenda and he doesn't even consider women to be human beings who are worthy of respect! Not only has Owens missed the proverbial boat, but I think that one of the blades from the boat motor may have sheered one of her brain stems!

Continuing:

> **She has said that abortion is "extermination" of black babies** … She has advocated for **an end to all welfare programs** … She attended the opening of the United States embassy in Jerusalem … She is critical of the press and open borders policies … **She has called for the immediate deportation of all undocumented immigrants** … In May 2018, Owens praised Louis Farrakhan's tweet endorsing Donald Trump with a description of "a really big deal" and "relevant." … Afterward, Owens received **criticism from conservative figures** for praising Farrakhan - who has a history of anti-semitic remarks - Owens deleted the tweet (Wikipedia, 2018 – emphasis added)

And so it goes. Abortion is about the extermination of the control that men want to have over women's bodies, period. It is an option when two people in hedonistic and sex-crazed America make a major mistake concerning bringing a life into the world. As for deportation of all undocumented immigrants, that is a racist policy and it should begin with people like Donald Trump's wife who got to the U.S. by way of Canada through a series of manipulations of the immigration system.

When Owens praised Farrakhan, that is when she tore her panties. Even if Farrakhan endorsed Trump (for reasons different from hers), she forgot one thing: Jews control the electorate and their money and the power of AIPAC (the American Israeli Public Affairs Committee) dictates who says what and when they say it. That means that the previous paragraph statement about "conservative figures" criticizing her actually meant "Jews criticized her." And they also control the radio waves, the major TV stations, the film industry and social media.

The Jemimas just keep on coming. Candace Owens, like some of the others, is a true beauty. But we all learn, sooner or later, that "all that glitters ain't gold." The only thing about Candace Owens that is remotely related to gold is that when it comes to being opportunistic, she is a "gold digger."

REV. AL SHARPTON, HOST – CNN's "POLITICS NATION"

Ever since the assassination of Dr. Martin Luther King, Jr., in Memphis in April of 1968, there has been a mad dash between Al Sharpton and Jesse Jackson to become "the leader" of black people. Both men have failed abysmally. Sharpton has managed to stagger his way through boycotting and protesting and land a television show on CNN called, quite inappropriately, "Politics Nation."

Again, Sharpton hails from that Jesse Jackson mold: pimp the name of Dr. King, land some speaking gigs, scare peckerwoods into boycotting their corporations and then sell out for a show on MSNBC.

But the reason and basis for this section of the book on sellouts and toms is not his long track record of joining protests so he can get a photo opportunity, but the way he acted back in 187 during the case of a young girl named Tawana Brawley. This, in my view, went a long way toward establishing his "hallelujah huckster" credentials and catapulted him to the top of the list of uncle toms and sellouts that this book is about.

The December 22, 2012 article about the Brawley-Sharpton incident is headlined, "25 Years After her Rape Claims Sparked a Firestorm, Tawana Brawley Avoids the Spotlight." Sharpton's presence helped make this case one of national prominence because of the lack of proof and some serious allegations lodged against a prosecuting attorney. But let me not get ahead of myself.

The article starts off:

> Twenty-five years after the spotlight first glared on Tawana Brawley — **a black woman who as a teen claimed she was raped by a gang of white men, smeared with feces and stuffed in a garbage bag** — she's desperately struggling to stay hidden from public view. "I don't want to talk to anyone about that," Brawley, 40, said recently after The Post found her in Hopewell, Va., where she lives in a neatly kept brick apartment complex with signs warning of video surveillance cameras. (Garland, 2012 – emphasis added)

The description of the incident was bad enough. But I was teaching at Milwaukee Area Technical College when the news broke and I opened the paper and read about the incident. My first response was the same as it is today: nobody raped this little girl. This is a lie. You will see how I came to my conclusion later in this analysis, and keep in mind the rape, the smearing with dog shit, and the use of the garbage bag.

Continuing:

> By all appearances, her life — so chaotic a quarter-century ago — now seems normal.Brawley, using aliases such as Thompson and Gutierrez, **now has a young daughter**, a neighbor says, and works as a licensed practical nurse at The Laurels of Bon Air in Richmond, **where co-workers were clueless about her past**. (Garland, 2012 – emphasis added)

So because of a fear of her father (I'll get to that in a minute), this girl made up a lie. To begin with, I think Tawana was a ho from the outset. She was worldly, cute and built like a brick shit house. Keep that in mind – she was no innocent virgin who was "defiled." That fear of her father now has her maintaining anonymity and living under various aliases to this very day. So anybody who thinks that child abuse is not important is out of their damn mind. It can traumatize a child long past adulthood. And now she's a single parent herself. What is she going to teach her daughter?

Moving on:

> On a recent Friday, Brawley, noticeably heavier and dressed in pink scrubs, emerged from her apartment at about 6:30 a.m. with a small child and a man wearing red hospital scrubs. The two left in separate cars — Brawley in a Chrysler Sebring and the man and child in a Ford Taurus. She arrived at work in Richmond about 30 minutes later, and the man pulled in minutes afterward. (Garland, 2012)

Of course she's noticeably heavier. She got paid from that "scam." Once Sharpton and the others teamed up, she became a national superstar. And money to someone whose never had it translates into: food, food, food. Not only that, but she got pregnant by some guy and that's not easy weight to lose. The man described above is probably a boyfriend who came in for a booty call and works at the same place she does. He talked her out of her panties and that's the way it goes in the big city.

Now pay close attention to the place where Tawana moved to and lives:

> Hopewell — where Brawley has lived for at least a year, according to a neighbor — has the highest rate of violent crime per capita of any city or town in Virginia, local cops say. Plagued by drugs and guns, it had five murders in the last three weeks. Jittery residents call police at even the slightest suspicion. (Garland, 2012)

In other words, it's a ghetto. This is what she was accustomed to. She was a ghetto star in her own right. And the fact of the matter is, it is probably an area that she was accustomed to from her days as a child because of its proximity to where she grew up. Check out the following:

> State records show "Tawana V. Gutierrez" and "Tawana V. Thompson" have held the same nursing license since 2006. The Virginia Board of Nursing confirmed issuing it to a "Tawana Vacenia Thompson Gutierrez."Brawley maintains a PO box in Claremont, Va., under the name Gutierrez, according to sources.**That town is a 45-minute drive from Hopewell and is the residence of her stepdad, Ralph King, who spent seven years in prison in the 1970s for killing his first wife**. (Garland, 2012 – emphasis added)

Reliable studies show that an abused child often gravitates toward the abuser. Could this be the case? Why live so close to her father? Now, you can see that he did time for killing his first wife. Tawana knew about that and he probably beat her ass when she came in late or did anything he didn't like. He may have sexually abused her, who knows? What I do know is that it takes a whole lot of fear to go so far as to run away for four days and then, as a cover or alibi, cut your body up and then tell a massive lie blaming it on a rape by four white boys. More on that in a minute.

The father was a brute and he was violent. According to the article, "Locals in the rural mill town described King, who lives in a ramshackle house near the end of a dead-end street where dogs run wild, as a nasty man and said they hadn't seen Tawana in years."He's real mean," one man said. King declined to be interviewed." (Garland, 2012) So he lived in a slum akin to where Tawana had moved to. He was a poor man and was frustrated and violent. This is not the kind of person who should be raising any child, especially a young girl who is blossoming into womanhood. Tawana lived in fear more likely than not.

Here is the story she (and Sharpton and others) told the world:

> A quarter-century ago, Brawley, **then just 15**, told a story incredible for its sheer brutality. **After she went missing for four days from her home** in Wappingers Falls, Dutchess County, Brawley **was found in a trash bag on Nov. 28, 1987, dazed, covered in feces and with the words "n—r" and "b—h" scrawled in charcoal on her body and "KKK" carved into her shoe.** Initially, Brawley said little, simply nodding or writing notes when investigators questioned her and revealing that **she had been abducted by two white men in a dark car who drove her to the woods, where four other white men were waiting.** Details were in short supply. Tawana **couldn't offer names or even a description of the attackers who ravaged her for four days.** (Garland, 2012 – emphasis added)

She couldn't provide names because the men didn't exist! But I'll tell you what: whoever was taxing that ass for four days probably made her feel like it was four men! I bet she had a ball: four days of screwing, probably drinking and getting high (they didn't perform a toxicology screen, did they?) and then having to come up with an excuse. Because the guy (or guys) she was screwing were typical teenage cowards, they weren't going to step up and tell a violent old man, "Hey bro. Uh… we was fuckin' your daughter for the past four days so here she is, unharmed. Bye!" No. They put it all on her. A little cutie pie out there to fend for herself – the polar opposite of Judge Faith other than the beauty aspect.

So now, almost two decades has passed since the assassination of Dr. Martin Luther King, Jr., when the poverty pimps like Jesse Jackson, Andrew Young, Ralph Abernathy and others crawled from under their rock and began trying to cash in on King's name. Sharpton, wearing a James Brown hairstyle (and dropping James' name whenever he could) was right out there "talking loud and saying nothing" (as Brown would put it). And since these pimps never met a cause célèbre that they couldn't resist, jumped at the Brawley situation:

> The case attracted attorneys Alton H. Maddox and C. Vernon Mason, and the then-**little-known Rev. Al Sharpton**, who used it to catapult to the national stage. Less than a week after Brawley was discovered, Fishkill Police Officer Harry Crist Jr., 28, was found dead in his apartment. Soon, Brawley's **advisers** would name Crist as a suspect in the rape. And when Dutchess County prosecutor Steven Pagones offered an alibi for Crist, **Pagones suddenly found himself also accused**. (Garland, 2012)

Pointing fingers without a scintilla of evidence. And Mason and Maddox should have known better. Maybe they got a shot at Tawana themselves, who knows? What I do know is that what they were doing was taking shots at powerful men with only little Tawana as a shield. After all, she would get the blame if push came to shove, right?

More specifically,

> Sharpton and Brawley's lawyers claimed — without proof — that Pagones kidnapped, abused and raped Brawley on **33 occasions**. They also **fingered state trooper** Scott Patterson, a friend of Crist and Pagones, who found Crist's body. (Garland, 2012)

Also involved in this, but never mentioned, is the media's fanning of all this bullshit. How can you blame men like this over thirty times for raping a child and not be seriously questioned or ignored? No evidence at all? That's the basis for a libel suit! But as we say in the journalism business, "If it bleeds, it leads," and if what Tawana was describing was accurate, there was a lot of blood during those four days. And every pedophile and pervert of any repute seemed to take a bizarre interest in the case. For instance,

> Brawley became a cause célèbre. **Bill Cosby posted a $25,000 reward** for information on the case; **Don King promised $100,000** for Brawley's education; and **boxer Mike Tyson** gave her a $30,000 watch to ease her pain. (Garland, 2012 – emphasis added)

And here we are three decades later and Cosby, who rarely does anything for black people (other than the ones who attend his homoerotic college, Morehouse College in Atlanta or his wife's alma mater, Spelman) and who toured the country castigating black families, comes up with 25,000. Knowing what we know about him now, he was never concerned about Tawana as a woman because we see what he ended up doing to women (with the help, I believe, of his psychiatrist friend Dr. Alvin Poussaint who could write prescriptions for the drugs that Cosby gave to the women he assaulted).

Don King? When was the last time you saw him with a black woman? In fact, his wife Henrietta died at the age of 87 (she was one year older than King) and she was white. So why would he get involved with the education of a young black woman when his history shows his only concerned for blacks were the exploitation of black boxers ("The Thrilla in Manilla," "The Rumble in the Jungle") and his financial abuse of former heavyweight champion Mike Tyson? And that money for education – all she got out of any education at all (if she ever received the money) was an LPN, a nursing degree. Yay!

And this brings us to Tyson himself. Just four years after the Tawana Brawley incident – July of 1991 to be exact – he was charged with raping a young woman during a beauty contest. And how is a $30,000 watch gong to ease the pain of this young girl? She probably pawned it and split the proceeds with Sharpton, Maddox and Mason.

But the case grows increasingly bizarre:

> **But a grand jury found in 1988 that Brawley was never raped and the whole incredible case was all a hoax**. The panel, which heard from 180 witnesses over its seven-month investigation, found evidence that Brawley **ran away from home and was hiding out in the vacant apartment from which her parents were just evicted** and that she spun her yarn to avoid being punished for staying out late and missing school. **Many believe Brawley feared her stepdad King's wrath and needed an alibi for her absence.** (Garland, 2012 – emphasis added)

There you have it. A young girl with her "own" apartment, missing for four days and probably fuckin' up a storm! Of course it was a hoax. Her father was such a loser that he couldn't do anything about an eviction and from the way the article outlines it, there was a "mother figure" at the house as well. Was it the father's wife? Was it Tawana's mother? The answer is that her mother helped her concoct the lie! While Tawana was on the run, her mother met with her at the old apartment and Tawana told her about the lie. Her mother covered her. But at any rate, it doesn't matter: in either case it is clear that Tawana did what she wanted to do, when she wanted to do it, and threw caution to the wind. And it is also clear that her father was so abusive that this 15-year old girl had to concoct this outlandish lie (probably with the help of the boys who were screwing her) and once it hit the media, the shit hit the fan.

The key lies in the statement that, "Many believe Brawley feared her stepdad King's wrath and needed an alibi for her absence." That's a helluva "wrath" to fear, let me tell ya: and I'm a male! When it was threatened that daddy was going to get in our ass once he got home, we kids were shaking like a Chihuahua trying to shit out a peach seed. Those old school father's didn't play that shit. When we called them "whippings," we weren't bullshittin': a belt, a razor strap, a switch from a tree outside – which you had to go and fetch and other forms of brutality in the name of "discipline." Perhaps her father went too far and then again, there is no mention of her having any brothers or sisters.

But she was young and stupid. She couldn't even get the shit right. Check out the following facts of the case:

> The hateful words scrawled on Brawley's body were upside down — likely written by Brawley herself, and traces of the charcoal-like material were found under her fingernails, the grand jury found. Brawley showed **no signs of genital trauma or exposure**. No semen was found. The feces on her body was traced to her neighbor's dog. One witness said Brawley was seen climbing into the garbage bag. (Garland, 2012 – emphasis added)

Obviously if the words were scrawled upside down, someone would have to be standing over her head and writing them. Perhaps she was giving someone some head while he etched out the evil words, right? No. she did it herself. She didn't even wash her hands – she just left the charcoal under her fingernails. No sign of anyone screwing her and no signs of getting head. The dog shit was traced to the neighbor's mutt. My question is, the neighbor who saw her climbing into the garbage bag: why didn't that muthafucka call the cops *at that time?*

If there was no sign of genitalia trauma or exposure, then why would Sharpton and company continue to promote the "rape" hoax? Where were the medical reports? And yet Sharpton – the man who has now wormed his way into his own television program on MSNBC and the one who invited Judge Faith onto the program – dug himself deeper and deeper. That may explain how he lost all what weight: he was suffering from fear! Check out how he made a bad situation even worse:

> These days, Pagones, still a lawyer but now a principal at a New York-based private-investigation firm, is trying to forget the name Tawana Brawley. But he can't."It'll come up randomly. It'll come up when something happens with Sharpton," he told The Post. In **1998, Pagones won a defamation lawsuit against Sharpton, Brawley and her lawyers. Maddox was found liable for $97,000, Mason for $188,000, and Sharpton was ordered to pony up $66,000, money that was paid by celebrity lawyer Johnnie Cochran and other benefactors.**Brawley was ordered to fork over $190,000 at 9 percent annual interest. None of that has been paid, which brings her total bill to $429,000. (Garland, 2012 – emphasis added)

Sharpton was such a leech that he had to get "financial assistance" from Johnny Cochran and "other benefactors." He talked all that shit and couldn't even pay his bills. Of course Mason and Maddox were probably insured. But because of the grandiosity of these three clowns, that young sister stuck with her lies and had to pay up $90,000 – which she has not done YET! Now the bill, because of the interest accrued, has risen to almost half a million dollars.

What has Sharpton done to allow this important story to slide under the radar? Whose ass has he kissed to get a TV program on a prominent news network called "PoliticsNation," which is really nothing more than his bloviating and babbling and asking loaded questions from guests who are so far to the left that they make Huey Newton look like a Mormon!

> Pagones, who served as Dutchess County assistant district attorney until 1990, continues to search for her."Through her silence, she's as guilty of libel as Maddox, Mason and Sharpton," he said. "The only way to hold her accountable — at least at this stage — is financially.**"Pagones contends that after all these years, Brawley still should publicly state he did not rape her.**"I absolutely think she was manipulated by Mason, Maddox **and Sharpton**," he said. "But even if at the time she was being victimized by them, 25 years have gone by. At any time she could have told someone, 'I want to tell the truth.' To me, she's no longer a victim." (Garland, 2012 – emphasis added)

She's changed her name, but thanks to the article being quoted from, she was eventually located. Sharpton, in the meantime, has cut and run. And rightfully so:

> **Pagones blames Sharpton more than anyone else for his troubles**. "I don't ever expect him to say he's sorry, but he should at least come clean and admit that, after the trial, that now he knows Steven Pagones had nothing to do with Tawana Brawley," Pagones said. Pagones is correct: **To this day, Sharpton remains unapologetic**. (Garland, 2012 – emphasis added)

Of course he does. It was Brawley's lie, not his. He just rode that lie to national prominence by playing the role of super negro. Maddox was disbarred from practicing law in 1990 and Mason was disbarred in 1995 for, get this, "66 incidents of professional misconduct against 20 clients"! All three men were scam artists who got paid but in the end only two of them – Maddox and Mason – was actually punished for that national hoax. Sharpton got away scott free.

His refusal to apologize for his lie? Check out the "reverend's" explanation:

> "**Does Donald Trump** owe the Central Park Five an apology? He advocated in the Central Park case what he believed, **I advocated what I believe**," he told The Post, referring to Trump's full-page ads demanding the death penalty for five teens accused — and eventually exonerated — of raping a jogger in Central Park. Pagones remains undaunted. (Garland, 2012 – emphasis added)

It is so appropriate that Sharpton would compare himself to Donald Trump. The article appeared four years before Trump would run for and win the Presidency, but if there is one thing that the American public has learned it is that Trump is a pathological liar. Want proof? On May 9, 2018 CNN reported the following:

> The Washington Post's Fact-Checker blog has been keeping a strict count of President Donald Trump's many misstatements, untruths and outright lies. And, over the weekend at a rally in Michigan, Trump hit a(nother) milestone: **He topped 3,000 untrue or misleading statements in 466 days in office**. That means that, on average, **Trump says 6.5 things that aren't true a day. Every. Single. Day.** (Trump is actually picking up the pace when it comes to not telling the truth; he has averaged nine untruths or misleading statements a day over the past two months, according to the Post's count – emphasis added)

That's a lot of lyin', folks. And there you have it – Sharpton earlier comparing his situation with the lies of Trump. And as the old saying teaches us,

"Dress a liar as you will/A liar is a liar, still." And I'm willing to bet that since King was assassinated in 1968, Sharpton has told as many lies as Trump, hands down. As the saying teaches us, "Dress a liar as you will/A liar is a liar, still."

IMAN

Another confused beauty that clearly falls into the category of an "Aunt Jemima."

My dealings with her relate to something I read about three decades ago, around 1979 or 1980. Iman had just married one of my favorite basketball players, Spencer Haywood. I admired Haywood because he sued the NBA and won. But that's not the issue here. In an interview, I read where Iman was asked about her relationship with Haywood, with whom she has a daughter, and she said he was "tall, dark and handsome." And then this dumb bitch told this white reporter that "he had the biggest penis I had ever seen."

I share this with you because it clearly establishes the mindless lengths that a Jemima will go through as she works to curry favor with the white establishment. She has changed her beautiful Somali name from Zara Mohamed Abdulmajid to its current form, given to her by her grandfather.

At any rate this woman is now deemed a "pioneer in the ethnic-cosmetic market" and is the widow of English rock musician David Bowie, the white man she married in 1992. The second mark of a Jemima. Supposedly she is a Muslim and can speak five languages, which are Somali, Arabic, Italian, French and English. Notice that of the five three are European – as are her values, mindset and orientation as you will see.

She has been thoroughly "whitenized." Put another way,

> While still at university, Iman was **discovered by American photographer Peter Beard**, and subsequently moved to the United States to begin a modeling career … Her first modeling assignment was for *Vogue* a year later in 1976. She soon landed some of the most prestigious magazine covers, establishing herself as a supermodel …During her 14 years as a high fashion model, Iman also worked with many notable photographers, including Helmut Newton, Richard Avedon, Irving Penn and Annie Leibovitz …Iman credits the **nurturing she received** from various designers with having given her the confidence to succeed in an era **when individuality was** valued and model-muses were often an integral part of the creative process (Wikipedia, 2018 – emphasis added)

Her assimilationist track has landed her a major cosmetics business and clothing line, as well as her highly regarded charity work. She has appeared in some very forgettable movies, but what I remember are the times she appeared on NBCs "Miami Vice" and clearly showed that she could not act worth a damn.

At any rate, she continues to make zany remarks. She was married at age 18 to a black man who was a Hilton executive, then was divorced two years later. When she got to the states she used to date Warren Beatty, then married Spencer Haywood, had a child with him and after two years f marriage they split, then she marries Bowie and becomes stepmother to Bowie's son, Duncan Jones.

She's a Jemima, but less so that the others. She fought against blood diamonds that were being mined in Africa, for instance. She's a Muslim which to me, is just the flip side of the coin, with Christianity being the "religious scam" on the other side. She was married to Bowie for 24 years and in my view, the fact that she is always surrounded by white folks is what influences much of her thinking.

But another dimension of Iman's selling out has to be mentioned: her African background. These sistahs, no matter where they hail from, can be seduced by the glitz and glamour of all that the white man and his racist nation, America, have to offer. Most black people seem to fit this mold – the lure of the filthy lucre. Iman has no real talent but, like Beverly Johnson and Naomi Campbell, gets by on her natural beauty. But a Jemima is a Jemima is a Jemima.

EZOLA FOSTER

Ezola Foster is the only one of the Jemimas in this book who actually had a shot at a high-ranking political office. But the man she ran alongside was as racist and backwards as President Donald Trump. You've heard of him – Patrick Buchanan. A veritable redneck, he chose her as his vice-presidential running mate, but let us not get ahead of ourselves. Her comments and views are what makes this Jemima one of the higher-ranking sellouts on my list.

Now it gets really interesting. This white man who talks all that shit about minorities being the problem decides that he's going to choose a black running mate! Check it out:

> As his running mate, Buchanan chose African-American activist
> and retired teacher from Los Angeles, Ezola B. Foster. Buchanan
> was supported in this election run by future Socialist Party USA
> presidential candidate Brian Moore, who said in 2008 he supported
> Buchanan in 2000 because "he was for fair trade over free trade.
> He had some progressive positions that I thought would be helpful
> to the common man" ... On August 19, the New York Right to

Life Party, in convention, chose Buchanan as their nominee, with
90 percent of the districts voting for him.

Let me state at this juncture that when white people select black people as running mates, it means that the black person is mentally as white as the white person. Ezola Foster was certainly no exception. As one source documents it,

Pat Buchanan selected Foster as his running-mate after several other candidates such as Jim Traficant of Ohio and Teamsters Union president James P. Hoffa declined his offer. Foster, who had supported Buchanan's campaigns in 1992 and 1996, quit her own speaking tour to join the race. While Buchanan was hospitalized during part of the campaign, Foster was the ticket's mouthpiece, campaigning through television and radio appearances. This was the first time in history that an African-American had been nominated for Vice-President by a Federal Election Commission-recognized and federally funding political party, and the second time a woman had accomplished this (Democrat Geraldine Ferraro being the first) … (Wikipedia, 2016).

Rarely have such "Jemimas" see the public in such a manner other than Hollywood. When a black woman is "trusted" enough to be a mouthpiece for a conservative white boy, you know she has to be a sellout, a water-carrier, a flunky – a willing thrall.
Check out Foster's "credentials":

Foster was chosen because of her conservative credentials and speaking ability; she called Lyndon B. Johnson's Great Society social policy "Marxist". Buchanan critics saw her as an affirmative action selection because she had never held a political office and is African American …(Wikipedia, 2016).

Throughout our history as a people there has always been some crazy ass "nigger" who the white man dubs a savior of our people. The more insane or stereotypical the person was, the more whitey propped him or her up. In our recent history the names Ward Connerly, Clarence Thomas, Michael Steele, Alan Keyes, and Dr. Ben Carson come to mind. Ezola Foster is of that ilk. If you think that today's black conservatives are backwards, their predecessor was this black woman, Ezola Foster. Known for saying dumb shit, following are some of the positions she's held. To begin with,

- Left Democrats & GOP because of differences of belief. (Aug 29)
- In the race to win. (Aug 29)
- Encourages attending John Birch chapter meetings. (Aug 29)

- No rift in Reform Party; no change in platform. (Aug 29)
- Worker's Comp claim not based on real mental disorder. (Aug 24)
- Foster was president of California John Birch Society. (Aug 14)
- Calls black leaders "snake-oil peddlers". (Aug 12)
- Foster denies reports of divorce filing. (Aug 12)
- Ran for office as both Democrat and Republican. (Aug 11)
- Strongly defends "family values". (Feb 14)

It should be clear that this is one confused bitch. But it gets worse. Check out her record as it relates to civil rights:

- Homosexuality is biologically & psychologically damaging. (Aug 29)
- Racism is out of govt; now focus on people. (Aug 29)
- Supports display of Confederate flag in southern states. (Aug 12)
- Against racial preferences. (Aug 12)
- Confederate battle flag should be honored. (Aug 11)
- Against gay rights & women in military. (Aug 11)
- Accuses Jesse Jackson campaign of using fascist slogans. (Feb 14)
- Democratic party policies are motivated by racial hatred. (Feb 14)
- Reparations bill for descendants of slaves is socialist. (Feb 14)
- No pro-gay groups & no AIDS educaiton at RNC. (Feb 14)

Just like Trump had the sellout Ben Carson and then hired beautiful black female Amarosa Manigault (for window dressing), the point is that she joined a long list of white men and "negroes" who literally had been throwing herself at him ever since she appeared on "The Apprentice." Others like Herman Cain often come out of the woodwork, as did Paris Denard, Michael Steele and a number of sick reverends and celebrities like NFL Hall of Famer Ray Lewis, rapper LL Cool J and former boxer Mike Tyson.

Like Candace Owens, we have a Jemima who has "flipped" several times. Prior to 1984 she was a Democrat; from 1984 to 2000 she was a Republican, and from 2000-2002 she was a member of the Reform Party. Now the name of her party is the Constitution Party – whatever the hell that is.

She started off like some of the others, as a "conservative political activist and writer. She was president of a group called Black Americans for Family Values, which I equate with the existence of the 2018 version, Blacks For Trump." She literally started from the bottom before dragging her way up the conservative system. As Wikipedia (2018) notes:

> Foster was born and reared in Maurice in Vermilion Parish in southwestern Louisiana and earned a master's degree from Texas Southern University in Houston, Texas. In 1960, she moved to Los Angeles, California, where she was employed as **a public high**

school teacher for thirty-three years—teaching typing, business courses, and sometimes English classes. She had sought public office prior to 2000—as a Democrat in the 1970s and as a Republican candidate for California State Assembly in 1986. (Wikipedia, 2018 – emphasis added)

All the time she was a political wannabe, but my concern is how many black minds did she poison by slipping her views into the curriculum when she taught for just over three decades. Like other Jemimas, she flips back and forth until she finds an ideological outlook or rich white man who will "adopt" her.

Moreover,

In the 1980s, she became an outspoken opponent of pornography, sex education, AIDS education and gay rights and **founded "Black Americans for Family Values."** She has been affiliated **with the John Birch Society,** founded after World War II by the late Robert W. Welch, Jr., to the dismay of Moderate Republicans. She was arrested in 1987 with several other women while disrupting the California state Republican convention to protest its recognition of the Log Cabin Club, an organization of gay Republicans. In 1992, **she was a staunch defender of the police officers in the Rodney King beating case and organized a testimonial dinner for Laurence Powell, one of the convicted officers, in 1995.** (Wikipedia, 2018 – emphasis added)

So this woman is not only a homophobe but she's out of her damn mind as well. Some of the stuff above I can understand because I understand the nature of the Jemima. But when she backed the officers who beat the shit out of Rodney King, this is evidence that her mindset and thought process is as white as they come.

But it is clear to me why she is involved in all this. She wants to stick out in the crowd. There are whites who, of course, hold the positions that are outlined above. But when a black woman does it, attention can be gained. And that is what she is all about: like most Jemimas they crave the television camera and the media and it is almost as if they can't live without it. That is why some of them begin as writers and bloggers, while others still seek some way to get on television or, as in the case of Whoopi Goldberg, walk about looking like the mate of "Manimal."

She seems to hate black people and other people of color as well – just like her white conservative "masters." Check it out:

In 1994, while teaching at Bell High School in Bell, California, Foster was a public advocate of Proposition 187, a California ballot initiative to **deny government programs of social services, health care, and public education to illegal immigrants**. Her position was

> extremely unpopular at the school where she taught, **which was 90 percent Hispanic.** In 1996, after she argued on PBS's *MacNeil/Lehrer NewsHour* that illegal immigration was responsible for the low quality of Los Angeles schools, **some of her colleagues at the school condemned her in an open letter.** Two days later, she attended an anti-illegal-immigration rally where several of her supporters **were attacked by members of the Progressive Labor Party, who allegedly wanted to harm Foster herself.** (Wikipedia, 2018 – emphasis added)

These Jemimas send up these kinds of "smoke signals" with their actions and statements that are aimed to document their commitment to the conservative movement. They know the white man will pick up on it and the conservatives are in need of "activist coons" who can show America that they are not the lily-white "no niggers allowed" party that they appear to be. Look at Ezola's visible (and life-threatening) positions.

She opposes social programs and other assistant for immigrants. They are not "illegal" because the white man says so. HE is the illegal immigrant, the great-great-great grandson of a slew of white illegal immigrants who came here and murdered off First Nation people. Now he points the finger at people of color whose ancestors were here before he was. And that is what Ezola is counting on: a white man who sees her for the brave "negress" that he can count on.

Foster was doing all this work in an context that was predominantly Hispanic. She was risking her life to defend the white man against her brown brothers and sisters. Now that's what I call true "Jemima-ism" – white nationalism in blackface.

As for the John Birth Society it is described by the Dictionary of Politics as, "an ultraconservative organization, founded in December 1958 by Robert Welch, Jr., chiefly to combat alleged Communist activities in the U.S." I have also heard that during the riots of the 1960s these were white boys who opposed the black movement because they felt that the turmoil was inspired by "communists." What is she doing hanging out with these dangerous white folks? And why would they accept her unless it was to use her for their own political ambitions?

And,

> Shortly thereafter, she left her job, **which she calls a necessity resulting from her treatment at work.** She went on **speaking tours for the John Birch Society** and took workers' compensation for an **undisclosed mental disorder**—which she describes as "stress" and "anxiety"—until her official retirement as a teacher in 1998. (Wikipedia, 2018)

How can you do the things this woman has done and make the decisions that she has made without feeling or experiencing "stress and anxiety" the entire time?

And as for leaving her job, she did that because she didn't want those Hispanics to start kicking her off in the ass! And finally, how can a black woman go around on speaking tours for the John Birth Society and do it with a straight face? Maybe the pressure behind all these anti-black contradictions is why she developed an "undisclosed mental disorder" – *paranoid schizophrenia!*

As is in the cases of most of the other Jemimas, the white media ate it up. They know that controversy is what people want to see and hear, so they bring this clown on their shows to say that no sane person, let alone a black woman, would ever say:

> Foster has appeared on *Larry King Live, CBS This Morning, CNN & CO., Nightline, NewsTalk Television, CNN Live*, MSNBC, *Politically Incorrect*, and various CBS, NBC, and ABC newscasts. (Wikipedia, 2018)

And so with national appearances that clearly exposed her conservative views (and consequent anti-blackness) this black woman was finally spotted, and history was about to be made:

> Pat Buchanan selected Foster as his running-mate after several other candidates such as Jim Traficant of Ohio and Teamsters Union president James P. Hoffadeclined his offer. Foster, who had supported Buchanan's campaigns in 1992 and 1996, quit her own speaking tour to join the race. While Buchanan was hospitalized during part of the campaign, Foster was the ticket's mouthpiece, campaigning through television and radio appearances. **This was the first time in history that an African-American had been nominated for Vice-President by a Federal Election Commission-recognized and federally funding political party,** and the second time a woman had accomplished this (Democrat Geraldine Ferraro being the first). (Wikipedia, 2018 – emphasis added)

All these black "firsts" and our people wear them like a badge of pride, as if they're saying "we'ze finally made it." You haven't made shit; how long did it take you before you became "the first," how many of our people died or were locked up in order to get that "first" to become a reality, and finally and most importantly, what good is it to be "the first" of anything in a system that only rewards cowardice, backwardness, acquiescence and "Aunt Jemima-ism"?

So Ezola got what she wanted: a chance to actually be a serious part of the electoral process. Her name is in the history books next to a man who was one of the staunchest anti-black conservatives to ever run for public office. But to the Jemima, even bad publicity is good because it's STILL publicity.

Why was she selected? One source claims,

> Foster was chosen **because of her conservative credentials and
> speaking ability;** she called Lyndon B. Johnson's Great Society social
> policy "Marxist". Buchanan critics saw her as **an affirmative
> action selection** because she had never held a political office and is
> African-American (Wikipedia, 2018 – emphasis added)

And there you have it. Of course she and Buchanan got their asses kicked and she continued to make one of herself when she appeared on several talk shows promoting the values of what was called the Constitution Party. But even Buchanan's co-hosts on the PBS program, "The McLaughlin Group", snickered at him and realized that he was just using this black woman to push his right-wing politics.

Ezola Foster is the prototype Jemima. Her last book, titled *What's Best for All Americans*, was co-written with another conservative and had a forward written by another conservative coon, Walter Williams. And so it goes.

O.J. Simpson, Hall of Fame Running Back, Sports Commentator

<u>PREFACE</u>

Karenga (1967) once wrote that, "The negro was made and manufactured in America." That is how I feel about O.J. Simpson. He always wanted to be white despite his upbringing in San Francisco and even while at USC he was a tom. He graduated and went to Buffalo where he was an even bigger tom. Despite being married to a black woman, he wasn't happy until he found a blond white woman, a gold digger, that he went bonkers over. And then when she found a white man who was really white by race (and not just by values and intention), he killed both of them.

I will always remember the eloquent description of the "house nigger" that Malcolm X provided us with, because what he wrote then describes to the core, the very essence of Orenthal James Simpson, a man who appeared to love the white man more than he loved himself. Note well the words of Malcolm:

> To understand this, you have to go back to what [the] young brother here
> referred to as the house Negro and the field Negro -- back during slavery.
> There was two kinds of slaves. There was the house Negro and the field
> Negro. The house Negroes - they lived in the house with master, they

> dressed pretty good, they ate good 'cause they ate his food -- what he left.
> They lived in the attic or the basement, but still they lived near the
> master; and they loved their master more than the master loved himself.
> They would give their life to save the master's house quicker than the
> master would. The house Negro, if the master said, "We got a good
> house here," the house Negro would say, "Yeah, we got a good house
> here." Whenever the master said "we," he said "we." That's how you can
> tell a house Negro. (Malcolm X, 1964).

White folks, partially out of ignorance, partially out of denial and partially because they are the products of the "negationism" that permeates their thinking and writing when it comes to the topic of enslavement, do not quite understand what Malcolm is talking about. So let me contemporize his designations and show how these same syndromes continue to exist today in 2015 America.

You see them in every city and scenario: the so-called "black leaders" (known back in the day as "negro leaders"). These people are either self-appointed or they somehow get the white stamp of approval from some white man. If they help out with an election, they'll get a position, a title and maybe a set of keys that don't fit anything. If they side with the white man publicly, they'll be rewarded. If they're ministers or represent a bunch of passive black people in some religious setting, they'll get paid under the table to continue to do the bidding of the system. Milwaukee is full of them, from the state legislatures to the common council; Dallas has them at the Congressional level as well as the county and city council; and Omaha even has a few. In all these cases these opportunistic people can openly sell out the black community and continue to get away with it. These are today's "house negroes."

Malcolm saw it in 1964 and called them on it by describing them to the grass roots masses:

> If the master's house caught on fire, the house Negro would fight harder
> to put the blaze out than the master would. If the master got sick, the
> house Negro would say, "What's the matter, boss, we sick?" We sick! He
> identified himself with his master more than his master identified with
> himself. And if you came to the house Negro and said, "Let's run away,
> let's escape, let's separate," the house Negro would look at you and say,
> "Man, you crazy. What you mean, separate? Where is there a better
> house than this? Where can I wear better clothes than this? Where can I
> eat better food than this?" That was that house Negro. In those days he
> was called a "house nigger." And that's what we call him today, because
> we've still got some house niggers running around here.(Malcolm X,
> 1964)

This can be seen in present-day terms, not only in the guise of "black Republicans" who carry water for the system, but even for the so-called leadership that continues to talk about black people and "our" system and talking about what we should do "as Americans." Is there any wonder why those people from other parts of the world who have it in for this country and its racist history now include US as a part of the problem? With the white-run media promoting images of us has happy and satisfied, the people of the world who suffer have begun to hate us as much as they hate the white man. They now lump all "Americans" into the same mold and it's because of that "house nigger" mentality that the black people who get on television continue to display. As far as the world is concerned, "the friend of my enemy is my enemy."

Malcolm's description continues:

> This modern house Negro loves his master. He wants to live near him. He'll pay three times as much as the house is worth just to live near his master, and then brag about "I'm the only Negro out here." "I'm the only one on my job." "I'm the only one in this school." You're nothing but a house Negro …(Malcolm X, 1964)

The previous descriptions describe O.J. Simpson to a "t." But black people are so full of shit that they act as if they have no standards. They continue to forgive and forget jive-ass preachers who continually bilk them out of their hard-earned money ever Sunday, they believe their sellout politicians who they never see until an election is pending, and they call for the cops when they should know by now that the police have no positive thoughts about black people, male or female.

And they loved O.J. even though he made it clear that he didn't want to have anything to do with a black person – except for those who were as big a toms as he was, like Marcus Allen and Al Cowlings. These niggas made some money and then moved up under white people into gated communities and then spent most of their time hunting down white bitches.

<u>INTRODUCTION</u>

In 1976, it was the great Ntozake Shange who woke people up with her play, "For Colored Girls Who Have Considered Suicide When the Rainbow is Enuf" who shook up male-female relationships among black people. Almost two decades later, in 1995, it was the O.J. Simpson "murder case," where he was accused of killing two Jews, that further shook up the country, along both the lines of race and gender.

Shange once said that, "If anything is life-changing, being the descendant of a slave is." As you read this brief essay, keep in mind that although institutionalized slavery may have been abolished, it is still alive and well in America. The "slave mentality" permeates the black community, and reactions to on-going attacks are met with prayers and picketing in public. Although other options exist, black people still want to suck up behind white people in a way that is most similar to the way that O.J. was lapping up behind Nicole.

As sad as it is to observe and then say, the slave mentality is alive and well and O.J. Simpson was living proof. Following is my evidence.

<u>OVERVIEW AND ANALYSIS</u>

He•do•nism/The doctrine that pleasure is the chief good in life; also a way of life based on this.

The need to "escape" from being married to Marguerite, the need to escape being "black," the love of white women, his overall lifestyle which may or may not have included cocaine abuse, and the power that money and status can bring to someone who was born without it all combine to create the kind of hedonistic lifestyle that O.J. apparently craved. But he was not the only one.

A lowly waitress, but a highly visible, one, Nicole also had hedonistic tendencies. She was working in an occupation where she met more than her share of men and, at 18, had a care-free attitude and goals that motivated her toward the same pleasure-seeking that O.J. practiced. She loved the fast life, as this book well documents, and *sexual conquests were more than just a means to and end;* at some points it appears that sex, no matter who it was with, was an end in itself.

The New Britannica-Webster's Dictionary defines an "anglophile" as, "a person who greatly admires English and English things." This is close enough for O.J.; what I am trying to describe here is a man who loves things that are white, white-oriented and white-directed. This was what O.J. was all about. He went after the whitest thing he could find: blonde hair, blue eyes and young (meaning that she had a long time to remain white.) He was in love. He was in lust.

He was out of his fuckin' mind!

An interesting study from 1968 may give us an idea of what was going on between Juice and Nicole. An article about "prestige dating" out of the University of Florida revealed that the degree of status homogamy increased with the seriousness of the involvement. Now this study dealt with university students and fraternities and sororites. But was Nicole not a mere teenager when O.J. first came across her? Was he not a status symbol? Were they not both wealthy? This then, is a status relationship from the outset: she a member of the "jet-set" and as far as O.J. was concerned, a paragon of whiteness (blonde hair, blue eyes) and he a highly visible paragon of what a black man in society is stereotyped to be: a gladiator, a "beast," as it were. Put into another mode, we can sit back and think about it like this:

> "The media portrays white women as beauty and the Black man as the beast. Both the beauty of the starlet and the beastly violence of the athlete are nurtured and even worshipped. For many players and spectators, sports are forms of sublimation -- psychological means of diverting aggressions and emotional tensions to forms that are considered more socially or culturally acceptable." (Davidson, 1994: 23 & 25)

There was a picture of O.J. and Nicole following their wedding. It was in Jet magazine with the caption, "Often seen together for several years, Simpson and Ms. Brown were recently wed." But it was the full page photo in the May 3, 1979 edition of Jet magazine that showed me that this bitch had O.J.'s nose wide open. The photo was titled, "O.J's Hot Date," and showed the two on the disco floor, O.J. skinning and grinning as usual and Nicole shaking her tits. The caption read: "With cameras and strobe lights flashing, O.J. Simpson and date, aspiring actress Nicole Brown, boogey to the disco sounds at Regine's in New York City. The rumor mill links the two romantically." (Jet, 1979: 32)

This was the second marriage for Juice, and as we now know, it was one that he was obsessed with. One article gives us even more family background:

> " ... the couple had two children, Sidney, now 9 and Justin, 6. On May 25, 1989, O.J. Simpson was ordered by a West Los Angeles municipal judge to serve two years probation, contribute $500 to a shelter for battered women, pay a $470 fine and perform 120 hours of community service after pleading no contest to charges of spousal battery." (Paddock & Warren, 1994: 14)

In other words, during this time, (February of 1989) O.J. got in her ass yelling, as he kicked her butt, "I'll kill you." How do I know? Because the police reports are made up of what SHE told them, that's how I know. *That white bitch, as far as she and the white public were concerned, was getting her ass kicked by a "nigger," not by her husband.* She was spending up his money and was the mother of two of his kids. She didn't bother to think about that. While O.J. thought he was white, she could see what he was: a black brute wearing out his size 11s on the crack of her ass. So she called the police, and O.J. ended up having to go to "counseling."

This white bitch was setting O.J. up all along. Take note that she married him just after he was inducted into the Hall of Fame. Take note that when they were in New York on that disco floor, Juice was at the top of his career as a sports commentator. That meant he was out of town a great deal doing football games. What was Nicole doing? And what made her an "aspiring actress"? What better way to make "contacts" than to start hanging out with a man who everybody knows and recognizes. What better way to gain credibility as a blonde, blue-eyed white woman (hardly in short supply in sunny California), than to link up with one of the few black men who white males admire and appear to have accepted?

And, in fact, my allegations can be verified by an article in a recent National Enquirer entitled, "Nicole--the Model Wife." Check it out:

> "Nicole Simpson was an aspiring model when she met O.J. -- and he helped the blonde beauty land her first modeling job. She posed for Mannis Furs in Beverly Hills about 10 years ago -- and as these photos show, Nicole was a knockout! "O.J. bought a couple of fur coats for Nicole, who was then his girlfriend, reveals an insider. "While talking to the store's owner, O.J. found out theywere looking for a new model. "O.J. said, 'Why not my girlfriend Nicole? She's trying to be a model -- and she's really pretty!' He said it almost as a joke. But the next thing she knew, Nicole was in front of the camera modeling ... " (Nelson, 1994: 32)

The couple divorced in 1992 citing "irreconcilable differences" after seven years of marriage. The "irreconcilable differences," in my view, was that O.J. was black and she was white; O.J. was in love with her because she was white, and she used that whiteness to take over his life and use him just as she had done and would do later on after their divorce.

When they split up, Nicole didn't sit around pining over Juice. After all, she got their $550,000 San Franciso condo, a payment of nearly $450,000, and $10,000 a month in child suport. Not bad for a former teenage waitress who did nothing more than bat her eyes in O.J.'s direction, huh? The divorce didn't leave Nicole sitting around, however:

> " ... Nicole was enjoying an active social life away from O.J. 'We're a little Melrose Place around here, and Nicole Simpson was Heather Locklear,' says local boutique manager Leslie Letellier. 'She was beautiful and flirtatious. You'd see her driving down this street looking hot in her white Ferrari.' Her vanity plates read L84AD8 -- late for a date..." (Schinderette, 1994: 101)

The word "flirtatious" in the statement above is a euphemism. The fact of the matter is that Nicole was behaving like the whore that she would have been had she not met and then married O.J. She was a waitress, after all; she was ten years his junior, and had probably never slept with a black man before. But now she had a reputation as having "tamed" one, and had done so to the point where he had made a public ass out of himself. For most men, this would mean, 'stay away from this bitch; Juice might be nearby.' But not to white men who associate her relationship with and her divorce from O.J. with raw, animal sexuality; and the temptation was too great for a number of them to resist, especially when they saw her scantily-clad, mini-skirt wearing ass out on the dance floor.

And, a bartender at the trendy Renaissance nigtclub in Santa Monica had this to say to *Globe* magazine:

> "She came in quite a lot and drank this expensive tequila ... She always dated different guys and came in with a new one nearly every time. She danced with different people. She wasn't short of admirers." (The Globe, 1994: 37)

"Dated different guys" is yet another euphemism. If she was with different men, it was by design; she was having a good time making up for the youthful life she missed as she was cranking out kids for O.J. (translation: setting him up). She had a right to do it: she was single, white, and a youngster, relatively speaking. But we should call it what we would call it if it was a hip-swinging young black woman riding around in a sportscar and entertaining different men: she was a stone ho'.

A whore with a lust for the fast life, the limelight, the glitz and glamour of the dance floor and with a body that wouldn't quit. This is what O.J. married, this is what he was obsessed with, and this is why he killed her.

But here is my point and one that people appear to be glossing over because they are trying to prove her to be the all-American mom: how is she doing all this dancing and partying and being a great mother all at the same time. Newsweek reported that,

> "She worked out frequently at The Gym, a neighborhood health club and on many evenings she hired a babysitter so she coulud go dancing with friends at clubs in Santa Monica, West Hollywood and Beverly Hills. (Turque, et. al. 1994: 22)

And you don't think Juice found out about all this shit? His child support money was enabling her to pay for babysitters so she could go out and party her ass off. Although she was entitled after putting up with his shit, we have to think the way Juice would think: all he was hearing about, and probably seeing if he was, indeed, following her around, was his ex-wife, in great shape, dancing with all kinds of men and partying as if she were single with no children.

And even with all that money, she still had bills. It was about money. As one article put it,

> "Despite being battered and bruised by O.J. Simpson during their stormy marriage, ex-wife Nicole Brown Simpson kept in constant contact with him after their divorce -- because of his money. 'When Nicole was married to O.J., she grew accustomed to a very lavish lifestyle,' says a pal. 'And when they got divorced, she wasn't ready to give that up.' ... 'For the average person that seems likke a lot ofmoney, the pal says. 'But for Nicole, who'd started dating O.J. when she was only 18, that amount wasn't nearly enough." (The Star, 1994: 36)

Continuing:

> "Because of her upscale lifestyle, there were mountains of bills. She'd bought a $700,000 townhouse at 850 S. Bundy Drive in the exclusive Brentwood community of Los Angeles. She owned a Ferrari and had recently purchased a brand-new $30,000 black Jeep Grand Cherokee. But instead of looking for work, Nicole preferred solving her financial problems by looking for a man ... 'Even after the divorce, O.J. would pay for things,' the pal reveals. 'He'd take her shopping, buy clothes for the children, toss her a couple of thousand here and there. Because of his bank account, she gave her children the best of everything." (ibid.,)

If he didn't know it from the outset, Juice had to now believed that his wife was nothing but a slut. And if he didn't know it before killing he, he will damn sure know what a chump he's been once he starts reading those tabloids and watching television. I can see it now: he knew, and he probably started thinking about all that time out of town, and all those games he had to cover as an analyst. He started wondering what she was doing when he was away, sometimes for days at a time. Being a sexist pig, it never occurred to him that while he was out of town trying to fuck every thing that moved, she might be doing the same thing. Juice knew she was a slut, and the fact that they were divorced didn't mean anything: he was paying her $10,000 a month and she already had her own money. She had a bunch of money and wanted to go back to dating people of her own race. O.J. couldn't stand it because he had tried so hard to be white. "Gee Minitly, for God's sake. It just isn't fair!!!"

> "One of those attracted to her, apparently, was Chicago-born Ronald Goldman, who moved to California seven years ago. The handsome 6'1" waiter had met Nicole at a local gym where ... Nicole made herself the center of attention to a lot of young starstruck guys. Ron was a naive and innocent guy, a real puppy dog, someone who wanted to be loved. Ron and the others sort of idolized her. She was a rich, bigger-than-life blonde, out of place with these young boys ... " (Schinderette, 1994: 102)

A fast, young white girl with two half-black kids, formerly married to a man who was away from home half of the year. Put two and two together. Just look at what she began doing once she and Juice were divorced. I contend it was an extension of what she had been doing all along, which is why Juice used to kick her ass. But Juice was sick and in love. And this proved to be his undoing.

Now, a theory. During O.J.'s preliminary hearing, a young man named "Kato" Kaeling testified. He lived on the premises in a guest house out back. Although I deal with him elsewhere in this book. let us merely put two and two together: he was a friend of Nicole's, but I don't think Juice saw him as a "friend." He saw Kato as "competition" for Nicole's affections. After all, Kato was an "aspiring actor" just like she claimed to be an "aspiring actress." They were both white and blonde. And, when Juice and Nicole divorced, she told Kato he could come live with her in her new home in a "guest room" that was downstairs.

Yeah, right.

When Juice wrote his so-called "suicide letter" (I outline it later in this chapter), he mentions a lot of people: golfing pals, close friends and former athletic companions. But he doesn't mention Kato.

I think Kato fucked Nicole while Juice was away on business. After all, he lived in one of the three guest houses on the premises (Juice's daughter Arnelle occupied one and the maid lived in the other) from January of 1994 until June of 1994. Just because he and Juice went for a ride and had a burger the night of the murders doesn't make them buddies. As Juice figured it, Kato would make a convenient alibi. If I have these suspicions about Kato and Nicole, you know Juice had them. And proof that Juice was suspicious could lie in the fact that when Nicole moved and offered Kato to live in her house, Juice pulled him to the side and they "mutually agreed" that it wouldn't look right for Kato to do that, especially, according to Kato's testimony, since "Juice and Nicole might get back together."

This point proves two things: one, Juice knew Nicole was a whore and secondly, that he suspected that she either had already screwed Kato or would, if given the opportunity.

And this is where Juice's hypocrisy comes in. He wants to date, fuck and "pal around" with every bitch he can get his hands on, but he doesn't want Nicole to do it. Typical sexist asshole. But don't just take my word for it.

Information provided by the newspapers and TV shows also stated that Juice was a cockhound and, although he wanted to fuck everything with a hole in it, he didn't want Nicole out doing anything. Even after the divorce, Juice was still stalking Nicole while, in my view, using his new white girl, model Paula "Polo" Barbieri, as a front. After all, he didn't want the public to know that he couldn't bounce back after the divorce.

So even though it was Paula who he was with (at a posh charity function) the night before the murders, it was Nicole who was on his mind. In fact, one smut magazine claims that Nicole was jealous of Paula and reported the "final argument" Juice and his "ex" would ever have, this way:

> "It was O.J.'s romance with model Paula Barbieri that finally destroyed his dream of remarrying Nicole. On the evening of June 11 -- the night before Nicole's murder--he escorted Paula to a black-tie charity dinner also attended by several of his ex-wife's friends. And when a pal told Nicole the next day she exploded, said O.J.'s friend. "Nicole called O.J. and screamed: 'I've had it with you! I can't believe you took that bitch out where you knew my friends would see you! You're not enough of a man to treat me right. We're finished!' Then Nicole told O.J. she didn't love him or need him, said his friend." (South & Lewis, 1994: 28)

This then, was why Nicole sat apart from him the night of the recital and didn't invite him to the family dinner that followed the recital. But it also proves that Juice knew where the dinner would be -- at Mezzalune's, the same place Goldman worked.

In my view, Juice found out about Goldman, and his name might have even come up during the conversation just outlined. As a matter of fact maybe Nicole saw to it that her mother's glasses were "misplaced" on purpose, which would serve as a reason to call the restaurant and ask that they be delivered. No wonder Goldman insisted on delivering them to her. No wonder he went home to change first. Whether or not Juice was following her is debatable, but one thing's for sure. He caught them in what he thought was "the act," and murdered them both. Right there.

The media continued to refer to Goldman as just 'a friend.' I disagree; Nicole was fucking Goldman and Juice found out. In fact, one source said that Goldman had been seen driving Nicole's car and would go to the house and play with Juice's kids. So I believe that if Nicole hadn't fucked Goldman up to that point, she was sure going to that night; if for no other reason than to get revenge on Juice and Paula.

But Juice got the last laugh. For now.

Meanwhile, Juice is hanging with Paula as more or less a "front." On June 22nd, she was interviewed on "DayOne," and had a high-pitched voice, sounding like some misguided, naive little girl. Still, she was pledging that O.J. "was not a violent person" and that "there will be some people who will have a lot of apologies to make when this is over." To this day, Paula stands by O.J. and believes him innocent of the murder of a woman who she (Paula) had to dislike. But the plot thickens.

Now while all this shit is going on and of course, it's getting back to Juice through the grapevine, Nicole is supposedly telling people that she and Juice are going to get back together and Juice is hoping for another chance as well:

> "Despite their stormy relationship, Simpson was frequently seeen driving up to Nicole's home in his Bentley to take his kids on outings, and in recent months he was said by friends to be actively courting his ex-wife again. Just six weeks ago, Simpson and Nicole vacationed together in Mexico. About a month ago, at a local grocery store, Nicole struck up a conversation with an acquaintance and reported that, 'we're getting back together.' ((Schinderette, 1994: 101)

I believe this was a front. Nicole had been seeing other men, but was telling people that she and Juice were going to get back together just in case Juice ran into them. After all, the man was stalking her: she had to be careful not to intentionally make him mad or look like an ass to people around the neighborhood where she lived (remember: Juice only lived a short distance away.) So Juice is taking this bitch on vacations in Mexico, gambling trips to Las Vegas, skiing jaunts in Aspen, Colorado, and she's running game. And Juice found out about Goldman, who was a good-looking young white boy. Translation: fucking Nicole's brains out.

And according to some of the information that was shared in court, Juice snuck by the house one evening and looked through the windows and caught Nicole sucking Goldman's dick.

Juice snapped.

CONTEXT: THE ISSUE OF DOMESTIC ABUSE

Nicole Brown was not the "domestic" type. She set OJ up and exploited his immaturity and stupidity and was presumed to be a "housewife" because they got married. But the lyrics from Dr. Dre's 2008 cut, "Housewife" do lend some validity to the type of woman Nicole was, and sets the stage for this kind of discussion on domestic abuse:

Now this this is one of them occasions
Where the homies not doin it right
I mean he found him a ho that he like
But you can't make a ho a housewife
And when it all boils down you gonna find in the end
A bitch is a bitch, but a Dogg is a man's best friend
So what you found you a ho that you like
But you can't make a ho a housewife (wife)

I mostly sold dick while I packed a gold clip
Worked my money-maker, she got paper, she bout to trip
(Where the fuck is my money?) I cannot G guilty
You pimpin strong, but comin home, to sheets that be filthy
She on the dillzy, I take advantage
All up in them panties, I got this bitch speakin Spanish
I'm mannish - get yo' nails out my back
Slut I'm bout to nut and get up, go scrub yo' cat
Learn the player rules, this is how I play a dude
Might not be a freak, but she got on the choosin shoes
Dollar signs are folded, I can't control it
Tryin to leave her, beeper just exploded
She sweatin me, won't let me, broad turned fraud
Now she on this dick huh, got her turnin tricks huh
Man it's a trip I don't trip I'm in yo' Lexus flexin
I left her up in Dallas, Texas - assed-out

Now this this is one of them occasions
Where the homies not doin it right
I mean he found him a ho that he like
But you can't make a ho a housewife
And when it all boils down you gonna find in the end
A bitch is a bitch, but a Dogg is a man's best friend
So what you found you a ho that you like
But you can't make a ho a housewife (wife)

Naw "ho" is short for honey, almost had to wail her like Bunny
Tellin tales of bein pregnant, catchin Nordstrom sales with abortion money
I spotted her, seen her with my nigga when I shot at her
Now we got beef, he caught up in the ho's erotica

Exotic - she's psychotic, rockin his Nautica
Soon he'll need antibiotics (sucka bitch)
Name a sexual disease, she got it like Sam Goody
You be like, "Damn how could she hit me off with chlamydia?"
Fool I pity ya
We live in the city of ballers
With more bouncin than a Zapp, she will doo-wah-diddy-ya
Prettier to grittier, the wittier can get her
To the Hotel, Niko, on some Sauve shit like Rico
That's when I caught a Vision like Coleco
A high-post ho, a perfect way for me to keep dough
Huh, have her sellin ass on Bronson Ave. and Pico

At the ho-tel, mo-tel, or the Holiday Inn (say what nigga?)
I said if that bitch keep fuckin up (beotch) then we'll fuck her friends
I said I dip, dive, what can I say?
Niggas need to stop fuckin with O.J
Some niggas bang Blood, some niggas bang Crip
And bitches ain't shit but hoes and tricks
I had to dream of hoes, I had to scream at hoes
I seen my hoes in all kinds of clothes
Lil' Almond Joy, I truly enjoy
If you blew my balls, right through my drawers
Come back to the mansion, chill at the spot
From the way she was blowin, I know she does it a lot
I have a eight-and-a-half, nine-and-three-quarters
The ho started callin when I started boss ballin
Gimme some head, gimme some ass (uh-huh)
Gimme some cash, pass it to Daz
Pass it to Snoop, or pass it to Nate
See hoes eat dick like eggs and steak
It ain't shit new, I thought you knew (what?)
I knew you would, you wish you could
Break a G down, break me down
But I'mma see you on the rebound (what what?) D.P. style

Now this this is one of them occasions
Where the homies not doin it right
I mean he found him a ho that he like
But you can't make a ho a housewife
And when it all boils down you gonna find in the end
A bitch is a bitch, but a Dogg is a man's best friend
So what you found you a ho that you like
But you can't make a ho a housewife (wife

With that having been said, and with my having made it clear that my belief is that Nicole never had any intention of remaining "faithful" in her marriage to O.J. and that the kids they had were just more nails in his coffin because there are hundreds of thousands of women out there who intentionally set men up with pregnancies so that they (the women) can gain some financial stability.

At any rate, this back and forth between men and women is the undergirding of a system of patriarchy – rule by the male. As Smith (1990) explains it,

> A patriarchy may be thought of as having two basic components: a structure, in which men have more power and privilege than women, and an ideology that legitimizes this arrangement . This system ... perhaps the most pervasive and tenacious system of power in history ... characterizes most societies, past and present, albeit with significant variations in particular historical epochs, under different modes of production, and across cultures, classes and other social structures ... " (Smith, 1990: 257)

Ann Goetting of the University of Kentucky provides a generic outline of what the situation is when it comes to the plight of women and the issue of men abusing them:

> "There has been a renewed interest in the status of women in this country since the early 1960s, and with it has emeged considerable reserach attention devoted to women as victims of violence. In the context of this observation, it is of interest to note the virtual absence of scholarly effort directed toward the study of what may be considered the most serious form of interpersonal violence against women: that is, homicide. This is true even though over one in every four reported homicide victims (25.2% in 1988) is a female) ... What is particularly surprising is that even less is written about women as victims of homicide than about homicidal women; this is so in spite of the facts that women far more frequently are victims than perpetrators of homicide, and much more information is available to researchers on homicide victims than on offenders..." (Goetting, 1991: 159)

During the 10 years from 1976 to 1985, a total of 18,417 people are estimated to have been killed by their spouses in the United States ... Estimated numbers of victims were 10,529 wives and 7,888 husbands. Hence, for every 100 men who killed their wives, about 75 women killed their husbands. (Wilson & Daly, 1992: 189) More recently, according to figures provided by the US Justice Department, one of every 185 women -- a total of 572,032 -- are victims of domestic abuse every year. (USA Today, 1994: 3A). Data from the FBI back in 1991 claimed that at least one woman is raped every six minutes, battered every 15 to 18 seconds and killed every six hours -- usually at the hands of a man she knows. (Walker, 1991: 1)

And guess what? the rates for white women are about the same as the rates for black women. So this societally accepted myth of the "black wife beater" is more bullshit: white boys are doing it too, but they live in the same neighborhood as the reporters and the attorneys (just like Juice did), but their abuse is swept under the rug.

Avni (1991) gives us more data regarding battered women:

> "Public attention was first drawn to the plight of battered women in the early 1970s, starting in England with the pioneering work of Erin Pizzey (1974) and quickly spreading to the U.S. A. The awareness of this problem led to the mass establishment of shelters for battered women ... " (Avni 1991: 137)

In the case of O.J. Simpson, he was much older than Nicole, being her senior by more than ten years. Wilson and Daley in their study of spousal killings *found that Canadian spousal homicide rates increased as the couple's age disparity increased.* This was true for wives and husbands, regardless of who was the older party. This information was also found to be the case in a study conducted in the United States by Mercy and Saltzman (1989). The facts then, are these:

> "Men often hunt down and kill spouses who have left them; women hardly ever behave similarly. Men kill wives as part of planned murder-suicides; analogous acts by women are almost unheard of. Men kill inresponse to relevations of wifely infidelity; women almost never respond similarly, although their mates are more often adulterous. Men often kill wives after subjecting them to lengthy periods of coercive abuse and assaults; the roles in such cases are seldom if ever reversed. Men perpetrate familicidal massacres, killing spouse and chilren together; women do not. Moreover, it seem s clear that a large proportion of the spousal killings perpetrated by wives, but almost none of those perpetrated by husbands, are acts of self-defense. Unlike men, women kill male partners after years of suffering when they feel trapped, and because they fear for their own lives ... " (Wilson & Daly, 1992: 206)

Now, check out the following information, documented by Walker (1983), and Hofeller (1982): the husband's suspicion of his wife is the most obvious expression of the patriarchal approach. This variable was found in researches in different parts of the world as a dominant, intensive and uncompromising characteristic of the battering husband.

They could have added another variable: hypocrisy. Why? Here is how one article put it:

> " ... Others saw no evidence of violence but sensed that O.J. was a dominating, jealous personality temperamentally unsuited for the spirited, gregarious Brown ... It was also no secret that Simpson enjoyed the company of beautiful women on the road." (Turque, et. al. 1994: 19)

A hypocrite; O.J. was playing around with every women he saw and wanted while, at the same time, never allowed Nicole the privacy or privilege to do so. And this is why Nicole took those ass-whippings on such a regular basis. Again, don't take my word for it: let the scholars in the field inform you that,

> "'It is not true that life is one damn thing after another, it's the same damn thing over and over.' With these few words, Edna St. Vincent Millay described a phenomenon well known to victimization researchers: Victimization all too often seems to produce yet more victimization. (Mandoki & Burkhart, 1989: 179)

The ABC Evening News recently (June 27, 1994) reported the extent of domestic abuse as a sidebar to, of course, the O.J. Simpson controversy. What is interesting is that it used the city of Milwaukee as its topic area. In that city, some 8,000 cases of domestic abuse were reported in 1992. ABC did not mention, however, that in Milwaukee, there are 18,000 more black women than black men between the ages of 18 and 44 -- child bearing years.

These incidents then, are important to understand, not to merely record in order to have something to hang over the head of the black male. Since disproportionately high percentages of those being charged in Milwaukee with domestic abuse are black males (another fact that ABC omitted), and knowing how many more black women there are than black men, this brings us to an important point to consider for ourselves and for the African-American community in general: black men are committing domestic abuse out of frustration, not superior numbers.

It should also have been noted, that in a disporportionately high percentage of those Milwaukee cases, most of those involved in "domestic abuse" were not married couples rather, they were boyfriend/girlfriend or the male who was present was the father of one of the children. This then, is another important contextual point: despite the absence of wedlock, a socially sanctioned sign of long-term commitment, African-American men are still disproportionately abusing our women. My conclusion is that we are doing it "just because we are men."

These two facts, in and of themselves, pave the way for an examination of domestic abuse which is somewhat different when we make cross racial comparisons. I contend that black men lash out at black women because black women know that, indeed, this man used to be a "slave" to the white man, and that it is another man -- the white one -- who is the source of their comfort and life-chances (i.e., heat, electricity, gas, housing, clothing, employment, luxuries, leisure, etc.)

This may be sub-conscious on the black woman's part, but the black male knows it all too well. We know because we continue to refer to whitey as "the man." If he is "the man," then certainly that leaves very little for us to be. In fact, Dr. Frances Cress Welsing offers us some insight in this area when she contends that there are five levels of life: man, woman, boy, girl and baby. And if the peckerwood is "the man," then the only thing left for the black male is "boy" or "baby." She then documents cases of this where we refer to our houses as "cribs," where our women affectionately call us "baby" and where, on occasion, we may call her "mama."

This may sound like a stretch of logic but, when compared with what I am about to document, it enables us to better understand the frustration of low-income males, of African-American males, of males who have "made it" but still feel impotent when compared with what society defines as the "ultimate male" in terms of success -- the white man. O.J. Simpson, as I hope to show, falls into this latter category.

And this brings us to Nicole's role. Nicole, perhaps without knowing it, was also guilty of abuse because she believed O.J. when he agreed to her "we will see other people" rules. O.J. never accepted it, but he didn't appear to be weak; after all, if Nicole wanted to see other people, he would look like "less than a man" if he couldn't convince her that he, too, had some resources he could call upon. He found a nice-looking alternative in Paula Barbieri, but it was just a "front"; all the time he was still obsessed with Nicole.

Nicole should have read an article by Toni Grant which appeared in a 1988 issue of *Cosmopolitan* magazine. In that article, titled, "Handling Your Hero," the writer contends that no woman can hope to manage or understand men without realization of the basic male fear of castration, and that men's concerns center around penis size, potency and staying power.

When O.J. lost Nicole, he may have felt that he lost his sex appeal, his allure. Although he messed around with other women even while married to Nicole, she was his standard of beauty: blonde hair, blue eyes and white skin. She was his ideal. He was merely pretending like he was messing around in a misguided attempt to re-affirm his manhood. His sexuality was probably at its peak when he was with her. He could have other affairs but only because he could pretend that they were Nicole. When they split up he had to look elsewhere for an ideal and evidently could not find it.

He was, in a manner of speaking, castrated. He was rendered socially impotent because now he had once again joined the ranks of the divorced. His "staying power" in terms of being able to maintain a relationship was again called into question. First Marguerite (his black wife) and now Nicole.

Then, to make matters worse, rumors began to circulate that Ronald Goldman, a younger man -- indeed, a *whiter* man -- was driving around in Nicole's car; was playing with the children. Translation: *replacing Juice in the minds and hearts of his family.* This was more than Juice could stand. A younger man who had a racial advantage on Juice, one that no matter how much Juice "tommed," he could never overtake -- this was too much and something had to be done. This then, is the psychological reasoning behind Juice doing what he did. At least, this is how I see it.

Juice lashed out at what he felt was the source of his impotence: Nicole, and a male who held a racial, social, and (at least after the divorce) personal advantage over with his ex-wife.

O.J.'s 'Suicide Note': An Analysis

The letter to Nicole is even more evidence that Juice felt he was white, that he was out to lunch and even more, that he is no "role model" for any youth, let alone African-American kids. The letter follows, with my comments appearing throughout as designated:

"To Whom It May Concern:

First, everyone understand, I have nothing to do with Nicole's murder. I loved her, always have and always will. If we had a problem, it's because I loved her so much.

Later in this letter he contradicts the claim of having nothing to do with her murder. The prosecution is going to eat him alive. This letter is nothing more than a pre-chase smokescreen to establish that he is "not sane." But look at the letter as we go through it and you can see that O.J. is thinking very clearly. Probably with the assistance of his buddy, Al Cowlings, but thinking clearly nonetheless.

He says that if he and Nicole had a problem, it was because he loved her so much. This is "spouse abuser logic," in my view. "I kicked her ass 'cuz I luvz her"; "if I can't have you, no one else will." This is the kind of sick bullshit that leads to stalking, obsession and the kinds of behaviors that O.J. exhibited even after this white girl clearly didn't want to have anything to do with him. Juice was in over his head and the white girl knew it; he thought he had things under control. *But in reality, she was in full control of that relationship.* Until the end, that is.

Moving on, the excommunicated ex-athlete writes:

> Recently, we came to the understanding that for now we were not
> right for each other, at least for now. Despite our love, we were different
> and that's why we mutually agreed to go our separate ways.

In my many years, most "mutual agreements" that I have had in my relationships were based on one of us establishing, first of all, that there was a problem. In the case of Juice, he wants us to believe that they BOTH arrived at this conclusion. But how could they? Even if they did, why was he the one hiding in bushes and stalking her, and she appeared to be having the time of her life? Why was she filing complaints and he not filing any?

If they "mutually agreed" to go their own separate ways, why were they out together earlier in the day before Nicole and Goldman were found murdered? If they were in such "mutual agreement," why did she still have the kids at her house when Juice only lived a few minutes away? Why didn't they sit together the night of the murders when both attended their daughter Sydney's dance recital?

Juice is lying because Nicole is not around to defender herself. She laid down the rules and wanted to see other people; her role as an "aspiring actress" was probably something she wanted to pursue. Juice was already on television and headed back to NBC for another season of football analysis. Meanwhile, Nicole was languishing because Hollywood suffers from no shortage of blonde, blue-eyed white women who will do *anything* for a role in a movie or a TV program.

And how interesting it is that these two individuals who chose to marry outside of their respective races come to the conclusion, after seven years of marriage that "they are different." Of course they are different: he's a bootlicking negro and she's a white woman with blonde hair! In his case, he can only go so far up the ladder before the white man slams the door in his face; she can go as far as she wants because, thanks to her physical features and distorted values, she represents the American ideal!

> It was tough splitting for a second time, but we both knew it was for
> the best. Inside I had no doubt that in the future we would be clsoe friends
> or more. Unlike what has been written in the press, Nicole and I had a
> great relationship for most of our lives together. Like all long-term
> relationships, we had a few downs and ups.

"We both knew it was for the best." Yeah, right. Juice cannot possibly believe this bullshit he is writing because his actions prove just the opposite. He didn't agree with Nicole laying down the law. He wanted her back and was working toward that end. Meanwhile, Nicole was busy trying to boost her career *by any means necessary.* And she couldn't do it with this black man breathing down her neck. So she decided it was time to let Juice know where he could go. He had a girlfriend and she understood. But Juice couldn't bear the thought of Nicole being with someone else. Fatal attraction like a muthafucka.

Back to Simpson's letter:

> I took the heat New Year's 1989 because that's what I was supposed
> to do . I did not plead no contest for any other reason but to protect our
> privacy and was advised it would end the press hype.

Give me a break, Juice! He pleaded guilty because he was kicking Nicole's ass all over that house, and she had the good sense to document that ass whipping with a phone call to 911! He had no choice but to admit it. Even if she did start the fight (which he alludes to later in his letter), she's a little white woman. No judge, not a white one at least, is going to believe that this nigga who made a living running all over huge linemen and defensive backs, was "attacked" by Nicole. So he pleaded "no contest" because there is never a contest when a black person goes up against a peckerwood in the peckerwood's court of law. Who in the fuck does O.J. think he's foolin'?

But remember: this asshole is supposed to be "insane," right? Seems to me like his memory and his analysis of his "legal and moral responsibilities" seems to be functioning pretty well!

Moving right along, the daffy defendant continues:

> I don't want to belabor knocking the press, but I can't believe what is
> being said. Most of it is totally made up. I know yhou have a job to do, but
> as a last wish, please, please, please, leave my children in peace. Their
> lives will be tough enough.

He can't believe what is being said. This proves that my earlier allegations against this Uncle Tom were correct. Juice felt that he was "above the law"; he felt he had made it. He had practiced, and succeeded at assimilating culturally, maritally and structurally. He felt he was on "the inside"; he thought he was a member of "the inner circle." He could not have been more wrong. The media is run and controlled by peckerwoods. White people who, in general, do not like black people, in general. Regardless of what O.J. *thought* he was, he was just another nigger in their eyes. And their writings proved that this is and continues to be the case.

225

Finally he realizes that his kids' lives will be tough enough. I guess so: black daddy, white mama, daddy hidin' in bushes and shit, and the mama fuckin' who knows who! I guess it will be tough for these little blonde mulattoes to get on with their lives. And since they'll be living with Nicole's family, life is going to be all that much more fucked up because those crackers don't give a fuck about those kids. They will raise them as "dark skinned honkies." And then they'll go to school and get called "nigger" all the same.

Yeah, Juice. A fine time for you to realize that getting a white bitch pregnant has its social and cultural costs. Yeah.

> I want to send my love and thanks to all my friends. I'm sorry I can't name every one of you, especially A.C. Man, thanks for being in my life. The support and friendship I received from so many: Wayne Hughes, Lewis Markes, Frank Olson, Mark Packer, Bender, Bobby Kardashian. I wish we had spent more time together in recent years. My golfing buddies, Hoss, Alan Austin, Mike, Craig, Bender, Wyler, Sandy, Jay, Donnie, thanks for the fun.

Just the fact that he would attempt to mention them shows that he didn't have too many friends. And if he really cared about them why mention them now that his ass was in a sling and he was being sought after by the police and just about every law enforcement agent in California. He picks this time to fake a suicide letter (if that's what it was supposed to be) and then start dropping names. And almost all of them are white, as if to disassociate himself from niggas is, somehow, something that should be bragged about, or that might save his ass to those who listen to the letter and think, "golly gee wow: he sure knows a lot of us honkies, doesn't he, dear?"

What an asshole!

Moreover, most of those mentioned above are most likely white males. Continuing with the letter from the nitwit from "Naked Gun":

> All my teammates over the years, Reggie, you were the soul of my pro career. Ahmad, I never stopped being proud of you. Marcus, you've got a great lady in Catherine, don't mess it up. Bobby Chandler, thanks for always being there. Skip and Kathy, I love you guys. Without you I never would have made it this far.

This is more evidence of my earlier allegations. Other than Cowlings (who is probably an Uncle Tom if he is O.J.'s "best friend" because like takes to like), Ahmad Rashad, Marcus Allen and maybe a few others, Juice was whitey's "boy."

Later on, he tries to give Marcus some advice about his woman. She's probably white, too. And besides that, Juice is in no position to give out tips on women: he can't even hold on to his own!

And he talks of being "proud" of Ahmad Rashad. Man, how can you be an Uncle Tom and be proud of a serious black man who cares about his people the way Ahmad Rashad does? First of all, Rashad changed his name so that he could reject the slave name of his former slave master? How could O.J. be proud of that fact if he, in fact, didn't do it? Furthermore, Rashad is a proud black man who has a sense of purpose, identity and direction -- three things that Juice lacked! And finally, Rashad found it in his heart to marry a black woman -- formerly Phyllicia Allen -- and a fine one at that. The same thing that Juice could have done if he could take his eyes of "Missy Ann" long enough. How could be be proud of the personification of "blackness" if he, himself, is the exact opposite?

But that's how it goes. Anyone with eyes can see that the white boy cannot afford to pay his mediocre gladiators (mediocre in comparison to ours) what he can pay the black athletes -- *but he can get the money back through her!!!*

And just look at a partial list of the millionaire black men in entertainment and sports, who are pouring money into the white man's woman and screwing up the race: George Stanford Brown, Mike Singletary (former linebacker, Chicago Bears) , Anthony Miller (wide receiver for the San Diego Chargers), Robert Parish (Boston Celtics), Sidney Portier, Dennis Rodman (San Antonio Spurs forward), Reginald Lewis (Asian wife), Lt. Robert Goodman, Redd Foxx (Asian wife), Billie Dee Williams (Asian Wife), Reginald Lewis (multimillionaire, now deceased-- Asian wife takes over his company, TLC), Ben Vereen, Cuba Gooding, Jr., Montel Williams, Sammy Davis Jr., (the first time around), Dorian Harewood, Gregory Hines, Ike Turner, and the list goes on and on.

Not to leave out the "sisters" married to white boys: Whoopi Goldberg (twice), fine ass Alfre Woodard, Nell Carter, Roxie Roker, Mariah Carey, Ann-Marie Johnson, Stephanie Williams, Iman, Lena Horne (the first time around), Pearl Bailey, Minnie Ripperton, Naomi Crawford, Tookie Smith (Robert DeNiro's concubine), etc.

Ain't that a bitch?

But in the case of the so-called "brothers," the white man is lusting for power and creating ways to get through life *without* his woman because he knows WE want her so badly! Those microwaves ovens, vaccuum cleaners, electronic kitchen aids and the like are not for her -- they are designed to make bachelor life more convenient for *him* !! Once he gets rid of her pale ass, he can jack off in a test tube if he wants to conceive children or, if he wants live pussy, he can get in his BMW and cruise through the ghetto! Very simple, No ties, no paperwork, no confusion, no nagging and no hair in the fuckin' sink.

Those who do tolerate her presence at the side of the black male will know that she will, indeed, be busy shopping, going to movies, the theatre, buying cars, clothing and jewelry in HIS neighborhoods and at HIS malls and mega-stores. Shopping with the money that these *high-priced coons* have given her as an "allowance."

How "far" does O.J. think he has "made it" with his ass in a sling with the criminal justice system? He hasn't gone anywhere; he's like a rat on a cylinder -- movin' but not goin' any place. Juice *thinks* he made it far because he is measuring his success by how closely he has been able to approximate what the white man has: let's see, white mansion, white condo, white beach house, two white Ferraris, a white Ford Bronco, television visibility and --- a white girl! "Lordy Day, I'ze done made it!!"

In an older article titled, "The Social Characteristics of Entertainers," Willhelm and Sjoberg found, among other things, that while the entertainment arena has provided an alternative avenue of upward mobility for many disadvantaged groups, both economic and religious, in American society, other patterns also emerged. One of those findings is outlined below:

> "Entertainers seem to be unstable persons from the viewpoint of the ideal norms of American society. Their instability seems related to their social origins and to the fact that they have experienced social origins and to the fact that they have experienced upward social mobility. It also appears that personal instability is functionally related to success in entertainment, and in turn the demand of the occupation itself reinforce this instability."

"Instability" certainly defines Juice's childhood and, of course, his college career. And there can be no doubt that it would also be a factor in his decisionmaking ability: should he allow Nicole to prosper on her own and date and perhaps marry other men? We now know what the answer to that question was, don't we?

Furthermore,

> " ... the social origins of entertainers may partially account for the nature of current entertainment in America.Nowadays entertainers generally must appeal to the interests of the general populace, and to do so it is highly advantageous to have experienced in extreme form many of the problems with which the mass audience is concerned."
> (Willhelm & Sjoberg, 1958: 76)

As a football player, he has to have some kind of tendencies toward pain or violence and, as a result, the isue of experiencing "in extreme form" the problems of which society is concerned certainly fits. This is a violent society; football is a barbaric sport which epitomizes that violence.

If those guys were really his "friends," they would have talked him out of marrying Nicole. They would have said to Juice, "look man: you don't need to get married right now. You're still in your prime. You've already been divorced once, and you really need to wait around and find you a fine *sister* to share all this with."

Nope. When Juice flashed this bitch at his "friends'" parties, they probably pulled him to the side and said, "I heard that, brother--get them draws!" Or, "hey man, how is the pussy?" And Juice was probably so busy skinnin' and grinnin' that he didn't notice that Nicole had a hidden agenda until it was too late.'

Next, the hypocrite from Hertz shows how pitiful he really is in his relationships before and since Nicole:

> Marguerite, thanks for the early years. We had some fun. Paula, what can I say? You are special. I'm sorry. I'm not going to have, we're not going to have a chance. God brought you to me. I now see. As I leave, you'll be in my thoughts.

Fine ass Marguerite. Beautiful Black woman. Went to college. Stabilized his life and his family. Body like a muthafucka. Mother of his oldest son and daughter. A good sister who was with him since early in college and even before that. And this muthafucka gives her five funky words in a "goodbye" note. What kind of sick Uncle Tom bullshit is *this ??* He gives Paula, nothing more than a concubine, more lines than he does Marguerite, who bore him two sons (one died after drowing in a swimming pool).

Thanks Juice for giving black women all over the country the ammunition they need to lump all of us menfolk into one big fuckin' category of cockhounds and lovers of white women: "see how y'all are?" "Yeah, that's what ya won't, huh?" And so on and so on and shoo-be-doo-be-doo-dah.

And speakin' of "everyday people," let's deal with this Paula Barbieri. Who was she but just another white woman that O.J. found after he and Nicole divorced? But at least Paula had dark features and does come close to favoring a light skinned black woman or a Latina. But when all is said and done, she is, indeed white. Paula was wasting her time on and with O.J.; he was just faking an interest in someone else while, at the same time, kissing Nicole's ass: taking her to parties, award ceremonies and to restaurants. If Paula was so "special," why didn't Juice marry her? Why didn't she move in with him? Why didn't he move in with her?

The answer is clear. *Paula is this niggas "alibi."* He can pretend that he loved her and, while he was banging her, probably had the blonde in his mind all the time. A "chance to do what", Juice? To fuck one more time? To sit around and listen while you talk about Nicole? A chance to be your concubine while your ex-wife, Nicole, is fucking out of both draw-legs?

God brought Paula to O.J. How timely. God waits until a blonde white woman fucks him out of his money, house and kids and then decides to bring him another woman (probably also white.) So because he is sick, he blames it on God. No, Juice, God didn't bring you shit: God is the one who made it possible for you and Nicole to split up. God saw you headed down the path of Obsession. No Juice -- the *Devil* made you do it -- in more ways than one!!!!

If anything, Juice, God saw you making an ass out of yourself. If a white bitch came along that you got to like, it was you, Juice, not God, who enabled you to latch onto her. But you were using her Juice; you knew Nicole didn't want you back and you needed to show the public that you were, after all, a mature man who could get on with his life. Bullshit. You were and continue to be an obsessed fanatic who loves white women more than you love yourself.

And now, you're paying for it. Then, the henpecked Hall of Famer decides to turn philosophical:

> I think of my life and feel I've done most of the right things. So why do I end up like this? I can't go on. No matter what the outcome, people will look and point. I can't tgake that. I can't subject my children to that. This way, they can move on and go on with their lives.
>
> Please, if I've done anything worthwhile in my life. Let my kids live in peace from you, the press.

Juice subjected his children to the media from the time they were babies. Front page of one edition of Ebony, taking them to games and preening and posing with them at games. He wanted the media to know that he had children. Now, he expects that same media to show him mercy after he has butchered the mother of two of those children? This is nothing more than an attempt, by Juice, to take the attention off of what he did and to make it appear as if he has compassion for what his children will think. *Maybe if you hadn't damn near cut of the head of the mother of your two youngest kids you might have a case.* But you DON'T, muthafucka, so forget it, okay?

Afrocentric scholar LaRue Nedd writes that, "if you do the right thing, you get the right results every time." You simply cannot do the right thing and get wrong results. Therefore, how in the hell can Juice talk of doing "most of the right things" and now we see him behind bars, pretending to be gypped, having committed murder, having married out of his race and basically having turned his back on the black community all of his life?

The begging and pleading reminds me of how Cosell dogged him in his book, *Like It Is,* and told how Juice was begging for forgiveness. Now if he will beg an ugly Jew like Cosell for forgiveness, can you imagine what Nicole must have had to sit around and listen to? Can you imagine the "degradation ceremony" that Juice put himself through to win back his number one white ho'?

Now, he's concerned about his kids. He wasn't concerned when he was stalking their mama. He wasn't concerned when he was kicking her all up in her ass and threatening to kill her. He wasn't concerned when he was sticking that knife in her ass. But now he cares about his kids. But it was his kids, asleep upstairs in Nicole's home, that led me to believe that Juice killed her. There was no burglary, no jewelry missing and no kids taken and held for ransom. There was no robbery of Goldman and that rich bastard had to at least have some major credit cards on him. No. Just two dead white folks sprawled out on the sidewalk.

Juice did that shit and he knows it. He can play deaf, dumb and blind for all I care. And guess what? I think that Al Cowlings helped him do the shit. He had to have help because while he was kicking Nicole's ass or slicing her up, Goldman could have ran. They say Goldman put up a fight. That means that Nicole could have run. Juice killed both of them as they stood there fighting him. He was mad because she was defending Goldman and Goldman was probably talking shit to impress her and let her know he wasn't scared of this "nigger."

So Juice fucked 'em both up. For good. And so he winds down the letter which he wants you believe is his last word on this planet:

> I've had a good life. I'm proud of how I lived. My mama taught me to do unto others. I treated people the way I wanted to be treated. I've always tried to be up and helpful, so why is this happening?

Just the fact that he's "proud" of how he's lived proves he's an Uncle Tom. He obviously has no regrets. He's happy. He's licked boots and carried water all his life, degraded himself in movies and now he's cut his wife's throat and the throat of a man he perceived to be her lover, and all of a sudden he talks about how happy he has been in life. Juice: don't make me barf.

Then, he wants to bring tomming ass mama into it. If he cared about her, he would have considered how she would feel when he started bringing those white girls by the house. Maybe she liked it, but I don't know very many black mothers who approve of that kind of shit. But take note of the tack that Juice begins to take in his well-written, concise, clearly-thought out letter that was read to millions of people by yet another of his white buddies, Robert Kardashian.

With "philosophy" out of the way, he now digresses back to his version of "sounding insane." First of all, if he were out of it, how would he even be able to reflect on his life? If his mother taught him to "do unto others," then he is admitting he killed Nicole: she fucked him, and he fucked her; she cut him off and he literally tried to cut off some of her shit. He then asks, "why is this happening?" I'll tell ya why it's happening, O.J.

It's happening because you are a pimple on the asshole of humanity. It's happening because you weren't raised right, O.J. Your mama was black and so was your first love and first wife, Marguerite. But that wasn't good enough for you was it, nigga? Naw, you had to become famous and decide that you would divorce Marguerite and then move on to the white bitches.

Well buddy, you got your fuckin' wish. And all the dick suckin' and pussy lickin' in the world can't bail you out, can it? All the fuckin' in the world can't explain what you did, can it? Because in either case, you're still gonna come out lookin' like a pussy whipped punk. And guess what? That's what you are you bootlickin' sonofabitch!!!!

Here is where he fucks up and shows sanity, reflection and compassion:

I'm sorry for the Goldman family. I know how much it hurts.

How could you know "how much it hurts?" How much what hurts, Juice? How much those knife wounds in their son's body hurts? How much the slashes on Nicole's throat hurt, knowing that it was Goldman's presence which led to the multiple deaths that you, Juice, are responsible for?

This single sentence, at least in my view, indicts O.J. for the murder of Nicole Brown-Simpson. If he didn't do it, then why would he apologize to the family. Does he know who DID do it if he did not? He is obviously apologizing for himself. He did it! He knows he did it, and that is why he got in that Bronco and split with his buddy, Al Cowlings! In order to establish insanity, you have to have evidence. The letter was supposedly O.J.'s ticket out of the gas chamber: but his single sentence, which obviously got past Cowlings and the white boys involved, *blows everything!*

At the time of the writing of this note could have issued an apology to the millions of black people he's disappointed over theyears as he turned his back on them, refused to help black children, refused to build a single black school and generally worked to become as acceptable to white folks as he could. His apology to the white man Goldman and his family, especially the father who hated his guts, shows that what I allege is true. He would rather issue an apology to a woman who didn't want him, her family which despises him and will never accept his apology, than to apologize to the race that backed and supported him.

Then, he moves to make more "sane and rational" statements regarding his relationship with the woman he killed. Check it out:

> Nicole and I had a good life together. All this press talk about a rocky relationship was no more than what every long-term relationship experiences. All her friends will confirm that I have been totally loving and understanding of what she's been through.

How could all of "her friends' confirm total love and understanding when Juice didn't display any? Total understanding begins with respecting the woman's wishes that she don't want to see your black ass no mo'!! Nigga, wake up! Secondly, how does he know that they can confirm anything -- he's been "temporarily insane," remember? How can he talk of people confirming what he felt unless he could explain how and what he felt to them. And if he was able to do that, all he has done in this paragraph is establish a rationale for obsession and stalking: while Nicole is out on the town dating and probably assuming that O.J. and Paula are doing the same, this nigga is sitting around with Nicole's friends talking about "total love and understanding."

How gypped can one muthafucka be??? His obsession is made most clear as he attempts to assume the role of the "unwitting victim" in this next section:

> At times I have felt like a battered husband or boyfriend but I loved her, make that clear to everyone. And I would take whatever it took to make it work.

> Don't feel sorry for me. I've had a great life, great friends. Please think of the real O.J. and not this lost person.

Oh, so now there's two of you sick muthafuckas, right? The "real O.J." and the misguided asshole who wrote that letter are one and the same. The only difference is now, for perhaps the first time, O.J. sees himself the way the white man saw him: as a misguided lost Uncle Tom worthy of exploitation. Look at what the Zucker brothers did to him in those insulting "Naked Gun" movies (analyzed elsewhere in this book). And O.J. accepted it. Crying on the telephone and begging Howard Cosell, of all people, for forgiveness. Giving out Uncle Tom advice to young people and now all of a sudden, he sees his life for what it is: a vacation in the fuckin' "land of the lost"!!!

Nicole's friends probably knew that she was wild and that she physically attacked O.J. The cops probably knew as well. But as with battered women, there comes a time when you make the batterings public. You don't wait until you strike her and then try to explain to the cops; you document what she did just like she did. Nicole was smart: she had O.J. by his balls (literally and figuratively) and he knew it. That's why she didn't file any restraining orders; she wanted just enough ass whippings to justify leaving O.J. because then, she could prove that he was what the legal system calls "an habitual offender"; furthermore, such abuse, on a regular basis, would justify a larger divorce settlement, prenuptial agreement or not.

Therefore, the paragraph above is an attempt to make him look victimized.

But, like his sexual skills no doubt, the attempt is feeble. Like his ejaculation, his conclusions are premature. He then concludes his attempt at soliciting pity:

> Thanks for making my life special. I hope I helped yours.
>
> Peace and love, O.J.

"Thanks" to who, Juice? And what makes your life any more "special" than any other professional athlete's? And whose life could you have possibly helped other than the people who are worse off and more "tommish" than you which, I hope, are few in number?

If this isn't a pitiful uncle tom, then tell me: what is?

<u>REFERENCES</u>

Advertising Age. "How They're Squiring Juice Through Airports." September 29, 1980.

----------------------. "Hertz Claims World Lead." October 13, 1980.

Blackwell, James E. **The Black Community: Diversity and Unity.** New York: Harper and Row. 1985.

Block, Joseph. "O.J. Simpson." **Unique.** Vol. 1. No. 4. 1976.

Blosser, John. "Days Before Murder, O.J. Rents Sleazy Porno Flick Showing a Blonde Attacked at Knifepoint." **The National Enquirer.** July 5, 1994.

Clark, Maxine et. al. "Dating Patterns of Black Students on White Southern Campuses." **Journal of Multicultural Counseling and Development.** Vol. 14. No. 2. April 1986.

Cox. Oliver C. **Caste, Class and Race: A Study in Social Dynamics.** New York: Doubleday and Company. 1948.

Daly, Martin and Margo Wilson. "Killing the Competition: Female/female and male/male homicide. **Human Nature**. Vol. 1. 1990.

Davidson, Harry X. "Beauty and the Beast: O.J., Black Men and White Women." **The Final Call**. July 20, 1994.

Downey, Maureen. "Many Black Women Resent 'Their' Men Marrying Whites." **The Korea Herald**. February 2, 1993.

Muhammad, Richard. "Farrakhan Blasts Media Bias, Exploitation of O.J. Simpson." **The Final Call.** July 20, 1994.

Mullen, Paul E. "The Crime of Passion and the Changing Cultural Construction of Jealousy." **Criminal Behavior and Mental Health.** Vol. 3. No. 1. 1993.

Murstein, Bernard, et. al. "Physical Attractiveness and Exchange Theory in Interracial Dating." **Journal of Social Psychology**. Vol. 129. No. 3. June 1989.

Nelson, Jim. "Nicole -- the Model Wife." **The National Enquirer.** July 5, 1994.

Oliver, JoAnn. "With Malice Aforethought: Dahmer's Control of the Judicial Process." **The Milwaukee Courier.** February 22, 1992.

Omaha World Herald. "'The Fall of an American Hero': O.J. Arrested at Home After Dramatic Chase." June 18, 1994.

--------------------------------. "O.J. Pleads Innocent, Doesn't Request Bail." June 21, 1994.

--------------------------------. "Simpson, Cowlings School Pals." June 18, 1994.

--------------------------------. "Police: Oiler Took His Life After Mishap." December 14, 1993.

--------------------------------. "Incapacity Defense is Foreseen: Prosecutor Says Simpson Might Use Mental State as Excuse." June 20, 1994.

----------------------------. "Even L.A. Finds O.J. Script Unimaginable." June 20, 1994.

----------------------------. "Simpson Enters Not Guilty Plea." June 20, 1994.

----------------------------. "O.J.'s Case: New Twists, A Mystery." July 3, 1994.

----------------------------. "Simpson's Child Reported in Coma." September 20, 1979.

----------------------------. "Clinton Calls Simpson Case a Terrible Tragedy." June 20, 1994.

----------------------------. "First Battle At Hearing: O.J.'s Hair: Number of Strands for Tests at Issue." June 30, 1994.

----------------------------. "Study Says Minority Students Mix More Than Whites." April 4, 1994.

----------------------------. "Two Proms Mark Split Over Race in Alabama." April 24, 1994.

----------------------------. "Interracial Marriage: Last Bastion of Legal Racism Fell in '67, But Some Still Object." June 14, 1992.

----------------------------. "Simpson Is Charged in Slayings: Weapon, Ski Mask Reportedly Found." June 17, 1994.

----------------------------. "Suicide Watch is Under Way at L.A. Jail." June 19, 1994.

----------------------------. "LAPD's Bad Call May Be Understandable." June 19, 1994.

----------------------------. "O.J. Shook Hands, Then Surrendered." June 19, 1994.

----------------------------. "Simpson's Actions, Words Offer Clues." June 19, 1994.

Paddock, Richard C. and Jenifer Warren. "Simpson Survived Rough Start." **The Omaha World Herald**. June 19, 1994.

Parker, Linda Bates. "'My Dad is Black, My Mom is White'." **The Black Collegian.** September/October 1992.

Poussaint, Alvin F. "The Black Male-White Female: An Update." **Ebony.** August 1983.

Rich, Melissa K. and Thomas F. Cash. "The American Image of Beauty: Media Representations of hair Color for Four Decades." **Sex Roles.** Vol. 29. Nos. 1-2. July 1993.

South, Scott J. "The Racial Patterning of Rape." **Social Forces.** Vol. 69. No. 1. September 1990.

Star, The. "Playboy O.J. Even Stole Best Buddy's Girlfriend." July 5, 1994.

-------------. "The Last Run." July 5, 1994.

Stelly, Matthew C. "The Process of 'Samsonization': A Socio-Political Theory." **The Omaha Star.** December 22, 1983.

------------------------. "The Situation May Be Insane, But Dahmer Ain't!!!" **The Milwaukee Courier**, August 3, 1991.

------------------------. "Dahmer II: More Notes on 'The Brew City Butcher' **The Milwaukee Courier.** August 10, 1991.

------------------------. "Dahmer III: More Notes on Brew City's 'Bone Ranger'" **The Milwaukee Courier,** August 17, 1991.

------------------------. "The Dahmer Trial, the Families and Lessons Learned: Critique and Commentary." **The Milwaukee Courier.** February 22, 1992.

-----------------------. "Entire City Shocked By Murders." **The Racine Courier.** July 27, 1991.

-----------------------. "Police, Residents Shocked By Murder Mutilations." **The Milwaukee Star.** Vol. XXVIII. No. 30. July 25, 1991.

----------------------. "Noise in New Kemet: Nuisance Law and Loud Music in the Inner City." **The Milwaukee Courier.** July 6, 1991.

----------------------. "A Tribute to Glenda Cleveland: Honored Citizen Teaches Valuable 'Racial Lessons' to Milwaukee." **The Milwaukee Courier.** September 14, 1991.

----------------------. "Incarceration VI: 'Fear of a Black Planet' or Fear of 'Black Planning'?" **The Milwaukee Courier.** November 10, 1990.

------------------------. "An Institute Would Benefit Everyone--Artison and Arreola: Models of Integrity for Racist Milwaukee." **The Milwaukee Courier.** September 14, 1991.

Stewart, Sally Ann. "Neither Side 'Gives Inch' on Simpson." **USA Today.** June 29, 1994.

------------------------. "'War Is On' In Simpson Murder Case." **USA Today**. June 29, 1994.

Tinney, Steve. "DA's Key Witness Living in Fear as She Tells: I Saw O.J. Flee Scene." **The Star.** July 5, 1994.

Todd, Judith et. al. "Attitudes Toward Interracial Dating: Effects of Age, Sex and Race." **Journal of Multicultural Counseling and Development**. Vol. 20. No. 4. October 1992.

Tucker, Dorothy. "Guess Who's Coming to Dinner Now?" **Essence.** April 1987.

Turner, Renee D. "Interracial Couples in the South." **Ebony**. June 1990.

White, Garland et. al. "The Impact of Professional Football Games Upon Violent Assaults on Women ." **Violence and Victims.** Vol. 7. No. 2. Summer 1992.

Wiley, Ralph. **What Black People Should Do Now: Dispatches from the Near Vanguard.** New York: Ballantine Books. 1993.

Willhelm, Sidney and Gideon Sjoberg. "The Social Characteristics of Entertainers." **Social Forces.** Vol. 37. No. 1. October 1958.

Williams, Celeste. "Quiet Life Shoved Aside After a Call of Concern." **Milwaukee Journal.** August 4, 1991.

----------------------. "'They're Real Human Beings': Comic Book on Dahmer Sparks Protest." **The Milwaukee Journal.** June 14, 1992.

Williams, Joe III. "No Mix Dating Allowed." **The Los Angeles Sentinel.** April 7, 1994.

Wilson, Margo and Martin Daly. "'Til Death Do Us Part." in Jill Radford and Diana E.H. Russell (eds.) **Femicide: The Politics of Woman Killing.** Boston: Twayne Publishers. 1992.

--. "Who Kills Whom In Spouse Killings? On the Exceptional Sex Ratio of Spousal Homicides in the United States." **Criminology.** Vol. 30. No. 2. May 1992.

Wilson, Thomas C. "The Asymmetry of Racial Distance Between Blacks and Whites." **Sociology and Social Research.** Vol. 70. No. 2. January 1986.

Wright, Richard. **Native Son**. New York: Harper and Row. 1940.

----------------------. "How 'Bigger' Was Born." in Abraham Chapman (ed.) **Black Voices.** New York: New American Library. 1968.

Omarosa Manigault-Newman

During the December 13, 2017 telecast of "CNN Newsroom with Brooke Baldwin," the news came heavy and hard about the "drama" around Omarosa's "resignation" from the White House. It didn't sound like a resignation to me.

This is the same bitch I saw on "The Apprentice" and when I saw her for the first time I said to myself, "she's sucking Trump's dick." Later on, after Trump had won the presidency she was on television and said something to the effect, "Every critic, every detractor, will have to bow down to President Trump. Everyone who ever doubted Donald, whoever disagreed, whoever challenged him. It is the ultimate revenge to become the most powerful man in the universe."

There is no doubt that this woman has "game." She can seduce any man by appealing to his ego, which is probably how she trapped Michael Clark Duncan, that huge Uncle Tom who appeared in such degrading movies as "The Green Mile" and then played the Kingpin in the Ben Affleck flop, "Daredevil." After he croaked she has apparently latched on to some other hapless coon, John Allen Newman who is, get this: a pastor from west Florida. One pimp marries another.

She had her wedding at the Trump Hotel and then had the nerve to bring her wedding entourage to the White House for photos. More on that debacle later.

General John Kelly was brought into the White House to screen Trump's visitors. Even cabinet members had to go through Kelly and when I heard that I immediately knew that Omarosa's days were numbered. And sure enough, Kelly – on the record for not liking black women – made it clear that she was persona non grata and asked what she actually did to earn her $180,000 a year salary. More on this second situation in a minute.

According to April Ryan of Urban American Radio Network, General Kelly said he had "a tense exchange with her twice." When a white man says that it means that she was cussing his white ass out and he became afraid because as quiet as it's kept, white men are far more afraid of black women than they are of black men. They consider black men as sissies because of the degrading things they have been able to get black men to do. They have no respect for them. But that black woman, that sassy fireball – that's what the spineless white boy, regardless of rank or status, is truly afraid of. So he fired her.

According to Ryan, " It was a dual firing resignation." Ryan said that General Kelly grew tired of Omarosa's antics. Since the days of former sissy Rance Priebus, nobody really knew what Omarosa's duties were. She told Priebus at one point that she didn't have to listen to him. In other words there was something going on between her and Trump that gave Omarosa the impression that her shit didn't stink, that she was above the rules and protocols. And recall my initial impression of her: she and Trump had a salacious background while she was on "The Apprentice".

April Ryan, in her report, said that her White House sources told her that Omarosa "stirred things up." She said that Omarosa was a "mood changer." If Trump was doing something, Omarosa would march into his office, show him a newspaper clipping or say something that would set him off. On the streets we call this an "instigator." In black politics we refer to her as a "provocateur." Omarosa's "walk right in" access to Trump and the Oval Office was changed when General Kelly was brought in.

In addition, it was reported that Omarosa "did not have warm feelings with others, and she would cause problems within the White House. She would come and go whenever she wanted to. Now back to the wedding.

Not only did this bodacious bitch get married in the Trump Hotel (I doubt if she got a discount), but then had the gall to bring the bridal part into the White

House to take pictures. She didn't ask permission and violated every protocol and one source said she "trivialized the White House" in doing so. Hell yeah: a bunch of black folks walking around taking pictures like they were at Disneyland, all on the invite of a woman who didn't have a lick of juice.

During the back-and-forth after her resignation she was telling reporters and anyone dumb enough to show interest in her story that she "helped elect Donald Trump" and that she "brought the black vote." That bitch didn't deliver a single vote except for her relatives and that dumb hallelujah huckster who was dumb enough to marry that slag. Black people didn't even like her. In fact, after the Charlottesville incident where Nazis and the Klan waged war on regular citizens, Trump defended the Nazis and Omarosa defended Trump!

Then there was the escapade at the National Association of Black Journalists meeting where she got into it with Ed Gordon, the moderator. She was heckled throughout by black people who knew she wasn't about shit. She embarrassed herself and even in front of all those black people she continued to kiss Trump's ass. Trump didn't show up, but he had a more than willing thrall ready to mock his every word.

And if America saw her as a villain when she was on the apprentice, why assume that black people couldn't see through her as well? We have a bunch of lyin' ass bitches in the 'hood who do the same shit that Omarosa was and continues to try to do.

On MSNBC's "Deadline: White House," Symone Sanders said that "high drama individuals are tolerated, but not her." Of course not. She's black. Despite her belief that she is some kind of "exception," nothing could be further from the truth.

With that having been said, let's dig a little deeper and get another look at one more Trump hire that got into a position and immediately began to think that they were not only above the law, but in Omarosa's case, could do what they wanted to do because she was "Friends" with Trump (read: concubine).

According to reports, after being told she was canned, Omarosa tried to go to Ivanka Trump (Donald's daughter) and ask her if she could keep her job. Ivanka must have told her to fuck off because then Omarosa tried to go straight to Trump, through the President's quarters. Alarms went off and from there she was escorted off the premises and had her security access revoked. The key words here are "escorted off the premises." She claims that she will continue to be paid through January, but if her security clearance is revoked, that means that she's being paid with taxpayers dollars for doing absolutely nothing.

Meanwhile, Sarah Huckabee Sanders, the lying bitch who has the unenviable task of defending Trump's antics, said she didn't know how many African Americans are in White House, but was quick to add that, "We have a truly diverse team, we always want to continue to grow the diversity. She also claimed, "I don't have a number directly in front of me, [but we have] ... a diverse team at WH and in press office. We strive to grow to be more diverse ..." Such bullshit and it's not even convincing bullshit.

According to MSNBC, the 22 highest paid people at the White House are white and Omarosa is the only black woman on the list.

Now she's going around claiming that she has "a story to tell." She's talking about what she heard and saw at the White House and how much of it disturbed her and her alleged concerns for "my people" and "my community." This bitch doesn't consider herself a member of the black community, in the same way that Vanessa Williams turned her back and was dating white boys. But when that bitch did that Penthouse layout, butt naked, and white folks stripped her of her Miss America title, that cute green-eyed, yellow bitch came running back to black people.

Omarosa is either shopping a book deal, a reality TV show or some kind of movie. She's just as egocentric as Trump, but as a black woman she's going to have to take another road. She's pretty enough to go into movies, but her attitude is going to alienate her from the decision makers. She probably figures that if she gives them head then the least they can do is allow her into the hallowed halls. She still hasn't learned yet that white men are duplicitous – just like she is.

In the movie "Outlander," these Scottish assholes are supposedly immortal and down through the years they may meet and battle one another to the death. Their motto? "There can be but one." This seems to be the philosophy of white folks in general but in this case, the doctrine of Donald Trump when it comes to black people in high places. If there are going to be any at all they have to be easy to control, willing to jump through hoops and willing to turn their backs on their own people. And even those of this misguided ilk are suspect, which is why, "there can be but one."

Diana Ross

While many will argue that interracial dating and marriage are not signs of "selling out," I have to say that when one of the people is white, it most certainly is. People of color can intermarry and there's no major problem with me. But when that white man and woman tie the knot of matrimony, I hail back to the days when they were tying knots in lynch ropes and placing those ropes around the necks of black men and women. And as Malcolm taught long ago, "Of all our studies, history is best qualified to reward our research.

She may have been born in Detroit, but I don't see her as being OF Detroit. She just always struck me as an opportunistic bitch, Berry Gordy's former concubine, and a talented singer who didn't want to share the stage with the other members of The Supremes.

According to her bio, she was raised in a Baptist church and sang in the choir. But some of the biggest hos I ever bedded were the daughters of ministers or "sang in the choir." The choir was nothing but their cover for the lascivious acts they got away with behind mama and daddy's backs.

I go back to a 1973 Rolling Stone article about Diana titled "Diana Ross Goes From Richies to Rags: 'You Have to, Like, Glide …'" . And I will quote extensively from it and retrospectively analyze what it says. Remember that the article I am about to quote from is 45 years old, and the fact that Ms. Ross changed very little in terms of her uncle tomfoolery proves the true tenacity and trait of a Jemima.

And now, the article, the evidence – and the indictment:

> Diana Ross is going out of her mind. She just threw a glass of champagne in somebody's face, and now it's the bathroom scene in *Lady Sings the Blues*, and she's running amuck with a razor. Billy Dee Williams won't give her back her works and she's raving for a fix – snarling like a rabid bitch, teeth and nails and then she gets a cut-throat razor and goes for the throat and she means it. When they got through somebody asked Billy Dee if he thought Diana Ross could act. (Thomas, 1973)

That was not acting. I always saw Diana as some ghetto star, a street corner slut that Berry Gordy immediately spotted and decided to put on the corner. She comes across like somebody who knew she had talent, but also was always willing to do whatever it took to get it, and WITH whomever it took to get it. She was raised in a black community in Detroit, got exposed to Berry Gordy and Motown, and from there started meeting powerful white men – most of whom she probably screwed. At any rate, she saw that she fit the model of white man's version of beauty: boney, no tits, flat ass and eyes bulging out of her head. Not quite the standards that bruthas envision when they're thinking up their concept of "thickness."

But she sells an entirely different image to the white media and to those who want to see her as some kind of "rags to riches" story. For instance, the Rolling Stone reporter wrote the following:

> Here was this little slinky, not long out of the Supremes; and it's common knowledge the **Supremes were a consummate corporate invention, with Diana Ross in her ravishing wigs and dazzling shimmer and gloss, working the most amazing pair of livid red lips in America over a faceful of blinding white teeth,** animating and

> insinuating her 103 pounds of lean sheen – she's exquisite, polished till she shines. But the girl never acted in her life except for a couple of dumb skits on Johnny Carson, **and here she is with the audacity to impersonate the most beloved jazz martyr of all time**. There were a lot of people outraged. Diana got a lot of spiteful letters, **a lot of them from righteous old black jazz veterans.** (Thomas, 1973 1- emphasis added)

Why didn't those "righteous old black jazz veterans" inform Ross and the others that Billie Holiday was a dyke? Why didn't they do more than just mention the drug addiction, and where does Billy Dee's role fit in. Holiday, like Ma Rainey, Alberta Hunter, Ethel Waters and even Bessie Smith. They might have messed around with men but that was a front: these sistahs were dykes pure and simple. And so was Billie Holiday.

Furthermore, the article lists the Supremes as a "consummate corporate invention," which they were. They were shined up and taught manners. They paraded into white clubs and so on and with that Motown sound, won over millions of white listeners. Berry Gordy taught them how to be Jemimas of the highest order. But even after Diana left the Supremes, mostly because of ego, she continued to tom and kiss ass and that's how she landed that movie role that is the subject of this 1973 article.

Continuing:

> And tight up against her, here's Billy Dee Williams, coming off a big break in *Brian's Song* on TV, a hot new black leading man with ten or twelve years in the theater under his belt – a seasoned actor – so he had his doubts about her, too. And then early on in the shooting they come to the bathroom scene and Diana Ross throws this fit and Billy Dee had to fight for his life. I don't know, says Billy Dee, I don't know if she can play Billie Holiday – she *is* Billie Holiday. And Williams has got scars to prove it.(Thomas, 1973)

That "big break" in Brian's song showed the world that Williams could also be a tom. After all, he was playing the role of Gale Sayers, a bootlicker from Omaha, Nebraska who, like other Omaha athletes who turned professional (Bob Boozer, Bob Gibson, Ron Boone, Michael McGee) turned their backs on black people and never looked back. Sayers remained a tom long after his football days and although injury cut his career short, he wrote a book that showed how subservient he was in life. The title of his book was I Am Third. What he meant is that god was first, his friends and family are second, and he comes in third. The perfect formula for an uncle tom – and the subject of a movie to influence (one-way) integration.

I remember when it was aired. They showed this peckerwood Brian Piccolo playing running back and Sayers beat him out. But they became friends, and I am talking about the white man's version of interracial friendship. That means that they feel free to call you "nigger." And that's just what Piccolo did. And when he died from cancer, Sayers was right there kissing his ass and giving that speech that will go down in history. Mike Puma of ESPN documented the situation as Sayers, who had won the rushing title, appeared for his award at a ceremony in New York. Here is what that uncle tom said:

> "He has the heart of a giant and that rare form of courage that allows him
> to kid himself and his opponent -- cancer," Sayers told the audience. "He
> has the mental attitude that **makes me proud to have a friend who
> spells out the word 'courage' 24 hours a day of his life**. . . . I love
> Brian Piccolo, and I'd like all of you to love him, too. **Tonight, when
> you hit your knees, please ask God to love him."** (Puma, 1971 –
> emphasis added)

The movie that was made was called "Brian's Song." A third rate football player with a movie named after him, featuring a Hall of Fame running back that kisses his ass throughout the same flick. This movie catapulted Billy Dee Williams into the hearts of America, spreading that black-white integration friendship bullshit. And Billy Dee landed many a role after that, including the one of Lando Calrissian in "Star Wars."

I only add this information to show you how one tommish act can began another. Williams was a proven tom and Diana was as well. Put them together to earmark an important point and personality in black music history and you can distort that history will just enough bullshit to make that movie a hit. And there was the pimp to guide the Jemima "prostitute":

> Berry Gordy was there. It's his picture, he put in close to four million
> dollars of Motown money, **and Diana Ross is his most treasured
> possession,** so he stayed close to the production. **And when Billy Dee
> said that, Berry dug it right away.** You've seen the ads by now, just
> the slim bejewelled wrist clutching an old RKO mike, a handcuff
> dangling like a manacle, and in classy bold type on top it says: DIANA
> ROSS **IS** BILLIE HOLIDAY. (Thomas, 1973 – emphasis added)

Two uncle toms, the first one who is Berry Gordy claiming that Diana was his "possession" (pimp mentality) and the other one falling for the promotion of that pimp, teamed up on someone who was more than happy and willing to prostitute herself for fame, and the 1972 movie was a runaway hit. But it did a disservice to Billie Holiday despite the sound track. Adding Richard Pryor as piano man was a good public relations move, but totally irrelevant to the real life of Holiday or Bobby Tucker, who was the real "piano man." He wasn't beaten to death by some thugs – he died of a heart attack in 2008 – some 36 years after the movie hit the screens.

> Ralph Gleason goes along with that, and John Hammond, and a lot of those other respected old hepcats who should know, because they were there. **They saw Billie Holiday come painfully apart, stitch by stitch, and along the way, because she couldn't help it, she sang jazz better than anybody had ever heard before.** She broke all the rules – changed the whole idea of the singer in the band to where she was no longer just another sideman stuck back behind the clarinet player and taking 16 bars of swift vocal. **She became the star of the show. Everybody from Ella Fitzgerald on down has been trying to catch up with her ever since.** (Thomas, 1973 – emphasis added)

Respected old "hepcats"? This writer is a revisionist. These white boys sat back and copped dope for Billie to continue getting high. And when she was high she was at her best. The white boys knew what she was up to and kept hit hidden. That's what these "hep cats" did to her. She broke all the rules of right, and did so because she was a lesbian and an addict. Diana only played the dope user part of Holiday's life. And that part about Ella Fitzgerald trying to catch up: they caught up, alright. You see what the other women were about in their private lives. I can't say the same thing about Ella, but her third husband was a white man named Thor Larsen.

So much for the Jemima influence and the complicity of the uncle toms who inspire and motivate them.

> Billie Holiday sang with the best bands there were, Teddy Wilson and Benny Goodman and Count Basie, all of them, and she was the first to sing as zingingly as they played. She brought a high radiance and sophistication into those steamy little Harlem cellars and took it all downtown to the plushest nitespots and finally into the sacred hush of Carnegie Hall. She hid nothing. **All her devotees knew she was banged out on stuff up there, they knew where she went when she left the bandstand in between numbers and came back with a faraway gleam in her eyes and made every song she sang into a stylized personal confession of hurt pride and carnal knowledge**. For those that knew and adored her, she remains the immaculate and tragic aristocrat of jazz, the saddest story of them all. (Thomas, 1973 – emphasis added)

What did I tell you. The article refers to them as "devotees" but the fact is they knew she was going backstage for a "hit." She was fucked up by the time she got on stage, high as a kite. And this is the point that Diana drove home because I believe that boney bitch was a junkie herself at one time.

The rest of the article is the writer showing off his command of flowery language and descriptive uses of the Diana Ross situation. I left out the bullshit to get to the point that establishes the Jemima tradition. For instance, where it is written that,

> **… Diana Ross' achievement is not so much in bringing Billie Holiday back from the dead for a couple of hours in the dark; she has sought and found a Billie Holiday who never lived** – beyond all the blues. "I believe that if we had stuck straight to what we had in the book, we would've had a documentary about a lady that was just one tragedy after another. **I read between the lines and I tried to find that other side of Billie Holiday that wasn't in the book, that's not on the back of album covers.** I tried to find the person that Billie Holiday was at home, that very few people knew about." (Thomas, 1973)

The article says that Diana "sought and found a Billie Holiday who never lived …" Then it wasn't about Billie Holiday! Diana couldn't cut it and therefore the producers, writers and directors said, "Fuck it," let's just make a movie and tell people that it's "sort of" like the life of Billie Holiday. They'll buy it." And buy it they did. Peckerwoods, working with uncle toms, butchered what Billie Holiday was about and marched out this boney, bug-eyed prostitute who would do anything for fame and glory. That's why they omitted the lesbian part – had they included that the gay community, quiet as it was back then, would have nevertheless been up in arms. Don't forget a large number of those Jewish Hollywood movie moguls are gay.

The fluff piece in Rolling Stone claims,

> **But Berry Gordy believes in making people happy**. Not just because he's moved zillions of Motown 45s that way, but because he's a happy man, and he truly believes as an article of faith that what the world needs now is love – it's his *philosophy*. That's why he got Michel Legrand to write a heartstruck love theme for the picture. (Thomas, 1973) (Thomas, 1973)

Making people happy? He believes in making money, and he peddles just as many songs about grief and bitterness as he did about so-called happiness. And a lot of those pity party, woe-is-me jams were crooned by none other than Diana. For instance "Love Child," "I'm Living in Shame," "Last Time I Saw Him," "Good

Morning Heartache," "Reach Out and Touch," "Touch Me in the Morning" – do these sound like "happy songs" to you? Like Aretha, Gladys Knight and a slew of black female singers, they sung about depression and grief. They belted out lyrics written by men and in the process, they degraded themselves. And black people ate it up.

The Supremes were good but Diana was the star. According to the article and Berry Gordy,

> **The girls had been singing a little bit here and there, and on the block they met Smokey Robinson, and it was he that first introduced them to Berry.** The Primettes they were called, because back then about 1963 there was a brief period when brother and sister groups were very popular, and Motown had a new act called the Primes at the time. **The Primes changed their name to the Temptations, and the Primettes were left a little in the lurch, so they became the Supremes**. More or less on the spur of the moment, in 1964, the girls had "Where Did Our Love Go" and it was a smash. **"We did have a little school. For choreography. And we had a lady who taught the girls how to talk and act and sit nicely. . . ."** (Thomas, 1973 – emphasis added)

You see how it works. Smokey just so happens to "meet" these girls "on the block." On the "ho stroll" would be more like it. Smokey was probably out there hounding for pussy behind Claudine's back and came across these three cuties who told them they wanted to be stars. He had green eyes and light skin and of course he probably cut a deal. But the main thing is that he introduced them to a man with a pimp mentality, a man who took them under his wing, gave them an "identity" and had a woman teach them how to kiss ass and act as white as possible. They call it etiquette classes.

Check out the following:

> You can picture it, some stern old dowager in an enormous hat and too many bracelets putting these foxy little starlets through their paces – Diana is walking around the room with a book on her head. She slips both legs demurely to one side as she sits for that kind of question-mark symmetry of posture. "How many times must I tell you, when a lady mounts a grand piano, she does not climb, Miss Ross. She *glides*!" Whatever it was, the Motown charm school took the kinks out, and the Supremes came out just right, three little kittens with a lot of droll feline moves and long sharp nails, svelte, slinky and a little bit naughty, singing stuff like *Are you just a breathtaking first night soul-shaking one night love-making next day heart-breaking guy* . . . (Thomas, 1973 – emphasis original)

Charm school. Transforming street girls into "ladies." But Diana had game and she saw right away that if she gave away enough ass and batted those lovely eyes at the right person, she could get whatever she wanted. How do you think they went from "The Supremes" to "Diana Ross and the Supremes"?

The Temptations were producing hits and so was Stevie Wonder. But the Jemima had her sets sight on being *numero uno*,

> **… because right from the start Diana was very quick to catch on and she learned fast.** She'd sit there and watch what all the other acts did, some particular two-step reverse kick-and-swivel grandstand maneuver the Temptations might have, the way Stevie Wonder kind of half swallowed a key rhyme, **any little winning trick at all–then she'd get up there in front and steal their thunder.** Pretty soon she was getting down in her silver fishnets and going "A little bit softer now . . . a little bit louder now . . ." "She stole everybody's act," says Berry. **"When they came on, they looked ridiculous. They had to change their act every day. They all hated her."** (Thomas, 1973 – emphasis added)

She was a divider, a selfish egotist and an opportunist from the get-go. You see what Gordy just said about her: she was stealing from other groups and incorporating it into her own "style." In doing so that put the pressure on the other acts to revamp their own presentations. This is what Jemimas do: they disrupt in order to gain attention for themselves. That is what the women named in this book, from Candace Owens, Stacey Dash and Sheryl Underwood to Condoleezza Rice, Whoopi Goldberg and Omarosa Manigault do – they curry favor with men of power, usually men of another race, turn their backs on their own people, and then head out on their own hoping for individual glorification.

In the case of Motown and Diana's activities, "They came to BG and complained bitterly, and he straightened her out. But by then the Supremes had five hits in a row, and they were moving up in the Revue, right behind Smokey. They never did close the show, though" (Thomas, 1973) Berry didn't straighten anybody out. He was an expert at the bureaucratic style. He pulled her to the side, probably took her to a hotel, laid in bed with her and told her to slow down a little bit because "the hits will be coming." Then he went back and told the complainers that he "straightened her out." With all the backstabbing and sellout behavior that she continues to exhibit even today in 2018, does it seem that this Jemima was ever "straightened out"?

You see, as the racist reference in the article points out, "Berry Gordy and Diana were raised in the same part of **darkest Detroit**; they both remember the Shakers running the block – they were the local cut-and-rape street gang, and their chicks were called the Shakerettes. Billie Holiday was across town, at the Flame

Showbar, and Berry used to go there all the time." (Thomas, 1973 – emphasis added). So they were both street wise and transformed it into something that was marketable. Gordy had a pimp mentality and Diana had a prostitute orientation: they were a perfect symbiotic match.

Read carefully the following excerpt because the writer's racism shines through and so does the histrionic behavior of Diana Ross:

> When she first quit the Supremes, she got lonely – she used to go and watch them a lot. She'd always been the one in the middle and she had long ago stepped out front of the other two – there was that sudden switch she pulled one night on a television special called *TCB* with the Supremes and the Temptations, where they just flashed a series of shots of **Diana enraged and unbound**, her Afro humming with untold combustible voltage, each pose **more sultry and menacing** than the last, every one a snapshot of terrifying and **almost deadly Mau Mau beauty**–and then she was revealed in a single soft spot, in a shimmer of pristine silver, singing "Someday/there'll be a place for us." But there was comfort in the Supremes, and some people thought she was taking a chance shedding her cover. She came out with "Ain't No Mountain High Enough." (Thomas, 1973 – emphasis added)

What was just described is the behavior of a paranoid schizophrenic, someone who is a "shape shifter." She's a Jemima and is therefore an expert at flipping her allegiances and moon walking over to the highest bidder. The writer is describing her in such a way that she sounds far more dramatic than she is; she's just someone who doesn't give a damn about anyone but herself. And in the process of chasing that "gold ring" (read; closest white man), she will do what has to be done. I'm surprised she didn't raise up her dress and show her panties to the world!

The article continues:

> She's not so easy to push around any more either. One time in Las Vegas she saw Sinatra's show, and a few bars into "My Way" something was a little off, so Frank just said "OK! Hold it!" and he gave the band a little venom and then he started again from the top. **If Diana doesn't like the way her show is going, she's likely to flare up the same way one of these nights. BG says she can get real bitchy about it.** (Thomas, 1973)

This bitch ain't NEVER been "easy to push around." Any time it took place it was part of a scam, a plan to front like she was "boney and defenseless." Other than that, Diana was the kind of woman who would scratch your eyes out if you pissed her off. That scene with the straight razor that you saw in "Lady Sings the Blues" – that was the REAL Diana! Even the previous excerpt makes the statement that, "If Diana doesn't like the way her show is going, she's likely to flare up the same way one of these nights. BG says she can get real bitchy about it."

This was in 1973 when Diana was 28 – that means that today in 2018 this Jemima has reached the ripe old age of 73:

> Diana's 28 now, **married to a PR man called Bob Silberstein**, the mother of two kids, one 15 months and another, Tracee Joy, born a few weeks ago. It's been a couple of years now since she outgrew the Supremes and became Diana Ross full-time. And now she's a movie star as well, and there are precious few of those left, and none who are as well-bred for the role as Diana. (Thomas, 1973)

So she marries ANOTHER white man, and this time she landed herself a Jew. And a powerful one at that. Here is a snippet on how they "hooked up":

> In the 1970s, **he managed Diana Ross**, the Rolling Stones' Ronnie Wood … Billy Preston and Chaka Khan whom he discovered while managing Rufus. **Silberstein was born into a wealthy family of Jewish garment manufacturers in Elberon, New Jersey** … He graduated from West Virginia University and tried teaching. Silberstein was married to Diana Ross from 1971 to 1977 … They have two biological children together: Tracee Ellis Ross, and Chudney Ross … He also raised Ross' eldest child Rhonda Ross Kendrick, **whose biological father is Motown founder Berry Gordy.** (Wikipedia, 2018 – emphasis added)

Look at the spin this obviously white writer puts on the kind of two-faced bitch Ross is and downplays her "Jemima-ism":

> She is living proof that **stars who really shine are not born, they're professionally made.** After all, down in the ghetto in Detroit with six kids in the family and holes in the walls where the rain came in and roaches everywhere and Dad working two jobs at the garage – **a pretty little fox like Diana could've been a hooker, like Billie Holiday.**"I could've been, that's true. The girls that I did see that were prostitutes were beautiful ladies. They looked good. We kind of knew what they were doing but not really. They were nice people. **It was a profession, you know. It would've been easy for me.** (Thomas, 1973 – emphasis added)

Three points from the previous passage shows that the writer knows that Diana is a prostitute and furthermore that she almost admits it.

First, the claim by the writer that stars are not born but are professionally made. That is bullshit. If you have no talent then there is nothing to "make". Stars have natural talent and professional shylocks like her husband and others (and Berry Gordy) come along and pimp that talent, market it, roll it and control it. All "professionals" do is exploit that which they view as being marketable

Secondly, the writer describes Diana's lousy living conditions and then adds that, "a pretty little fox like Diana could've been a hooker, like Billie Holiday." Can you see how he's made the connection? Using terms like "pretty little fox," the kind of slang that a street playa would use. She had all the makings of a hooker, the location of a hooker and the attitude of a hooker. This leads to my third point.

He quotes Diana as saying, "It was a profession, you know. It would've been easy for me." If she saw all that then she went after it. It is only now, with the benefit of retrospect, that she tries to make it sound that as a poor child with no money, and with men walking by drooling over her, she simply shook her head "no" and looked the other way. Bullshit! She's all but confessed about how good the prostitutes looked and how nice they were. You know they gave her advice, a tip here and a tip there. And since she's a prostitute now that she's famous, you KNOW she must have been one when she was poor. Did she or did she not make a song called "I'm Living in Shame"?

The article continues:

> **Because it's difficult to figure out ways to get out of what the white man calls the ghetto. Either black people end up being the best in sports, or else it's show business.** You know, we all got rhythm. Or some of the girls **make their money to drive around in Cadillacs and have beautiful clothes by being prostitutes, selling their bodies.** I knew a lot of pimps. It's a possibility if I had've got strung out over one of these guys it could've been me. If I had fallen in love. . . ." (Thomas, 1973 – emphasis added)

What she said in that first sentence is all the most reason for her to take her boney ass out on that ho stroll. Getting out of the ghetto is one explanation that uncle toms and Jemimas use to rationalize their selling out. Look back to those lyrics to Lou Rawls' "Dead End Street" that I shared with you earlier. And once again she's focused on the nice cars and clothes that prostitutes have. Diana Ross knows full well what she was and what she still is: a gold-digging Jemima, with some talent, who will do what it takes to live as "white" and away from black people, as possible.

Raven-Symoné: Child Star and Co-Host of "The View"

The March 18, 2015 publication Business and Politics reported a story under the headline, "Actress sparks firestorm defending Michelle Obama-Planet of the

Apes reference on 'The View': 'Some people look like animals'. The article, written by Carmine Sabia, documented the following:

> Actress Raven-Symoné infuriated many African-Americans by defending the Univision host Rodner Figueroa over comments he made **comparing a makeup artists impersonation of Michelle Obama to a cast member from "Planet of The Apes" — comments that got him fired from his job.** Symoné appeared as a guest co-host on ABC's "The View" Monday when she made the controversial remarks. "He said that he voted for her later," the actress who played Olivia on "The Cosby Show" said. "I don't think he was saying it racist." (Sabia, 2015 – emphasis added)

When you read something like this, the only sane response is, "You stupid bitch!" I mean, comparing the beautiful Michelle Obama to an ape is like comparing an apple to a car engine! And if the peckerwood who said it believes that, then what could he possibly think of other black people? And what else could the comment be other than racist?

But it gets worse. Check out the following:

> That's like saying I'm not a racist but I have black friends," liberal co-host Rosie Perez fired back. "Michelle, don't fire me from this right now," Symoné said, joking about the first lady's possible role in Figueroa's firing. **"Some people look like animals**. Is that rude? I look like a bird! **So can I be mad if somebody calls me Toucan Sam?"** (Sabia, 2015 – emphasis added).

This little yellow bitch has always been precocious, since the days when the Cosby show exploited her. What happened was that she "auditioned" and her parents probably played up how "cute" she was. Cosby saw the skin color and the attitude and marched that little girl out there and gave her lines that made her sound like a miniature adult. Now she's grown and the bitch is walking around with multi-colored hair and is as confused as ever. She is a true sellout.

Before her stint on "The View" (she is no longer there), she had this show called "That's So Raven." The show should have been called "Check out them titties" because this bitch was built like a brick shit house. And she played it to the hilt! That show exploited the shapes of both Raven and her white co-host, Chelsea Daniels (played by Anneliese van der Pol) amidst all the hijinks and foolishness that permeated every show. It stayed on for four years, but don't ask me how.

Here's another series of comments made by the young Jemima:

> The former "Cosby Show" actress appeared on Oprah's "Where Are

They Now" and explained how she totally rejects labels. "I'm tired of being labeled," she told Oprah. "I'm an American, I'm not an African-American." Symoné went on to state, "I don't know how far back they [my roots] go … I don't know what country in Africa I'm from, but I do know that my roots are in Louisiana. I'm an American. And that's a colorless person." (Kenney, 2016)

Stacey Dash: "Clueless" Actress & Former Fox News Contributor

In my view Stacey Dash is the most physically attractive woman on this list. Not because she has green eyes or dyed red hair, but because of the symmetry of her face, her hour-glass figure and the way she carries herself. That's from the physical aside. But as the saying teaches us, "all that glitters ain't gold," and Stacey Dash proves this in spades. She is clearly psychologically damaged and her positions on certain social and political issues proves the point.

Let me demonstrate. Like many of the Jemimas featured herein, she began as a Democrat and then flipped to being a Republican. Like many of the Jemimas featured herein, she draws from an alleged traumatic experience and makes sure that it is a part of her public resume. Can you say "pity party"?

> **Dash has spoken openly about past traumas in her personal life.** She has at various times revealed that **she was molested as a child by a family friend,** was **addicted to cocaine in her teens and 20s**, and has a history of **being with physically and emotionally abusive partners** … Dash has attributed her openness with such topics to her desire to be honest with her children, feeling that being honest is the best way to protect them, **and to let them and others know that she is not a victim but a survivor** … She is supportive of the right to keep and bear arms, crediting a gun with saving her life **after being sexually assaulted at gunpoint by an ex-boyfriend, because she was able to retrieve her own weapon, a .22 revolver, and shoot at him, scaring him away**. (Wikipedia, 2018 – emphasis added)

So being a true Jemima, we begin with her views about Black History Month. In January of 2016 she began her attacks through an article by Kendall Fisher which appeared on Entertainment On Line under the headline, "Stacey Dash Doesn't Think Black History Month Should Exist, Wants to take BET Off the Air." Following are her comments and my analysis of them:

> Stacey Dash has her own opinions amid the controversy stemming from the all-white Oscar nominations this year. The Clueless actress sat down with Fox News' Fox & Friends and not only called the outrage over the Oscars "ludicrous," **but she also said African-American-targeted institutions—such as BET, the Image Awards and holidays honoring black history—should no longer exist, calling them an unprogressive "double standard."** (Fisher, 2016 – emphasis added)

What would this bitch know about that which is "progressive" when every woman in Hollywood is at the mercy of "auditions" that are conducted by lecherous white men? When their very profession is based on pretending to be someone else? If she has an opinion on anything "black" it is as an outsider, and what you just read is the opinion of someone who may have dark skin but wh is definitely outside of the race. When she describes herself she does so by placing her ethnicity and nationality BEFORE her racial background. That means that she is ashamed to be considered black. And that shame is evidenced by the comments you just read.

For her to believe that Black Entertainment Television (BET), the Image Awards and holidays are "African-American targeted" is a mistake. These black institutions and symbols are aimed at white advertisers, convincing them that by taking out ads aimed at the black community, you should do so by promoting them on programs that CLAIM to be black. But the fact is that these are not aimed at African-Americans; they are aimed at white people who, in one way or another, have bitten and bought into the black cultural market. Everything that's black ain't black.

And look what she does: she runs to the enemy of the race and degrades what she considers to be black institutions. Who would do that but a traitor, a "Jemima"? And it apparently gets worse:

> She explained, "**We have to make up our minds. Either we want to have segregation or integration.** And if we don't want segregation, then **we need to get rid of channels like BET and the BET Awards and the Image Awards where you're only awarded if you're Black**. If it were the other way around, we would be up in arms. It's a double standard." Later, she added, "**Just like there shouldn't be a Black History Month. You know? We're Americans. Period. That's it.**"
> (Fisher, 2016 – emphasis added)

As I wrote earlier, this bitch doesn't know the difference between segregation and separation. Segregation is what led to the need for things like BET and Black History Month, although both definitely fall short. Segregation is what led to the need for black businesses and black institutional arrangements. White people imposed the ghetto upon black people and we responded by doing for self. Separation was something that was an ideal by groups like the Nation of Islam and the Republic of New Afrika. But black people were so tommish – much like Stacey Dash – that we didn't want to "separate from that good ol' white man." So we settled for a segregated reality because it was the law of the land.

Now, having begged for inclusion and integration, the black community has to look up and deal with this green-eyed, high yellow bitch complaining about what few institutions there are that have the courage to put "black" in their name. While no threat to the white system, they are at least making an attempt at representing a symbol of pride. What does Stacey Dash do in that regard? She joins in with a movie that carries an indicator of what she is: "clueless.' She teams up with a white girl in a flick where she is basically the white girl's tagalong lackey. And then she joins the Fox Network, which hates both women and blacks, and then has the nerve to critique Black History Month?

Even white people have a problem with what she was saying. Check it out:

> The show's host, Steve Doocy, clarified: "Are you saying there shouldn't be a Black History Month because there isn't a white history month?" To which Dash replied, **"Exactly. Exactly."** After the Internet erupted over her commentary, she took to her blog and stuck to her word, promising she is "right" and again reiterating, "There should be no Black History Month." (Fisher, 2016 – emphasis added)

There is a white history month. And a white history year and a white history century. This country re-writes history every day of the year to make it appear as if it is greater than it really is. Just recently even Governor Andrew Cuomo of New York made the statement that "America is not so great." He said what black people already knew (as is usually the case with these white talking heads). Specifically what he meant was described as follows by the *New York Times*:

> Gov. Andrew M. Cuomo mocked President Trump's ubiquitous "Make America Great Again" campaign slogan on Wednesday, quickly drawing the ire of Republicans from New York to the White House for saying that America "was never that great." "We are not going to make America great again. It was never that great," Mr. Cuomo said. "We have not reached greatness. We will reach greatness when every American is fully engaged." Mr. Cuomo made the comment at the end of a 20-minute speech that focused heavily on Mr. Trump. The event was ostensibly a bill-signing ceremony for new penalties for sex trafficking in New York. (Goldmacher, 2018)

So who is closer to being right: some beauty who makes her living acting out lies on screen or the governor of the largest state in the union? Both are liars for the most part, but I'm going to lean with Cuomo's analysis of the situation, especially where it relates to race.

And she's just as anti-female as she is anti-black:

> Of course, her controversial remarks shouldn't come as much of a surprise … A few months later, in April, Dash also told Meredith Vieira **she doesn't believe that a pay gap exists between the sexes.**"I feel like it's an excuse," Dash explained to the audience. "It's the same thing with race, it's an excuse. Stop making excuses." **She continued, "If there are opportunities, seize them and be prepared for them and be the best if that's what it takes. If you have to be extraordinary, then be extraordinary…**If you want to be pissed off about it, then be pissed off about it and **work harder for it**. I don't think us complaining about it because there is a law passed that we get equal pay." (Fisher, 2016 – emphasis added)

How sick can one bitch be? What's she's saying is if the audition (in her profession) calls for you to suck dick, then do it! Cave in to the perverted whims of those Jewish directors, producers and script writers. And in that way you land the part and nobody feels "used." That's the unspoken message and, unfortunately, there are a number of "actresses" who cater to such a sick Sargeant Schultz "I see nuthink!" philosophy.

A similar article appeared on MSN.com with the heading, "Stacey Dash Becomes Her Own Joke at 2016 Oscars" as Chris Rock sarcastically introduced her as "the director of our new minority outreach program." She came out and fed into the sarcastic moment saying, "I cannot wait to help my people out. Happy Black History Month!" The sarcasm was deeper than most people realize: for Dash to refer to blacks as "her people" was an inaccurate statement based on what this Jemima has said about black people in recent years.

A month later, during a February 28, 2016 airing of Entertainment Tonight On Line, Dash began her litany of lunacy for the world to see. Following is the news report with my analyses filtering in and out.

The article, titled, "Stacey Dash Speaks Out on Oscars' Lack of Diversity: 'It's Ludicrous," focuses on comments made regarding the 2016 Academy Awards, began as follows:

> Stacey Dash has a lot to say about the lack of diversity among this year's Oscar nominees.On Wednesday, the *Clueless* actress and Fox News contributor expressed her outrage over the fact that, once again, only white performers made the cut while chatting with Steve Doocy on *Fox & Friends*."I think it's ludicrous," she said. **"Because we have to make up our minds. Either we want segregation or integration."** (ETonline, 2016 – emphasis added)

Ignorant black people are continually put in front of the microphone to spew forth specious and spurious opinions which are then pawned off as fact. In this case, Stacey Dash shows she doesn't understand racial issues even though she is a black woman in a white-dominated society and white-oriented Hollywood culture.

More specifically, you can see where she puts the black condition in the hands of her white master. When she says "Either we want segregation or integration," what she should be saying is that "either we want SEPARATION or integration." Segregation is decided by white folks and imposed on blacks, as is integration. Separation is what WE decide to do. Most Jemimas, like the title of one of Dash's movies, are "clueless" when it comes to political vision and therefore they should keep their mouths shut.

Kanye West: Hip-Hop Artist and Fashion Designer

Something is mentally wrong with this young black fellow. And that is why the Millennials, black and white, gravitate toward him. He marries one of the biggest whores in the world, Kim Kardashian (from a family of Kardashian whores who can always find and uncle tom Black athlete to marry them) and then has a child who he never mentions. He gets out on stage and makes outlandish comments that clearly establish him as a leader of the new wave Millennial uncle toms.

One article documents an example of that uncle tomfoolery:

> West sat down for an interview with Power 105's "The Breakfast Club" in January, **during which he suggested that classism is the new racism**. The rapper also explained to Style.com **that "racism and the focus on racism is a distraction to humanity.** It would be like focusing on the cousin from your mom's side versus the cousin on your dad's side. **We're all cousins. We're all the same race."** (Kenney, 2016 – emphasis added)

The dumber the uncle tom sounds, the more absurd the ideas that he or she promotes, the more space in the newspaper and time on the television and radio he or she will receive. Kanye West is a classic case in point, hence his inclusion on my list of new wave uncle toms.

Whoopi Goldberg: Actress, Comedian & Host on "The View"

Whoopi Goldberg is 62 years old and dresses like a pre-teen hobo fresh off the train from Greenwich Village. No slouchier a Jemima than she,that's for sure! Her real name is Caryn Elaine Johnson and she claims her mother told her to change her name to Whoopi Goldberg so she would be able to get tight with the Jews. Who knows if it's true or not, but the part about her hanging with Jews most certainly is. And Jews are about as white and racist as you can get when it comes to exploitation and making money off of black people (witness the music and film industries).

As a Jemima she has been well compensated, being one of only a few women (another one is Rita Moreno) to win an Oscar, a Grammy, an Emmy and a Tony. And there is another one she would win if it was awarded and that would be "Female Bootlicker of the Decade."

Most of her movies were bullshit except when she played the abused young sistah "Celie" in "The Color Purple," which was written by Alice Walker but directed by a Jew, Stephen Spielberg. By 1992 did you know she was the highest paid actress of that time?

But back to that name thing for a minute. According to one source:

> She has stated that her stage forename ("Whoopi") was taken from a whoopee cushion; "When you're performing on stage, you never really have time to go into the bathroom and close the door. So if you get a little gassy, you've got to let it go. So people used to say to me, 'You're like a whoopee cushion.' And that's where the name came from" … She said in 2011, "My mother did not name me Whoopi, **but Goldberg is my name, it's part of my family, part of my heritage. Just like being black."** (Wikipedia, 2018 – emphasis added)

Really? Not according to another sellout, Henry Louis Gates, Jr., Check out the following:

> Henry Louis Gates Jr., in his book *In Search of Our Roots: How 19 Extraordinary African Americans Reclaimed Their Past*, **found that all of Goldberg's traceable ancestors were African Americans, that she has no known Jewish ancestry, and that none of her ancestors were named Goldberg** … Results of a DNA test, revealed in the 2006 PBS documentary *African American Lives*, traced part of her ancestry to the Papel and Bayote people of modern-day Guinea-Bissau. Her admixture test indicates that she is of **92 per cent sub-Saharan African origin and of 8 per cent European origin** (Wikipedia, 2018 – emphasis added).

And there we have it, one more component of the Aunt Jemima repertoire, that "of denial." Just as the young Butterfly McQueen shouted out in "Gone With the Wind," "Ah don't know nothin' 'bout birthin' no babies!", coons like Goldberg find a way to make an association with whiteness: Stacey Dash is green eyes, Geraldine Alexis is fake green contacts and a white minister, all have a gimmick that links them with white folks. We can add Halle Berry, Venus and Serena Williams, Iman and a host of others to that list.

But this is about Whoopi, and her "Aunt Jemima" moment came during an event held for her at a Friar's Club roast. Following is the text of someone who attended although what happened made national news. I use the following excerpt because you get to see the words of the "tommish" Goldberg.

The article comes from a website called "Is It Funny or Offensive?" The title of the article: "The Roast of Whoopi Goldberg: A Look Back At Ted Danson's Blackface Performance." My analyses will filter in and out.

The article starts off with the sub-heading, "Friar's Club Flop?"

> May 18th, 2017 – Whoopi Goldberg and Ted Danson made a lot of headlines back in the 90s but perhaps none were more hard-hitting as those that followed October 8th, 1993. That Friday night, the two entertainers, who were recent co-stars and lovers, were in attendance at the Friar's Club roast held at the New York Hilton Hotel ballroom. Danson was roasting Goldberg. His makeup was blackface and his jokes included over a dozen uses of the n-word.

A dozen times with Whoopi sitting in the first chair right next to the podium where Danson was clowning up a storm, uttering the word "nigger" in a huge room full of entertainers, celebrities and corporate types. Nobody shouted him down. Nobody said, "Get your racist ass of the stage." The best that Montel Williams (another favorite "coon" of the establishment) could do was take the hand of his white wife and walk out.

Continuing:

> Noted film critic Roger Ebert covered the event, opening his October 10th column with: **"It's a tradition of the celebrity roasts at the Friar's Club that everything goes – that no joke is in such bad taste that it cannot be told. Friday, that tradition may have ended, as a roast for Whoopi Goldberg turned into such a tasteless display that some audience members hid their faces in their hands, and others left."** (emphasis original)

Ebert is right, and remember: he was married to a black woman, so you know he was pissed. Goldberg, the Jemima in question, just sat there. But worse than that, she defended the actions of Danson. Let's move on:

> More than 3,000 people were in attendance and the star-filled dais had over 100 celebrities including Halle Berry, Vanessa Williams, Anita Baker, RuPaul and Mr. T, Michael Spinks, Sugar Ray Leonard, and New York Mayor David Dinkins. Most reporting sets the reception of jokes at "stone faced" or "cringing" with talk show host Montel Williams turning his back and eventually leaving the event.

Look at all the toms and Jemimas who were present. I have no idea what RuPaul thinks he/she is, but whatever it is it's nasty. But Sugar "the coke head" Leonard was present, as was Michael "take the money and run" Spinks, former governor David "bootlicker"Dinkins, Halle "the zebra" Berry, and foxy and sweet Anita Baker (they ain't all bad). The thing is, nobody said a damn thing while Danson was acting a fool at the expense of black people.

And while all this was going on, guess what Aunt Jemimia Whoopberg was up to?

> Goldberg, however, smiled and laughed during Danson's roast and defended him both on the dais and in statements after extreme fallout from the *Cheers* star's decision to cross the line. **"Let's get these words all out in the open. It took a whole lot of courage to come out in blackface in front of 3,000 people. I don't care if you didn't like it. I did," she said at the roast. "If they knew me," Goldberg said the week after the roast, "they would know that Whoopi has never been about political correctness. I built my whole career destigmatizing words like 'nigger.'" (emphasis added)**

Look at those fucked up explanations for her tommishness. It didn't take a whole lot of courage for Danson to come out in blackface, no more than it takes that slouchy bitch to appear on the view five days a week looking like she just got gang raped by Ali Baba and the Forty Thieves! She said she liked it. That goes back to the "self-hate" section of this book and proves, once again, that black celebrities hate being black and only do so because they get paid for it. The only roles that black people get are roles reserved for them (with the exception of Denzel Washington, and he'll do anything for a dollar, just like Samuel L. Jackson).

She has never been about political correctness. I didn't like that term when I first heard it. Call me a nigga and I'm gonna kick your ass and I don't care what the conventions or social protocols of the time dictate. Social correctness? Calling us nigga IS socially correct for most peckerwoods, which is why the word is still being used! She claims she spent her entire career "destigmatizing" words like nigger, which is a damn lie: Her career is filled with nigger-like roles and stereotypes. Want proof?

How about flicks like "Ghost" (1990) where she played a spook (which is what they used to call black people back in the day), "Jumpin' Jack Flash" (1986), where her character admittedly "doesn't fit in" with the bank she works at, "Burglar" (1987) which is self-explanatory, or "Boys on the Side" (1995), playing a lesbian on a cross-country road trip with two white bitches? In most of her movies she just does walk-ons and plays herself. Now that must be for comic relief. If that ain't a Jemima-related job, then I don't know what is. She's never worked to "destigmatize" anything; if she has accomplished anything it is that she has brought utter shame to the locks that she wears, but that's just part of her "po' me, po' me" gimmick. Remember, all Jemimas have a gimmick.

Back to Danson and his being defended for appearing in blackface by the truly backwards Whoopi Golderg:

> Goldberg also defended the routine by sharing that **she had written some of Danson's remarks as a satirical piece** and tried to re-focus the attention to what he said at the beginning of the roast. "**Ted prefaced his remarks by saying to me, 'I love you, I'm proud of you, and I love being with you.' That's all being left out by people.**"

A truly sick bitch. She collaborated with his peckerwood to poke fun at black people. And then she falls for the okey-doke when he says that he loves her, is proud of her and loves being with her. That's the same thing that these white people utter to their pets at home; that's what the dickless corporate cockhound utters to his mistress before handing her a fistful of hundreds. He didn't love her because as you will see later, this bitch don't believe in marriage. And yet everyone she marries is a white man. Sounds a lot like Geraldine Alexis and some of the others, doesn't she?

But "Jemimas of a feather, flock together." Check out who got in on the act: "African-American model Beverly Johnson also defended Danson and the intent behind the roast. **"If you can't see the humor at a place where there's supposed to be over-the-line jokes, then there's something really wrong"** ((emphasis added). Say what?** This is the same bitch who was wining about the white man doing black models wrong when it came to covers of magazines, remember?

And since she wanted to poke her nose in the shit, let's look at what she has to say about race and racism before we move on with Whoopi's bootlicking ass. In an October 2014 internet article the beautiful super model Johnson said,

> "I lived a very sheltered life," she shared. "Of course, I'd been called the n-word riding my bicycle through the wrong neighborhood, but I really wasn't that aware of just the centuries of struggle that my ancestors had."Still, Johnson asserts, **it doesn't offend her when young stars like Raven-Symoné speak about eschewing the label African American,**

saying, "I think it's freedom of speech. I think it's her opinion of herself and who she wants to be." (Sprankles, 2014 – emphasis added)

Johnson was a culturally deprived "negro" and grew up the same way. She learned about her blackness late and how she skipped over the "Black is Beautiful" movement of the '60s I don't know. I do know that she was the first black woman to ever grace the cover of Vogue magazine and that didn't take place until 1974, more than enough time to know what Malcolm X, the Black Panther Party and Martin Luther King, Jr., were fighting for. Some Jemimas mature late; but even now she sides with the likes of Raven-Symone (you'll read about her elsewhere) and that can't be a good sign. That "she's who she wants to be" bullshit is one way that the majority of black people continue to get bamboozled by the white media elite. As Karenga (1967) once wrote, "Individualism means being yourself at the expense of others."

Moreover,

Johnson also empathizes with Raven-Symoné in a way, as she knows firsthand how a seemingly simple statement with no agenda can be blown out of proportion. "I just remember doing this radio show, and they immediately said, 'Well, how does it feel to be the top black model?' And I said, **'Excuse me, I'm really the top model in the nation!'"** she said, laughing. (Sprankles, 2014 – emphasis added)

Another element of "Jemima-ism": the belief that "we're all Americans and by golly we need to pull together." That kind of bullshit is what keeps black people trapped in mythology. And with that "I beez an American" belief system linked to that mythology of Christianity, can there be any doubt as to why black folks are so miffed and mummified in their dealings with each other?

The top model in the nation? That's like saying "I'm the head nigger on the plantation." The answer to both is, who owns the modeling agency, the magazine and the promotional elements? Who pays you to lay back, gap your legs, change your clothes in dressing rooms that are most likely "bugged" by horny white boys, and who are you modeling for? Black women can't afford that bullshit that those white boys have you trying on! Like any other prostitute, she sells herself and her body. And she loves it.

She adds,

"You know, because I was on the cover of *Glamour*, *Vogue*, Italian *Vogue*. And after that, it was this big hoopla. So I understand how the things that you can say can be taken out of context and that she's merely speaking what she feels — **that she wants to be labeled a human being," said Johnson.** (Sprankles, 2014 – emphasis added)

She shouldn't want to be "labeled" at all. If it's up to the white man, the only label you will be wearing is "human being/nigger." He defines things the way he wants them to be. And he gets people like Whoopi Goldberg (and Beverly Johnson, for that matter) to act the way he wants them to act. People like Raven-Symone say and do things assuming that they are "above" other black people. And in Raven's specific case, she's half peckerwood – just like Halle Berry, Barack Obama, Blake Griffin, Stephon Curry, and a host of other "celebrities" who get a break because they are part cracker.

But it's only "half a break" because you're considered "mixed race," and remember what Dr. Welsing said about that term "non-white." It means the absence of whiteness. So these Jemimas may be dancing jigs now, but their time will soon run out when a new nationality (Asians and Middle Eastern women, for example) come into vogue with just enough skin color, their own hair, and a willingness to do anything, and that mulatto will be replaced with the quickness.

Back to the Goldberg-Danson debacle:

> *The New York Times* interviewed Richard Greene, owner of Crown and Glory Hair Salon, for their coverage of the roast to get his take on how Danson and Goldberg's decision was playing at his predominately black, female business. **"A lot of people feel she's just covering up for Ted and not looking at it as an insult to a race of people," he said. "She may say, or think, that comedy has no limits. In reality it does, and what they did exceeded those limits."** (emphasis added)

You can explain it any way you want to. Whoopi Goldberg is a sellout and that night, in particular, made that fact crystal clear.

So acceptable is she by the white establishment that they made her the new co-host of ABC's "The View" in 2007 when Rosie O'Donnell was canned. She learned quickly that even as America's favorite Jemima, there were limits to what she could say. Wikipedia (2018) documents a couple of incidents:

> Goldberg has made controversial comments on the program. Her first appearance included statements taken by some to condone football player Michael Vick's dogfighting … In 2009, she opined that Roman Polanski's rape of a thirteen-year-old in 1977 … was not "rape-rape" … later clarified that she had intended to distinguish between *statutory rape*("unlawful sexual intercourse with a minor") and *forcible rape* … Goldberg was a staunch defender of Bill Cosby from the outset of his rape allegations, asserting he should be considered innocent until proven guilty, and questioning why Cosby had never been arrested or tried for them … After learning that the statute of limitations on these allegations had expired and thus could not be tried, she called for Cosby

to answer the allegations, and began advising women to come forward if
they are raped.

She was wrong in every instance, defending black men who also thought
they were above the law (Vick was a multimillionaire quarterback who couldn't
stop hanging with his 'homies' and doing gangsta shit like dog fighting and got
busted, Cosby drugged and raped those women and thought no one would ever
find out, and "rape is rape"). Her voicing those views also shows that she thinks
she's above the law – the basic belief of one Jemima after another.

The next Jemima is also in love with the media and is a self-made public
speaker.

Diamond and Silk, Conservative Pro-Trump Commentators

You may not have heard of them and if you haven't, you ain't missed much.
With the likes of Paris Denard and other negro conservatives kissing Trump's ass,
these two women may have been lost in the shuffle (no pun intended). But they
are mentioned here because their views qualify them for what can only be referred
to as "the Hall of Shame."

Known as Diamond and Silk (Lynette Hardaway and Rochelle Richardson,
respectively, they were raised to be bullshit artists because they had role models.
According to one source, "Hardaway and Richardson are the daughters of
husband and wife televangelists ... currently affiliated with Jericho Deliverance
Temple church in Raeford, North Carolina ... During a 2016 interview
with *Newsweek*, they were "reluctant" to give their ages but stated they are "old
enough to vote".(Wikipedia, 2018). Bullshit artists with something to hide – just
like their parents. Peddling that Christian bullshit to gullible black people just like
the two sisters, Diamond and Silk, peddle that conservative Trump line to anyone
dumb enough to accept it.

Who are these women, you may ask. In a nutshell,

> Lynnette Hardaway and Rochelle Richardson, popularly known
> as Diamond and Silk, are American live-stream video bloggers, social
> media personalities and political activists. They are known for their
> commentary in support of United States President <u>Donald Trump</u>.
> (Wikipedia, 2018) .

Two overweight women who choose names that are the opposite of what
their looks remind you of when you see them. They start off small, as most
bloggers do, and then figure out a way to get some major attention. I will share
with you how these Jemimas puled that off.

First, the usual bold-faced lies:

> The duo received media attention during the 2016 campaign and again in April 2018 when they reported that Facebook had notified them they were "unsafe to the community", and when they accused Facebook of blocking and censoring their Facebook page. There is no evidence that Facebook blocked or censored Diamond and Silk's Facebook page. In April 2018, Republican members of Congress brought up the duo's censorship claims at Mark Zuckerberg's testimony before U.S. Congress. (Wikipedia, 2018).

Since the Republicans have a history of lying, what these two skanks were able to do was right up the right wing alley. So now they had a little fame from white men (the target of all Jemimas) and they were on their way.

These bitches were insane from jump Street. They reacted to Trump the way someone with a white mindset would react – and that is how Jemimas think. Note fhe following:

> Formerly Democrats … their switch to the Republican Party occurred when they saw Trump announce his candidacy on television. **According to Hardaway, "When he announced and we heard everything that he stood for, it was on and poppin', and we've been on the Trump train ever since." …** They came to wider prominence in 2015 as supporters of then-presidential candidate Donald Trump after posting a video **criticizing former Fox News host Megyn Kelly for asking what they considered irrelevant questions during the first Republican presidential debate .**(Wikipedia, 2018 – emphasis added)

Of course they were "formerly Democrats" in the same way that these Jemimas – all of the ones that I have covered in this book – were "formerly black" before they turned into some kind of "Afro-Saxons" (as Nathan Hare would call them). These coons switched because that is where the money is at and Obama could not run for office again. So these opportunistic negroes made their move.

Now they say that when they heard Trump outline "everything he stood for," they were on the "Trump train." These bitches were out to get paid and get on television no matter what the cost. In America, negative publicity is still publicity, and with their look – two fat women with attitudes – they would be able to provide plenty of "comic relief" to the political scene, and provide it they did.

By questioning the blond and racist Megyn Kelly, they again showed the Republicans that they would attack anyone who attacked Trump. Like the true lapdogs that they apparently hope to be, Diamond and Silk were a part of the "cast of clowns" that the Republican Party had lined up as representing black folks: Paris

Denard, Omarosa Manigault, Ben Carson, and a few others. But these Jemimas combined street lingo with politicl commitment and were able to finagle appearances on some major television programs.

> Although **officially unaffiliated with the Trump campaign**, they urged support for Trump via **social media efforts and rallies and traveled to three states for the campaign …** The duo first joined Donald Trump as the "Stump for Trump Girls" on stage at his Raleigh, North Carolina, rally on December 4, 2015 … They later warmed up the crowd at the Trump rally on January 2, 2016, in Biloxi, Mississippi … They initiated a "Ditch and Switch" campaign to encourage Democrats to register as Republicans … and created a website explaining to voters which states had closed primaries and when the deadlines were for changing party affiliations .(Wikipedia, 2018 – emphasis added)

These "toms" were putting in work! Trump doesn't claim them. They don't have any kind of executive clearances. They're just two fat black bitches who work for chump change and appeared on stage as Trump was campaigning in front of lily white, racist audiences with few if any blacks in sight. For instance,

> On November 2, 2016, Diamond and Silk appeared with Lara Trump, wife of Eric Trump, in Winston-Salem, North Carolina, on behalf of the Trump campaign … **They were paid $1,274.94 for field consulting work by the Trump campaign …** They regularly appear on Fox News shows including *Hannity*, *Fox News Sunday*, *Watters' World*, and *The Ingraham Angle*, and Fox & Friends … as well as ABC's *Nightline* … **Hardaway is notably more talkative, while Richardson often just expresses agreement …** .(Wikipedia, 2018 – emphasis added)

Bums performing "stunts for bumps" like two crack head bitches willing to perform any sex act for a hit off the pipe (which is also known as "the glass dick"). They were where they had to be, and that small amount mentioned that they were paid was probably pulled out of Eric Trump's wallet. These women were the laughing stock. And that explains their "regular appearances on the TV shows mentioned above.

Both can't be talkative. But as it is with all good comedy teams, one has the charisma and the other is the stooge. Martin and Dean featured Deano while Jerry made an ass out of himself; Abbott and Costello featured Costello, but it was Abbott who was the brains of the outfit; Laurel and Hardy were together 28 years and Oliver Hardy was the logical one who made an ass out of his hilarious sidekick, Stan Laurel. And now we have Diamond and Star.

But it is their views on race and related issues that shows that these Jemimas are on the same level as Whoopi Goldberg was the time she showed "understanding" for Ted Danson's blackface appearance at the Friar's Club roast. These women don't necessary go full bore to the right, but their stands on issues show an abysmal ignorance of what is going on racially and politically in this country. As Wikipedia (2018) explains their "racial views,"

> Following the controversial Unite the Right rally held in Charlottesville, Virginia, on August 11 and 12, 2017, Hardaway and Richardson, appearing on *Fox & Friends*, were critical of both the far-right and far-left groups taking part in the event. Hardaway criticized Neo-Nazi groups and the Ku Klux Klan for "spewing hate and ... creating violence" declaring "all of them should be condemned and denounced. Period". In the same interview, she also said she does not "... like Black Lives Matter and Antifa." They further noted that they feel statues of Civil War Confederate soldiers should be kept in museums .(Wikipedia, 2018)

I am in agreement that those civil war statues should not be torn down, but my reasons are different. I want them to remain so that future generations of white and black people can see the racist assholes who were responsible for murdering off First Nation people, enslaving black people, and making life hell on earth for the rest of this nation. But as for that other shit, these women merely stated the obvious, which was more than what Trump would do. But they made it appear like there was "problems on both sides" in the same way Trump did.

> Hardaway and Richardson, in December 2017, expressed support for Omarosa Manigault Newman following her controversial firing as White House liaison and assistant, faulting the treatment of her by African Americans and the media generally: "What I find appalling, to my brothers and sisters [is] how you ... can laugh at, pick at, gloat at somebody because they either left the White House or you listened to a salacious story that Miss Piggy went around, running around telling everybody." (Wikipedia, 2018).

With Omarosa in the White House, Diamond and Silk probably figured that they had a way to get next to Trump. But they found out that he doesn't like any black people, male or female, and after getting rid of Omarosa he called her a "dog." That's his way of calling her a "bitch," since a female dog is a bitch. He also referred to black NFL players as "sons of bitches" so what does that make their mothers? And yet Diamond and Silk stood silent until another member of the "Jemima Clique," Omarosa, got canned in shame. Then they call Sarah Huckabee

Sanders, Trump's spokesman and flunky, "Miss Piggy", as if name calling is going to do anything but piss off their master all that much more.

And,

> In the same live-stream, they criticized *Good Morning America* anchor Robin Roberts for saying, "Bye, Felicia" to Newman during a segment on the ABC show which aired on December 14, 2017 … Addressing Roberts' remarks, Hardaway said, "How is it that you want the community to come up and then when a sister is sitting at the table, 'Well, she didn't represent us'? Are you crazy?: .(Wikipedia, 2018)

And don't get me wrong: Robin Roberts and her CBS counterpart Gail King are two more Jemimas that skin and grin and scratch when don't nothin' itch. These Jewish men who run these stations know what they're doing and they don't respect any women of color. Les Moonves is married to Julie Chin, this Asian woman who as TWO shows on CBS ("The Talk" and "Big Brother") and he still fucked around behind her back. NBC offers their own version, Hoda Kotb, and she and Kathy Lee Gifford sit around babbling with one trying to "out-white" the other. ABC has bisexual (my opinion) coon Michael Strayhan.

So all the major stations (Fox totally belongs to Trump and all the hosts kiss his ass and don't need or want any black input) know the value of the Jemima and Diamond and Star are simply trying to get their piece of the rock. But I first suggest that they each drop about 50 pounds, put down the mayonnaise sandwiches, and engage in some serious study before getting on the air wasting valuable time and teleprompter space exposing their ignorance.

Diamond and Silk lied on Facebook and continue to take chump change to attend events. To sum up, note the following:

> Artist and activist Bree Newsome has described Hardaway and Richardson as "a modern-day minstrel show" and stated in an interview that the pair's presentation relies on "stereotypical images of black women". Columbia University professor Keith Boykin argued that if the pair, "the way they speak, the way they talk and act and behave, were saying anything that was contradictory to Trump, the Trump supporters who defend them would be the first to attack them." Boykin argued that conservatives give attention to Hardaway and Richardson because they "only want to listen to the people who reaffirm their narrow, limited vision of what blackness is all about and how black people should perceive white people and specifically how they should perceive Donald Trump." .(Wikipedia, 2018)

The saying in the street is "you gotta bring ass to get ass." That means if you're going to bring it, then you better have your shit together. These two

Jemimas do not. When you're a Jemima, you don't have to be concerned or worry about what black people think of you; your job is to curry favor and kiss the ass of the system. And that is what Diamond and Silk and the rest of the women in this book do.

Robert Griffin III, Washington Redskins

White people in general, but their "reporters" in particular, have always been instigators; some would call them provocateurs. In other words, they like to keep shit going. If they are covering a story that has to do with race, they will find a way to fan the seeds of discord in some way, with the goal of "exposing" the individual or individuals involved for their racial views. This informs the higher ups of whether or not this person is a "safe" or "acceptable" black or if this individual is someone to be feared, ala the more confrontational brothers like the members of the Nation of Islam, the New Black Panther Party or, heaven forbid, the NAACP!

On the morning of December 13th, I was watching "First Take" as I do each morning after watching two half hour airings of the comedy, "Wings" that comes on another channel. After changing over I noticed that once again, Stephen A. was not in the studio but was being telecast from someplace else, probably Miami or New York.

The show was going smoothly and then the subject of Washington Redskin quarterback Robert Griffin III came up. It seems that at a December 12th press conference, Griffin was asked about his race and being a quarterback in the NFL. This goes back to what I was saying early about these white reporters doing whatever they can to play games with the political viewpoints and the futures of black athletes. They know these black men are sellouts and bound by contracts to always be on their best behavior. They apparently cannot have any relevant political viewpoints because few of them every express any.

At any rate, during the press conference, Griffin was asked about his race and being a quarterback in the NFL. Griffin stated, among other things: *""For me, you don't ever want to be defined by the color of your skin,"* He then added,. *"You want to be defined by your work ethic, the person that you are, your character, your personality. That's what I strive [for]. I am an African American, in America, and that will never change. But I don't have to be defined by that."*

In my view this statement is bold because most black athletes would not have even acknowledged that much. And when Griffin said he doesn't have to be defined by being black, all he's doing is showing his own abysmal ignorance of race relations in this country (but reflect back on the influence and impact of the military on his life, as outlined in the previous section). Maybe HE doesn't define himself in those terms, but white boys sure do. To them he is a BLACK quarterback, and he's treated as such; the commentators imply as much as they go out of their way to not use the word black. It's as if they're saying "he's one of us."

In fact, Stephen A.Smith – house negro extraordinaire -- often makes it clear that he believes that Andrew Luck is the better choice for quarterback even though Griffin is the superior athlete. This is the same view that the white man has: Luck, who is white and tall, fits the bill as a quarterback; Griffin is a world class sprinter who has a cannon for an arm and therefore, "gets the job done." This seems to be what is always implied.

So then we fast forward 24 hours to the "First Take" show and Rob Parker is asked, "What does this say about RGIII?" Such a stupid question could be nothing more than a set up because the answer spoke for itself. And yet the question was posed, by Cari Champion, to get a response from Parker who everybody in the studio knows has a history of speaking his mind, dealing with race issues, and not biting his tongue just because a few white people might be around. And he fell for the trap, hook-line-and-sinker.

Here is how Parker responded.

> "This is an interesting topic. For me, personally, just me, this throws up a red flag, what I keep hearing. And I don't know who's asking the questions, but we've heard a couple of times now of a black guy kind of distancing himself away from black people. I understand the whole story of I just want to be the best. Nobody's out on the field saying to themselves, I want to be the best black quarterback. You're just playing football, right? You want to be the best, you want to throw the most touchdowns and have the most yards and win the most games. Nobody is [thinking] that. "But time and time we keep hearing this, so it just makes me wonder deeper about him, and I've talked to some people down in Washington D.C., friends of mine, who are around and at some of the press conferences, people I've known for a long time. But my question, which is just a straight honest question. Is he a brother, or is he a cornball brother?" Is he a brother, or is he a cornball brother"?

To begin with, Parker tempered his remarks by saying, "For me, personally, just me." Isn't that good enough, or is Parker not supposed to have the same opinions as Smith and Bayliss? Every day, you can hear the latter two pontificating, even delving into social psychology, to address issues that is really nothing more than their assumptions, guesswork and suppositions that are rooted in conjecture. They are both articulate, so it sounds good, but there's little that is objective about what either Smith or Bayliss say? So then, why should Parker be held to a different standard when he made it clear it was HIS opinion?

I, too, sicken of black men having to apologize for being black. Griffin wants to be known as "a quarterback" and acts as if he isn't black. That's why later on Parker would interject that Griffin had a white fiancé and was a Republican. These pieces of information shed light on the way that Griffin thinks about himself – he thinks IN SPITE of the black community and not IN RELATION to it.

The way that Griffin answered that question bought back memories of a scene from "Guess Who's Coming to Dinner," which starred Sidney Portier, a black doctor who was about to marry a white woman who had nothing on the ball. This is one similarity between Griffin and his white fiancé: she's a nobody and he's an athlete, they met in college, as did Portier and his white woman and I am sure these white girls knew that these brothers had a bright and wealthy future ahead of them. This is what they do. Now they've got somebody that will not only marry THEM, but also help out their family as well – the way that O.J. did when he hooked up with his white woman and helped her family out financially.

Anyway, the scene from "Guess Who's Going to Dinner?" takes place in the library/office of the father's home. Portier is talking with his father and his father is concerned about his marrying a white woman. The father gives him some advice and speaks his mind and then, when it's Portier's turn to respond, he says, "That's the difference between you and me. You see yourself as a black man, and I see myself as a man."

What kind of bullshit is this? What he's saying to his father is, "you see yourself as a black man, and I see myself as a white man." What else could it be? Is he not black? So if there is a differentiation to make, it means that he is a "different" kind of man. This is the same thing that RG III was saying and Parker spotted it right away. Were it not for Warren Moon, Marlin Briscoe, Jefferson Street Joe Gilliam, Doug Williams and the long line of BLACK quarterbacks that came before him, Griffin would not have been given the time of day. These were the brothers who showed the white man that they were MORE than his equal. The fact of the matter is, the black quarterback has revolutionized the position and the white man, although begrudgingly, is having to accept it. And Griffin – along with black quarterbacks Cam Newton (Carolina Panthers) and Russell Wilson (Seattle Seahawks) – are just what the white man ordered.

So there was no need for Griffin to kowtow because he's calling the shots. He could have said something of relevance because he's doing that team a favor. But no, he wanted to distance himself from other black people and he didn't want to be seen as black because, after all, the woman he claims to love and has pledged to marry – is a white girl. And how would that make HER feel? She has all the proof she needs that he's black, you can believe that. But he need not get political lest he be looked down upon by other whites. He's in an all-black city, on a team that is at least half black, and he (Griffin) nevertheless chooses to make that distinction. I'll say it: he's an Uncle Tom.

If Parker had stopped at that, it would have been consciousness raising enough and white folks probably could have overlooked it the way that they overlook some of the diatribes uttered by Stephen A. Smith and Skip Bayliss. But no, there was more. After all, Parker is not a regular on the show so when he does appear, he tries to make it count: complimenting Cari on how lovely she is, engaging in banter with Smith who always seems to have something insulting to say about Parker's wardrobe.

So following is the coup de grace – the stroke that kills.

When asked to explain what he meant when he said that Griffin wasn't "down with the cause" by both Bayliss and Cari, Parker said, *"He's not real. OK, he's black, he kind of does the thing, but he's not really down with the cause. He's not one of us. He's kind of black but he's not really, like, the guy you want to hang out with because he's off to something else."*

Most of the friends I've had in life were not conscious and, just because I was more aware and gifted than they, did not stop us from associating. Parker cannot come out and call Griffin a sellout, but that appears to be what he is. He's from Texas, a state filled with mealy-mouthed, white folks loving black people. He's got a white fiancée and he claims to be a Republican. How much more of a reactionary can you be? I don't want to "hang out" with him either, and Parker is right: the reason is "because he's off to something else." He actually said, "He's off INTO something else," and that something else is white folks.

But Parker just kept on talking – as if he owed Skip, Cari and Stephen some kind of explanation. Stephen had already jumped ship on him and let him know that the race of the fiancé and the like were issues he (Smith) wasn't concerned with. Just a month ago he was on the air crediting Parker with being "a mentor" for him. But I can see Stephen A. Smith's point: what little voice black people have on the air is well represented by him, so he has to keep his mouth shut on such issues or he will be judged by the company he keeps. So when he talks personally, it's about his family, his sister's biscuits, Skip's wife and that kind of thing.

On another point, the house negro Smith had already been canned once by the station. As it was reported in April 2008 by Raissman,

> Stephen A. Smith, who had a meteoric rise at ESPN, screaming his way into his own show, is out at the all-sports network. ESPN will not renew Smith's contract. His last day at the network, where he was a featured NBA reporter, will be May 1. "We decided to move in different directions," an ESPN spokesman said. Smith, a former Daily News sportswriter and ESPN could not come to terms on a

new deal. Industry sources said ESPN wanted Smith to take a pay cut.

Stephen A. is no stranger to dealing with political views having been ORDERED to take his off his website when he worked for the Philadelphia Enquirer a paper that, by the way, took away his title as sportswriter and made him a general editor because they said that at $225,000, he was making too much money. So it stands to reason that he would be gun-shy when it came to standing up for Parker (which I still think he should have done).

At any rate, here are more words uttered by Parker in regard to RGIII:

> Well because that's just how I want to find out about him. I don't know because I keep hearing these things. We all know he has a white fiancée. There was all this talk about how he's a Republican, which, I don't really care, there's no information at all. I'm just trying to dig deeper into why he has an issue. Because we did find out with Tiger Woods. Tiger Woods was like, 'I've got black skin but don't call me black.' (Wikipedia, 2012).

First, the Tiger Woods issue. Skip recalled that Parker told him, back a few years ago, that after Woods appeared on "Oprah" and made the statement that he (Woods) wasn't black, Parker said that he took all of his Tiger Woods memorabilia and donated it to the Salvation Army. Skip turned around and said that he was proud of Parker for doing that – as if Parker needed his white stamp of approval.

So it was alright to make that statement about Tiger. Now the second point regarding Parker's desire to "dig deeper" and "find out" more.

For centuries white people have been getting jobs, padding their resumes, getting grant money and making a name for themselves checking out, investigating and "finding out" about black people. Names like Thomas Kochman, John Howard Griffin, Grace Halsell, and many others come to mind. They have the right to find out whatever they want to because they choose to.

John Howard Griffin, a self-described "race expert" who changed his skin color to black and then made millions when he wrote *Black Like Me*, and Grace Halsell, a woman who did the same thing and then wrote *Soul Sister*, didn't give a shit about black people. They were showboating and thinking long-term: they knew there was money to be made.

These people were curious. Thomas Kochman goes around lecturing white people on how to talk to black people and how to translate what black people say. He had the nerve to write a book *Rappin' and Stylin' Out* and white folks swear by it. I exposed him once in Chicago when my fiancé and I attended one of his seminars and shut him up by asking, "If you know so much about black people, then you must know that by doing what you're going, you're talking a job away from a black person that these whites should be consulting." He couldn't say shit and after my question, the session was adjourned.

I say this to back up Rob Parker's "right to know." He's a reporter but he's also a "sports analyst," which is his title when he appears on "First Take." Parker has as much right to state his views as those white reporters did to ask Griffin that question about being a "black quarterback." It seems that the people at ESPN who suspended Parker forgot about how intrusive naïve white people have been, presently are, and apparently will always be.

Skip showed his racism when he bought up a subject trying to defend Griffin's being "urban" because he wore his hair in braids. And Parker played right along with it, although it's bullshit. Nobody wants to come out an Afro every day for a game – so you get your hair braided, plain and simple. And I'll bet you one thing: that white girl that Griffin is engaged to ain't braidin' it!

So when Skip makes the comment about the braids, Parker responds, thusly: *"Now that's different ... To me, that's very urban and makes you feel like...wearing braids, you're a brother. You're a brother if you've got braids on."* That is such bullshit because it implies that Griffin cares enough to be seen as "a brother" although when he gets the chance, he tells people something different, his choice of life mate tells people something different, his choice of political party tells people something different. I say he wears braids because he's with a woman that doesn't know SHIT about braiding hair and therefore he gets his sister or some relative to do it, pays them big bucks, and this keeps him from having to comb it out every night. Plain and simple.

Wikipedia claims that "Later, Parker was given an opportunity to clarify whether he was judging Griffin's blackness." And there is what he said:

> I didn't mean it like that … We could sit here and be honest, or we can be dishonest. And you can't tell me that people in the barbershops or people that talk, they look at who your spouse is. They do. And they look at how you present yourself. People will say all the time, you're not gonna get a job in corporate America wearing those braids. It happens all the time. Let's not act like it doesn't, because it does."

And Parker is 100% right. It's all about being honest and stating how you feel – something Skip Bayliss and Stephen A. Smith do every day on "First Take." But when you stop glossing over the periphery of issues and get down to the nitty gritty and start talking about the barber shop (the white man will be investigating these businesses next), then all of a sudden it's off base. How is what Parker said any different than the value judgments that Stephen A. Smith makes about pro basketball players and other athletes he has never met? The same for Skip? All they go by is what they hear the person say, what they read about or what they've seen. That is exactly what Rob Parker did.

And here is something that Parker said that wasn't addressed. While explaining why people admitting that they belong to the race was important, at one point he says, "I'm black, you're black (pointing to Cari Champion) and then he turned to Christian __ and said "you're mixed" and then went on to make his point. Mixed? Why was he willing to castigate Tiger Woods for denying being black but points to Christian and labels him "mixed"? Even if Christian is mixed, it's clear he's a light-skinned black man. Why wasn't this made an issue during the debate on race and one's political views as a result of race?

ABOUT ROBERT GRIFFIN III AND THOSE OF HIS ILK

A recent program aired on NBC-SN (December 15,2012) claimed that Robert Griffin III generated $250 million for Baylor University during his Heisman bid. We have long known of the exploitation of black college athletes by these universities, but even in that, what Griffin allegedly generated – and saw none of – is reason enough why white people would love him, cuddle him and once he turned pro and began making the real money, would question him about his views on race, just to make sure that he was truly a "reliable nigger."

The "ilk" or type that I am talking about applies to those who want to look at life descriptively and evocatively instead of analytically. They want to hunker down in suburban homes and lay back with their own families while other people starve. They want to use their power to define the extent to which people can voice their concerns about "the system." Griffin is like this because he is the product of two parents who spent time in the military and this fact in itself speaks volumes. I address this point later in this section.

Of Griffin's "ilk," then, means those who have been programmed. Either by an education system that paints American history all white, by a college system that offers Western Civilization and claims that the white man invented the world, programmed either by their churches that tell you to take your time and that God will handle it, by their parents who are passive and warn you to "don't talk too much – you'll make people hate you." And it goes on and on. Most black people have been programmed by whites and all whites have been programmed by their own. The product is an illusion of life that exists only in the minds of the "patriots" and those who are so starved for acceptance that they often doubt their own humanity.

According to CBS-DC.com, "The Parker controversy came about after Griffin responded to a question in a press conference on Wednesday after practice about Martin Luther King, Jr. To begin with, King has long been over-rated by black and white people. What he and those of his ilk marched for ended up biting us in the ass. With one-way integration (as I call it) came a number of black people being happy and duped, but we lost black-owned motels, movie theaters, and so on. This thing about King being a great civil rights leader may be true, but I liken civil rights to a pacifier: it may satisfy a need (keep the baby quiet), but it offers nothing nutritious and is only good for a short time.

In response to this question on King, the young black man who had made all this money for a Texas college responded, *"For me, you don't ever want to be defined by the color of your skin ... You want to be defined by your work ethic, the person that you are, your character, your personality. That's what I've tried to go out and do ...I am an African-American in America. That will never change. But I don't have to be defined by that."*

And that's what set Parker off.

Your work ethic? We are the descendants of a people who gave over 300 years of "work" to these white people, and it was work that we were not compensated for. When all the cotton had been picked and all the shoes had been shined, we became expendable, so they went out and got themselves some "new niggas" – the Mexicans. Here in Texas, where I live, I see these hard working Latino brothers building up an economy, constructing interstates, landscaping mansions and performing the same type of high quality work that we, as black people, must have done in the South when we were making the Southern economy the largest in the world.

Defined for his personality? What personality? You're not even allowed to be yourself in this country. Look at what they did to Rob Parker. If you show you have a personality – other than the laugh when ain't nothin' funny/scratch when don't nothin' itch type – than you will be isolated, alienated and, as in the case of Rob Parker, suspended with extreme prejudice. Is that why Griffin is smiling all the time? Is that the kind of personality he's talking about? Never speaking out on critical issues that impact on his "African-American heritage" but instead, chilling with his white fiancé, raking in a lot of money and then stating, for all young people to read (the few that can) that it's better to be known for what you do than what you are?

Defined by your character? How does he define that? The definition of character is, "the particular combination of qualities that makes someone a particular type of person." What "particular type of person" is RGIII? A military brat that was raised never to question authority, to follow orders and to "do a good job" no matter what it is you're doing? A football player with a bright smile? Someone who will risk injury playing a million dollar "game" in stadiums that most black kids can't afford to get into? A man who makes commercials for fast food outlets and other retail stores that, in turn, use that image to sell their crap to black customers? So he's a slave on all counts: football player, colorless citizen, no political views having lackey and someone comfortable using his visibility to promote all that is "American" (white).

Where was Rob Parker wrong?

That's just it. He wasn't. But the white industrial complex, of which ESPN is a key part (sports is a therapeutic catharsis, not a social engineer) is not about to have one of its leading puppets exposed on a talk show that spends its time glorifying black men who do NOTHING in their respective communities. Time spent arguing over who should be MVP, who should make the all-star team, who is going to be traded or drafted, and none of these "niggers" cares enough about the community to do something positive, other than to move their mother out of it. Griffin is not the exception. *He is the rule.*

After Parker's suspension was made public, ESPN came out with a statement of their own:

> Following yesterday's comments, Rob Parker has been suspended until further notice," ESPN spokesman Mike Soltys tweeted. "We are conducting a full review."

A full review of what? Where are the race experts? What will be the criteria for the review? If they didn't have a full review, then what was the suspension based on – a *partial* review? ESPN is full of shit: they make billions reporting on, analyzing and commenting on black athletes (we are the ones who get into the end zone, perform acrobatics on the basketball court and dominate sports, in general), but they want to tip toe around race when the issues become linked to the lives of those who they want to spoon feed (e.g., Robert Griffin, Michael Jordan, etc.)

All of these people are of the same ilk as Robert Griffin: the "ostrich-in-the-sand syndrome. Hide your head or do damage control when an issue comes up that is not of your liking. White people have a long history of this childish tactic, and yet they persist in imposing it on people of color who they don't like: those from the political left, black grass roots community organizers, civil rights leaders, and others who attempt to deal with this system's number one problem: racism.

Liz Raftery of *TV Guide* wrote that, "Parker went on to mention that Griffin is married to a white woman and is rumored to be a Republican." At no point did Parker say that Griffin was "married" to a white woman; he said that Griffin's fiancé was white. Raftery added that, "In full context, Griffin's initial comments were related to his passing game versus the running game. "That's the negative stereotype when it comes to African-American quarterbacks, that most of us just run," he said. "I like to think I can throw it around a little bit."

What Griffin said is true about perception that black quarterbacks run a great deal. But Griffin had an obligation to go into greater detail than to just flippantly add, "I like to think I can throw it around a little bit." What this young man is going to learn is that whether he runs it or throws it, he is in a system that will discard him like yesterday's tampon if he dares to act like the kind of black man that Parker is talking about; if he puts his hands on his white fiancé; if he speaks out about or against racist mistreatment of his fellow blacks in the Washington, D.C. inner city. To paraphrase Malcolm X, "I don't see any football dream; I see a gridiron nightmare!"

There are those who promote the kind of black person who is guilty of what could be called "avoidance." For instance,

> DeMaurice Smith, executive director of the NFL Players Association, told the Post in an email:"Robert can certainly take care of himself. Nonetheless, I hope that our men and for that matter, my own kids, will never beg for authenticity from someone who can only talk about the things that other people have the courage to do. People need to be held accountable for the offensive things that they say." (Boren, 2012)

If what Parker said was offensive to him, that was his opinion. But when it comes to "begging for authenticity, no one could be more guilty than an NFL player who struts around on the field every Sunday and then drives to his suburban home while the majority of his people starve and serve as the butt of jokes of the same white people who pay his salary. You don't think white people find it laughable the way these black athletes carry on with their money, jewelry, big cars? Then, many of them retire and end up broke. This, from a system, that set all this up.

Now I hear that these "negroes," the ones who DeMaurice Smith thinks have the courage to do so much, are now taking Viagra before games to "give them an edge." These are people of Griffin's ilk: think about yourself, make the "game" your life, do what you want to do and you'll get paid. The people who write about Parker are getting paid to do it; the people commenting on him via radio and television are getting paid to do it; the people who have positions like that of DeMaurice Smith get paid to support the same system that has priced football tickets so high that black kids can't get in to see a game.

They say, "like father, like son." Robert Griffin II told USA TODAY Sports on, "I wouldn't say it's racism. I would just say some people put things out there about people so they can stir things up."

How could it be racism? That man has served in the military, which means that he stared racism square in the face for two decades, and his wife stared it in the face for another four years. They should be able to recognize it when they see it. Instead, what do they do? They do the same thing that far too many black parents do: work on steering their kids around racism by pretending that it's a thing of the past and that it doesn't exist anymore.

White folks and black folks of this ilk want to "tiptoe through the tulips" of the race issue because if they discussed it, somebody would have to be held accountable. Typical of the criticisms by people of Griffin's ilk was an article by Farrar (2012) that asserted,

> But what Rob Parker said went far beyond the parameters of
> "opinion" and veered quickly into something that should have
> ESPN seriously considering whether they want Parker representing
> even their worst traffic jam of a media product (Farrar, 2012).

What was that "something" that Parker's comments veered into? White people are good at pointing out what they view as problems, but they usually fall short when it comes to solutions – that is, solutions that don't include their white stamp of approval.

In this case it is clear that Farrar (whoever he is) can't define any parameters in the first place. If it's a "talk show," then there are no parameters. Parker's website and slogan, which includes t-shirt insignias, states, "no way. No how." Maybe he means that he won't be taking any shit. At any rate, ESPN promotes the slogan on their website and they have to know that Parker is no "yes man." They (ESPN) also had to know that Griffin had a white fiancé. So how can a station that will do stories on the kinds of pets that athletes have, the impact of their mothers on the athletes' lives, kids that might also be interested in sports, kids with handicaps and so on, all of a sudden show a hesitancy to deal with race and the fact that disproportionate numbers of black athletes are marrying white women? More profoundly, that white women (read: Kim Kardashian) are "out there" looking for black men to bed and wed them?

Of all people, Cari Champion should have been sensitive to, or at least had something to say, about Parker's ref erence to RG III's "fiancé" being a white woman. But she didn't say squat. Read back to the earlier statement about how "First Take" hosts usually leave the show for greener pastures. Maybe this is what she wants or looks forward to and as such, realizes that interracial sex is not an issue that she wants to broach.

And people of this ilk – RG III's ilk – are people who will veer from the topic because if you do, you have to deal with black genetic superiority. That's why all of a sudden Christian Favrio, in Parker's own words, becomes "mixed." And that's why nobody's saying anything about the fact that those Latinos who are supposedly taking over baseball are BLACK Latinos. The white man and those of his ilk feel that they owe no one an explanation – apparently the same way ESPN and RGIII feel. A point that Farrar also displays in the following excerpt:

> Unlike Parker, I've met Griffin a couple of times. Not nearly enough to know him or his particular thoughts on any particular cause, but enough to know that he knows how to carry himself, and that he's never made any particular statement claiming that he isn't in line with whatever Parker seems to believe he's supposed to be in line with. His teammates respect him, his coaches can't say enough good things about him, and everyone I've talked to who spends any time in his orbit seems to believe that Griffin is absolutely all that he's cracked up to be (Farrar, 2012).

In other words, he (Griffin) has "the white stamp of approval." And when you have that, can you honestly expect white people to give a damn about whether or not you have "street cred"? In other words, once you're recognized as a reliable "house negro," the very idea of being deemed or considered a "field negro" is quite out of the question.

Charles Barkley, NBA Hall of Famer, Co-Host "Inside the NBA"

Don't get it twisted: there are many, many more men of this ilk and while the man on the cover, Mantan Moreland, was a walking stereotype from bugged-out eyes when he became afraid to his classic phrase, "feets don't fail me now," today's coons are more sophisticated and in fact, may well be in the majority. This especially applies to those who have received some semblance of fame or celebrity, locally, nationally and/or internationally.

But there are similarities between these three that can serve as a kind of matrix regarding the tendencies that lead to black men to sell out the race in such a manner. All three were born poor, all three were involved in athletics to some extent, but after that it was straight into the white man's system and his way of life. The academic careers of these men are lesser known than their respective professional credentials, so that is what I will share at this juncture.

Let us begin with the fattest of the duo, Charles Barkley:

> Barkley was born and raised in Leeds, Alabama, ten miles (16 km) outside Birmingham, and attended Leeds High School. As a junior, Barkley stood 5'10" (1.78 m) and weighed 220 pounds (99.8 kg). He failed to make the varsity team and was named as a reserve.

However, during the summer Barkley grew to 6'4" (1.93 m) and earned a starting position on the varsity as a senior. He averaged 19.1 points and 17.9 rebounds per game and led his team to a 26–3 record en route to the state semifinals …(Wikipedia, 2017)

Continuing:

Despite his improvement, Barkley garnered no attention from college scouts until the state high school semifinals, where he scored 26 points against Alabama's most highly recruited player, Bobby Lee Hurt.[9] An assistant to Auburn University's head coach, Sonny Smith, was at the game and reported seeing, "a fat guy... who can play like the wind".[10] Barkley was soon recruited by Smith and majored in business management while attending Auburn University (Wikipedia, 2017)

In other words, Barkley was viewed in the same way that the white farmer might view a pack mule. He was fat and strong and could rebound. He was a commodity to be used and exploited. As far as I can find he never got that college degree while attending Auburn for three years. His claim to fame was as an athlete and that brought him into contact with a number of white folks. A white woman hooked up with him, got pregnant and he married her as a result. He kept it quiet, made the professional ranks, and carved out a name for himself. After retiring he does sports analysis for TNT in Atlanta. A "boy" from the Deep South through and through, he is known for making remarks that white people find controversial, but in reality they are remarks that white people don't expect well trained "negroes" to say.

Mike Brown, the lesser known of the three Uncle Toms who are the subject of this essay. Although he coached LeBron James in Cleveland and went to a championship, he is now an assistant coach with the Golden State Warriors. As for his background and education, take note:

Brown was born in Columbus, Ohio, but spent periods of his childhood overseas. He graduated in 1988 from Würzburg American High School in Würzburg, Germany, where he excelled in basketball and football.[2] After studying and playing basketball for two years at Mesa Community College, Brown went on to the University of San Diego, where he played two seasons for the Toreros and graduated in 1992 with a Bachelor of Business Administration degree (Wikipedia, 2017).

Mediocrity at best, akin to that of Barkley. But at least he got a bachelor's degree after spending time at a community college. But remember that he spent time overseas and received his high school diploma from a school in, of all places, Germany. His "excelling" in football and basketball was against German competition of course, so he never came up against and "real" bruthas. In other words, it appears that he was assimilated through and through. He was more likely than not a military brat and one can bet that he never addressed directly any issues of race or racism. This explains why he turned out to be the narrow minded Uncle Tom that I describe elsewhere in this paper.

CHARLES BARKLEY, CO-HOST, "INSIDE THE NBA"

What people who are not black are going to have to learn is that just because you have dark skin doesn't mean that you're Black in the true sense of the word. As a cultural nationalist said long ago, "We say that Blackness is three things: color, culture and consciousness." Charles Barkley has one of these components but is sorely lacking in the possession or understanding of the other two.

Case in point: he likes to talk about race but at no point has he ever mentioned the fact that he is not only married to a white woman, but has a daughter who he also never talks about. He lives in Phoenix, which has about as many black people as there are Klingons on Earth, and in a community that is gated and lily-white. I doubt if he graduated from Auburn and often admits that he is lacking in intellectual ability, hence is ongoing insults against Shaquille O'Neal on "Inside the NBA" – Shaq has a doctorate.

Chasing white women is nothing new. Though married, he would often cavort openly. When I lived in Milwaukee I often heard about his escapades when the Philadelphia 76ers came to town to play the Bucks. During one of these "adventures," some racist white dudes – and there are many in downtown Milwaukee – confronted him on the streets in front of several white women (read: NBA groupies looking for a good time) and he knocked one of them out.

Most recently, though an NBA Hall of Famer and an announcer for TNT, this overweight oaf decided to use the national airwaves to knock the NBA. He has done it before, putting down particular games that he didn't want to watch, although he is paid to do so.

If you watch his analyses on "Inside the NBA" he spends most of his time insulting black players, many who were better than he was. He insulted LeBron James, who fired back and humiliated him so badly that I noticed that though attending the third game of the finals in Cleveland, Barkley sheepishly avoided LeBron while Shaquille freely conversed with the Cavalier star. He said that Warrior center Jeremiah McGee was "stupid" and he's made other insulting statements throughout the season. And yet he has nothing but praise for marginal white players like ZaZa Pachulia, Kelly Olynyk and Jonas Jerebco of the Boston Celics, and any small action he can find to give the white man props.

In this case, in June he was invited to attend a National Hockey League game, as he had continually praised the lily-white sport. Andrew Bucholtz of Turner Sports wrote, "*NBA on TNT* analyst Charles Barkley has been talking up his NHL fandom this year, first saying *"Thank god for the NHL playoffs, that's what I've been watching in the back"* on-air as a shot at the NBA playoffs, then calling in to NHL Network to discuss his hockey fandom (and call the Stanley Cup playoffs *"the best thing in sports"*), then saying on-air *he wanted to leave Game Five of the Boston Celtics-Cleveland Cavaliers Eastern Conference Finals* to watch the NHL game. On Monday, he took it to a new level, flying to Nashville to take in Game Four of the Stanley Cup Final.

See?

The hockey game was played in Nashville, known more for rednecks and racism than for anything remotely black. This is not Barkley's first escapade into whiteness: he also pays homage to NASCAR, which is the motorized personification of red neck culture. Add this to the fact that he has a serious alcohol problem, and Barkley is like the proverbial Oreo cookie: dark on the outside, white on the inside.

But there's more.

In September of 2017, this bald-headed bastard knocked the entire NBA by saying that the players were "babies." These men sometimes play two games in two nights, run up and down the court for 48 minutes, and this fat fucker couldn't hang when he played. He was fat, out of shape and hogged (no pun intended) the ball. Today's athletes realizes that they are modern day slaves and are therefore working to get their piece of the rock and feel that they're being overworked and risking their health. Injuries mount up which impacts on their livelihood and as a result, their longevity.

Uncle Tom Barkley, sitting comfortably in his TNT announcing studio, seems to get off dogging out black males who excel. He calls them babies because they don't want to be overworked. But this fat bean-eater complains when he's asked to come in on the set a few extra hours and put in work for an advertisement or some other easy ass job. He's typical of too many older athletes: jealous if the young brothers, especially now that their names and records are being forgotten, and so they lash out for publicity purposes.

REFERENCES

Kenney, Tanasia (2016, May 19). "12 African-Americans Who Adopted the 'New Black" Mentality. **Atlanta Black Star**. Retrieved from http://atlantablackstar.com/

CONCLUSION

I once read where Audre Lorde wrote, *"When I dare to be powerful – to use my strength in the service of my vision, then it becomes less and less important whether I am afraid."* This is a sensible way to live life because you can do so without walking in fear – the way black people in 21st century America have done and continue to do. The bootlickers mentioned herein, from their dumb statements to their counter-productive actions, are but a tip of the iceberg. Some group of black people voted for them, made them celebrities, buy their tickets, make them rich and powerful and convince white people that these black people are the best that the black race can produce.

www.ingramcontent.com/pod-product-compliance
Lightning Source LLC
Chambersburg PA
CBHW081608250726
48657CB00009B/2504